The Pottery Barn Rules

You Break It ... You Own It

Del Walters

WRIGHT
BOOK PUBLISHING

The Pottery Barn Rules

Wright Book Publishing books may be ordered through
booksellers or by contacting:

Wright Book Publishing
www.WrightBookPublishing.com
email: info@wrightbookpublishing.com
1.877.266.5920

Because of the dynamic nature of the Internet, any Web
addresses or links may have changed since publication and
may no longer be valid.

ISBN 978-0-9822822-2-9

Dedication

This book is dedicated to all of those who care about Africa. It is for the Hollywood actors whose voices cause the world to take notice to what is a most horrible wrong, to the churches whose pastors and parishioners provide badly needed spiritual support, and to the filmmakers who try to tell the story as best they can with little or no support from the filmmaking industry.

Africa was no accident. No continent can give the world the likes of Oprah Winfrey, Michael Jordan, Tiger Woods, Muhammad Ali, Michael Jackson, Jackie Robinson, Martin Luther King and Malcolm X to name a few, on one side of the Atlantic, only to suffer where the water breaks on the other side. No country can suffer so much, without so many trying to 'do it in' from outside its borders. I write this book as an African American, and as a person who believes that we are all in this global community together. It is not enough for us to vow to clean up the planet, if we lose those its people, those who 'live on it' in the process.

Finally, this book is for Robin. She is my wife, my strength and the single person who has made this journey possible. It is difficult to tell Africa's story. If it were easy Africa would not look as it does. The story of Africa is a battle against governments, apathy and in some cases, the African's themselves. It is also a battle against history, much of it incorrect, because so little of it was written by people of color.

From Cannes, France where we premiered the film version of this book, to every theater, community center and basement in cities across the country where it has been shown, Robin has been with me. Without her this book would not be possible.

For Robin

Foreword

Colin Powell, according to press accounts, turned to George W. Bush, who at the time was seeking to invade Iraq, faced the President, and said, 'You are going to be the proud owner of 25 million people. You will own all of their hopes, aspirations and problems. You'll own it all." He was warning the president of the consequences of invading and destroying another nation.

Powell then cited what has become known as the 'Pottery Barn Rule'…'You break it, you own it." In truth, there is no such rule, and the same can be said about what America invades and breaks. We, America, take what we want and leave behind those we have invaded, to find their own way. Tragically an uninformed media, fanned by the flames of racism, international ignorance and national pride, take up the cause when it is far too late.

Such is the case with Africa. The continent that lays before us today is a shadow of what it once was, and should be now. The invasions that were launched in the mid to late fifties by Presidents, who saw Africa's natural resources as their own personal piggy banks, have devastated the continent. No one revisits those days, instead journalist after journalist returns from Africa with horror stories about what Africans have done to each other. No one asks the simplest of questions. Was there an Africa before all of the killing? Did Africans dream of two cars in every garage, and education for their children? Do they watch the Olympics and wonder, when will it be their turn? Do they wonder where the guns come from that kill and maim so many? And if guns are responsible for most of the deaths, where did the Africans get the guns since no guns are manufactured on the continent itself?

Two men who offer no excuses are Randall Robinson and Roger Morris. Their credentials are without question. Both men graduated from Harvard and then went on to distinguish themselves on all things African.

Randall Robinson became famous worldwide when he led the push to end Apartheid and secure the release of Nelson Mandela from almost three decades of prison hell. Robinson says of the U.S. role in Africa, 'There is blood on America's hands."

Morris, who served on the National Security Councils of both the Johnson and Nixon administrations, speaks more apocalyptically. "I think that we are responsible for what has to be the greatest human rights disaster in the history of the planet. What do we owe them? (Africa) We owe them tremendous blood debt for what we allowed to happen…we owe them everything."

Africa has become a "shell game" of human misery. While the world focuses on one crisis, another country is being raped, usually for its natural resources. While we focus on Rwanda, plans are secretly being drawn up to destabilize Kenya; and while we focus on Kenya, the same is happening in Somalia, or Zimbabwe. This book is a close examination of the historical record. There is no conjecture, or farfetched hypothesis. What makes the contents so disturbing is the truth that lies behind them. The book also examines the one issue at the heart of Africa and its collapse…racism. We are fools to believe that racism did not play a role in Africa's collapse, or as Eric Holder, the nation's first African American Attorney General puts it, 'cowards'.

This book seeks to examine the cause and collapse of an entire continent. It will examine the one fact no one wants to explore; that being that Africans die simply because the people, who were born there, live there, and die there are black. There is no other plausible explanation. We, America, broke Africa, now it is time to fix it. If not, we own it. As you read these pages you will learn my own experience, my journey into Africa's steep decline, was not of my own doing. Some would argue it was preordained. Africa's demise began on the day that I was born, only I was among the last to know!

Chapter One

The Dark Continent

Notice how the brightest lights are in North America and Europe ... Africa is dark...

The Author

If a picture is worth a thousand words, then the picture on the next page is worth 20 million lives. It is a photograph showing how the earth looks from space. Notice how the brightest lights are in North America and Europe. The areas we call civilized. The homes are well lit so they can read at night, the streets illuminated so they can drive their cars and feel safe as they make their way home at night. It is no small secret the areas that are brightly lit are the world's superpowers. They have the biggest guns, and largest armies and the most sophisticated weapons.

No one ever asks where the raw materials to fuel the factories to build those weapons and illuminate their streets come from. Notice how the continent of Africa is dark except for a few bright lights around South Africa. This picture tells the true story of what happened. Africa is needed to keep our lights burning brightly. The parts of Africa where the lights are brightest also had the largest concentration of whites.

This single image shows what historians have been arguing for years, that so few take the resources of so many. It is living proof that greed often drives capitalism. Beneath each light is safety on city streets, comfort inside homes, furnaces that run, and plumbing that flushes toilets. Electricity brings with it traffic lights, and city lights, night clubs with neon signs and thriving industrial areas. Electricity is life. Africa is dark. Why didn't the astronauts who took the picture sound the alarm? The truth is, they probably didn't see it, and that is Africa's dilemma in a nutshell.

This picture is the backdrop for thousands of network newscasts including CNN's 'The Situation Room'. (1) Despite that, few ever question the images they see. Africa's collapse is happening in front of our very eyes. We simply choose to see what we want to see, and ignore the human suffering that makes it all possible.

NASA City lights

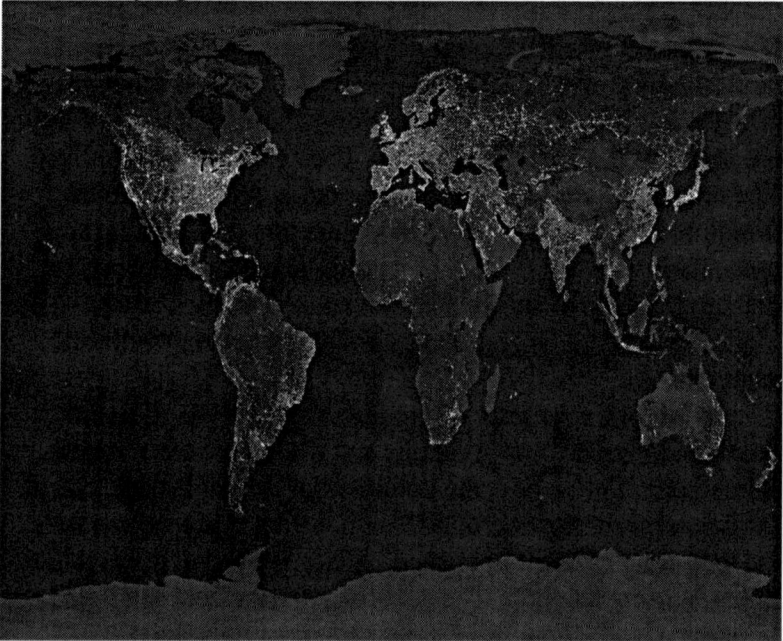

Notice the bright lights on the North American and European continents. Notice the darkness of the African continent.

Chapter Two

Birth Curse

"I was born on September 5th, 1957. That is the day my government declared war on my ancestors in Africa."

From the documentary: Apocalypse Africa Made in America

In my lifetime 20 million Africans have died from disease, starvation and war. By the time this book is published, that number will almost certainly rise. Imagine the horror, if you will, of learning that it all started on the day that you were born. Imagine learning that while you and your loved ones celebrated your birthday, the CIA and White House secretly set out to destroy the continent of your ancestors. Imagine growing up to be one of the few African Americans capable of uncovering the documents needed to set the record straight. Now, if you will, imagine that the ghosts of your ancestors were haunting you, demanding answers. There is but one question they might ask, why?

Wheeling, W.Va.

I was born on September 5th, 1957 in the small, mostly white, mostly working class, Northeastern industrial town of Wheeling, West Virginia. It was an unremarkable birth in an equally unremarkably city. It was the type of birth that history would have and should have ignored because most of the real news was taking place elsewhere...some of it a half a world away. Earlier that year, Jackie Robinson, the man who integrated baseball, announced he was retiring. It was big news for African Americans or Negroes as we were called back then. The other events somehow slipped under our conscious radar.

The other half of what was to become known as the Civil Rights/Pan African movement was taking shape on the other side of the Atlantic. They were two distinct movements, one involving us Negroes, while the other involved the Negroes we barely knew, Africans. Little did we know then, both had been targeted in a secret war that would claim millions of casualties, even though it was never declared.

In Africa, men like Patrice Lumumba of the Congo, tall and defiantly dark skinned with horn rimmed glasses that framed a stern face, and Kwame Nkrumah of Ghana, who was described by his contemporaries as brilliant, were the revolutionaries. They were also unsuspecting targets of the CIA. They were the men of vision that African historians dreamed they might one day compare to America's Jefferson, and Washington or Britain's Churchill. They were great men who looked out over the landscape of the African continent and demanded change. Those changes, which could not be obtained peacefully, they threatened to take by any means necessary, and that made them a threat to the most powerful country on the planet, America. Turning on the lights in Africa meant turning them off someplace else. Africa's time was over before it would begin. Lumumba, Nkrumah and the others went to their graves never knowing the truth.

Because these great men took their American educations back home to Africa to rebuild the continent they left behind, they were all the more dangerous. American educated Africans. Nkrumah studied at Lincoln University before going on to study the non-violent philosophy of Gandhi at the University of Pennsylvania. He envisioned an Africa that would more closely resemble today's European Union and saw an Africa where trading partners had sovereign borders. When combined, Africa would represent an economic juggernaut the world would have to take note of. Patrice Lumumba, on the other hand, lacked the formal training provided by degrees but made up for any short comings with cunning he gleaned from his European overseers. He knew what he wanted to do for the Congo and brought with him fiery rhetoric that left little doubt of his intentions. Both men, and a host of other African leaders, saw the U.S. as Africa's friend. That is where the comparisons between our revolution and Africa's, ends.

September 5th, 1957
Washington, D.C.

On September 5th, 1957, Dwight David Eisenhower was President, Richard Nixon was Vice President, and those who saw the world as their playground, were secretly hard at work. History would later record that on that day, the day of my birth, they were plotting to assassinate Patrice Lumumba and overthrow Kwame Nkrumah. How they did it has never fully been explained in part because so very few care. That they did it is not even the subject of debate. It is contained in great detail in thousands of documents. Those documents reveal that 1957 was a deadly year for Africa, in more than one way.

Sadly, for Africa, we were the British, and Africa's newly emerging heroes were already being marked for death. In secret meetings inside the White House, inside the CIA, and inside the highest ranks of government, their demise was being planned. However, there had to be a reason why. The answer was simple. They would be labeled as communists. The day was fast approaching when Nkrumah and Lumumba would be labeled as the African versions of Stalin and Lenin. That day happened on the day of my birth. On that day, Africa was on the move, and the world was at peace...or so it seemed. On September 5th, 1957 the country of my birth, declared war on the continent of my ancestors! The operation was code named, 'Project Wizard'!

1957, Hollywood

1957 was the same year that Tarzan exploded onto the scene across America in full color. A modern movie idol was about to be solidified, one that would become etched in the minds of every American for generations to follow. America could have chosen Nkrumah or Lumumba as the new face of Africa, but instead, it chose Tarzan...a white man, a European played by a German who could swim faster than alligators, out wrestle lions, and summon elephants with a blood curdling scream. America chose to paint an image of Africa as white, just as it did with Moses, Mary and Jesus. The image of Africa that would be painted would be one of a dysfunctional continent that haunts Africa today. In 1957, the year of my birth, America's image of Africa was solidified, and Africa was already starting to die. Between Eisenhower, Nixon and Tarzan, the continent didn't stand a chance. It was about to get worse.

September 5th, 1960

Three years later, on September 5th, 1960, the secret plot to destroy Africa was in high gear, even though it would be decades before anyone would learn the truth. 'Project Wizard' was the code name given to the CIA's plan to destabilize Patrice Lumumba's and his aspirations for the Congo. Hatched three years earlier on the exact day of my birth, there was now no turning back. Lumumba had been marked for death, the Congo marked for conquering, and Africans were collateral damage. That day, as I was blowing out the candles on my third birthday cake, with the CIA's assistance, Patrice Lumumba was jailed. Operatives, the documents would later reveal, had also set their sights on Kwame Nkrumah, who, by now, was expressing thoughts of paranoia, complaining of death threats, and telling others that the CIA wanted him dead. Other African leaders were also targets.

Tarzan was still in the theaters and I, like everyone else, was lining up to buy tickets. Patrice Lumumba was assassinated that January, but few paid attention. John F. Kennedy was elected and promising to send a man to the moon. Who cared about Africa? It was too far away, it was Africa, and after all, it didn't involve Tarzan. The United States was far from finished with Africa, and my 'birth curse' was about to grow more complicated.

On September 5th, 1964, my seventh birthday, the Unites States was secretly preparing to invade the Congo, by drawing up plans for one of the biggest military exercises in U.S. history. Lumumba was already dead, assassinated, but those still loyal to his cause needed to be crushed. Those rebels were holding a white missionary hostage, and there were fears the rebels would target all whites living in the country. Something had to be done. This time, the plan included the CIA, the United States Air force, and Belgium paratroopers. Because it would also become one of the biggest military cover-ups in history, the truth would remain secret for decades. When it was made public few if anyone, cared. The project, this time, was code named, "Operation Red Dragon." As for me, by now, I was swinging through the trees and beating my chest. I was becoming Tarzan.

A lot happened in the forty four years between that day and the day of my fiftieth birthday. Like most of my generation, I planned lavish celebrations, and secretly desired gaudy gifts. That was not to be. Instead forty-four years later on September 5th, 2008, I mourned the loss of twenty million lives. Lives lost on a continent where most of the people look like my aunts and uncles ... and me. Eisenhower is dead, as is Patrice Lumumba and Kwame Nkrumah. Lumumba was found tortured and burned beyond recognition, in a vat of sulfuric acid. The CIA was involved, but only on paper. No one ever confessed their sins. Richard Nixon became the most disgraced president in the history of the United States. Nkrumah died, still haunted by the demons placed in his brilliant mind by the CIA, and I became a journalist, a news anchor and an investigative reporter, working in Washington D.C. I was a journalist who made his living investigating past presidents. It was in that capacity that I came face to face with the man that the CIA sent to Africa to assassinate Patrice Lumumba. My life, and the

African Diaspora, was now one. As for Tarzan, he was on Broadway.

   Is it a 'birth curse' to have been born on the day when so much was taking place a half world away or just coincidence? Less clear are the consequences that so much coincidence brings with it. How can you claim to be an African American, and let the greatest crime of the 20th century go unexplored and unpunished? How do you turn your back on those who look most like you who die by the thousands daily? People ask me if this story is personal. I respond, "it is my destiny."

   I write this book because I am one of a few African American journalists bold enough to examine the government's secret files that expose the lies, corruption, and greed behind the destabilization of an entire continent. I write this story because I have to. Someone black has to defeat the myth of Tarzan.

Chapter Three

The Eight Stages of Genocide

"Classification: all cultures have categories to distinguish people into "us and them" by ethnicity, religion or nationality"

Gregory Stanton, President Genocide Watch:
The Eight Stages of Genocide

In 1996, Gregory Stanton presented his 'Eight Stages of Genocide' speech to the U.S. State Department. Stanton was seeking to explain how death in Africa occurred, specifically the senseless massacre of hundreds of thousands in Rwanda while the world watched and did little to stop the carnage. Stanton told those gathered that it didn't happen overnight and was instead the culmination of many factors. He argued that there are eight distinctive stages of genocide.

Stanton suggested that genocide is no accident and requires several carefully planned stages in order to occur. The stages, in order, are "classification, symbolization, dehumanization, organization, polarization, preparation, extermination, and denial."

As I was completing research for my documentary film, 'Apocalypse Africa, Made in America', I read Stanton's researched and realized those principles applied not just to Rwanda, but to Africa as a whole. We have classified Africa as a continent where "those people live" and, as was the case with the Jews or Gypsies, the name "African" carries with it a certain inescapable symbolism. Stanton goes onto say that groups subjected to genocide are dehumanized in writings and on the airwaves before being targeted by organizations set out

to destroy them. Like the Hutus and the Tutsis, African and
African Americans have been driven to think that there is
something "different," even though they, we, share a common
ancestry. The final stages need no explanation - preparation,
extermination and denial.

We are in a state of denial today when it comes to Africa. We deny that what we are seeing could've happened, or
have been caused by us, the industrialized, coffee drinking,
laptop using, and car driving world. We want to blame "them"
because it is easier than pointing the figure inward and examin-
ing the true causes behind Africa's collapse. We even debate
whether what has happened on the African continent, is indeed
genocide, even though millions have died during the debate. It
is as if they, the Africans, are to blame for killing themselves.

No, Africa was no accident. There is a cause, and an
effect, and a beginning, without an end. Just ask anyone if they
could name five countries in Africa, and then, when they have
given up, ask them to tell you the story of Tarzan. It is the
easiest example of dehumanization, cause and effect.

Chapter Four

Tarzan, King of the Jungle

Dehumanization: one group denies the humanity of the other group. At this stage ... hate propaganda is used to vilify the group!

Gregory Stanton, President Genocide Watch:
The Eight Stages of Genocide

I can remember, as a child, grabbing the rope we hastily tied around a tree that appeared sturdy enough to support both myself and the group I considered to be 'my gang'. I remember swinging without hesitation or fear to the next tree, landing on the branch, beating my chest, and screaming at the top of my lungs a horrid shriek that made me sound like an idiot. Actually, it made me sound like Tarzan. It mattered little that I was black and Tarzan was white, or that Tarzan made a living exploiting the people who looked more like me than anyone else on television, at the time. It mattered little that Tarzan made a living making my ancestors in Africa, and then me, look like idiots. I didn't care. I had chosen sides and I wanted to be on the side of the white man who could conquer an entire continent with a blood curdling scream that, I later learned, was actually yodeling...whatever that was.

After all, who wanted to be the Africans? They were pygmies with bones in their noses, who threw spears in the face of gunfire, got trampled by elephants and eaten by lions, all the while looking defenseless and stupid. No, I wanted to be like Tarzan, as did everyone other black child in my neighborhood. We wanted to be Tarzan, laugh at Cheetah, and, deep down, we desired Jane. The die was cast for me, my 'gang', and millions of other African American children like me, growing up in a 'Father knows best' white man's world. The die was also cast for Africa and none of us saw it coming.

I'm fifty now, and, as I mentioned in the opening pages of this book, in my lifetime, an estimated 20-25 million Africans have died from disease, starvation and war. Some say those numbers are conservative. They died while I lunched on 'Colonel Sanders' Kentucky Fried Chicken', or while I laughed at the antics of 'Buckwheat' and his gang of friends. They died through the fifties and sixties, and the seventies and eighties … of my life. They died through my childhood all the way through to my adulthood. They died while I laughed at Richard Pryor, Bill Cosby, Eddie Murphy … and now Tyler Perry. They died … while I laughed.

When I grew tired of Tarzan I embraced all things American. America had skyscrapers and fancy cars and history. Africa still had huts. America had Disneyland and Universal Studios where Tarzan had been replaced by Indiana Jones and the others who raided the tombs of my ancestors in the name of archeology. He was a descendent of Europeans and Europeans were educated. How was I supposed to know the difference? My ancestors came from Africa.

Even the biblical figures I would come to worship had their faces changed to reflect a culture that wanted everything about me, but not me. Wasn't Moses, Charlton Heston? They played his movie and others like it every Easter. They were movies that showed a white Jesus dying on a cross with white soldiers in darkened faces at his feet. Edward G. Robinson also played an Egyptian. Edward G. Robinson!

All I remember about Africa was death, disease and famine. As a result, it was easy to turn my back on a continent that never saw its destruction coming. Tarzan conquered the jungle without even firing a shot, and he conquered the minds of an entire generation of African Americans who beat their chests and wanted to be all things American. In the decades since little has changed. For proof, recently during a class I teach at Bowie State University, I showed one of the earlier Tarzan Movies and asked my students for their reaction. The class is all black. They watched, became bored, and then told me how 'technically' the movie was lacking. No one noticed that in the case of Tarzan, a single white man who ruled all of Africa, it seemed just a little out of the ordinary. Instead, they thought the movie was funny.

Recently I reviewed one of the scripts from a Tarzan movie and was stunned to see the way the Africans were described in writing. "Savages, half naked natives, stupid, cannibals," were just a few of the ways the Africans in the movies were described. The actors portraying those roles were asked to "mumble something in African'" as if black actors in Hollywood knew any African languages. Those languages were destroyed in slavery.

On page thirty of the script an Irishman named' O'doul' remarks that the natives look hungry. He jokingly adds he was hoping they were "vegetarians". One person in the group maintains they are "Zimbali." Instead another person his party remarks they are "Umbardi."

There is also the description of the 'Witch Doctor' in the script. He is described as holding a 'human thigh bone with a skull attached to it.' Hardly the type of person a western doctor would pattern himself after. There is no mention in the script of the many medical devices that originated in Africa long before 'the white man' arrived. Again, only savages. (2)

Prod # 4813

"TARZAN NO. 3"

filmed As "TARZAN'S SECRET TREASURE"

Due to the excessive expense of re-running entire
scripts merely in order to obtain consecutive page
numbers, the script with its changes will not be
re-run, but herewith in the front of the script you
will find a summary of the total number of pages
in the script.

dir: D. Richard Thorpe

MGM
5/20/41

Total number of pages in script,
including revisions to date,
and based on 62 lines per page: 117

Script completed 5/7/41

From. Myles Connolly
4/28/41

Script OK'd by.
Mr. B.P. Fineman

Tarzan No.3   30
Changes
7-15-41   120   WIDE ANGLE - JUNGLE AT OUTSKIRTS OF UBARDI
                VILLAGE

                Four white men with half a dozen blacks advance
                rapidly toward village which is already visible
                to them through trees. The maniacal uproar from
                the village grows in intensity and volume as they
                advance. Three of the men advance vigorously;
                the fourth, a slight, nervous man, timidly brings
                up the rear.

                The man in the lead is Medford, the guide - a
                white hunter who has lived in and off the jungle
                for years. On one side of him is Professor
                Elliott, a scientist, who heads the anthropolog-
                ical expedition.

                On Medford's other side is Baroni, a geologist,
                a cold-blooded realist with something of the
                manner of a professional soldier. The fourth man
                is O'Doul (pronounced O'Dool) an impish Dublin
                portrait photographer whose imagined love of ad-
                venture has brought him away from wife and home
                into a world he fears and despises.

         121   MED. CLOSE SHOT - EDGE OF WOODS AT VILLAGE

                The men come to a quick stop, stare tensely out
                at drama in village square.

                              Medford
                Juju.

                              O'Doul (scared)
                They're hungry-lookin' black divils. Is it - is it
                canninbals they are?

                              Baroni (to Medford)
                They look like Zimbali.

                              Medford (shakes his head)
                Worse! They're Ubardi!

                              O'Doul
                I was hopin' they'd be vegetarians!

         122   MED. LONG SHOT - VILLAGE SQUARE - FROM WHITE
                MEN'S ANGLE

                Through the pandemonium, a half dozen giant
                blacks carry a huge, wooden stake. The crowd
                opens for them, then closes around them.

Tarzan No. 3
Changes
5-21-41   123   MED. SHOT - WHITE MEN - AT EDGE OF WOODS   31

                              Elliott (staring ahead)
                    What is that, Medford?

                              Medford
                    A religious ceremony of some sort.

                              Baroni
                    We're in luck, Professor.
                              (to O'Doul)
                    Get your camera, O'Doul, and we'll take pictures
                    of it.

                              O'Doul
                    I'm all for movin' on. - I don't think we should
                    be interruptin' the h'athen in the performance of
                    his religious duties.

                         O'Doul starts back into woods. But a new
                         tumult from the village stops him. He
                         returns to group.

         123-X1   MED. SHOT - SQUARE - FROM WHITE MEN'S ANGLE

                         Tumult increases. Savages strap Boy to
                         stake but in confusion the action is not
                         clear to whites watching.

                              Elliott
                              (his hand going to gun on his hip)
                    It's some sort of human sacrifice!

                              Medford (restraining him)
                    Easy, Professor - this has been going on for
                    thousands of years and we're not going to change
                    it in five minutes.

                              Baroni (nods)
                    Right. Let's see it through to the finish.

                         Elliott's face suddenly goes taut with
                         horror. He takes a stride forward.

         124   MED. SHOT - SQUARE

                         The stake, with boy strapped to it, is
                         elevated and put in place.

                                        CONTINUED:

The 'Witch Doctor' mumbles something in African, according to the script, and arrives at a logical conclusion. The 'white boy' must be responsible for the mysterious death that is plaguing his village. Therefore the 'white devil' must be sacrificed to satisfy the gods

Little does he know hiding in the bush are the brave white men watching it all. At first they decide to do nothing. After all it is only a human sacrifice that is taking place. They chose not to get involved until they learn that the sacrifice is a *"White boy!"* Only then do they spring into action, doing whatever it takes to save one of their own. As long as the sacrifice involved Africans they were content to sit and watch. Only when the death involved someone white was action warranted.

Savages toss brush high around it. The witch
doctor takes a burning brand from altar, sets
fire to the edge of the brush.
Smoke billows up from fire as from green wood. The
blacks swing into a barbaric dance around stake.

124-X1   CLOSE SHOT - BOY

Seen through smoke. He's trying to be brave.

125   MED. CLOSE SHOT - WHITE MEN AT EDGE OF WOODS

Horror on all faces now.

                    Elliott (draws gun)
It's a white boy!

                    Medford (quickly)
Careful, Professor - they're crazy with juju.

                    Elliott (advances with drawn gun)
We can't stand by and watch this. Come on!

Baroni and Medford advance with Elliott, their
guns slung for action. Their advance weaves
through smoke blown from fire. O'Doul turns and
dashes back into woods. The blacks in party fade
with him.

126   FULL SHOT - ULANDI SQUARE

The savages dancing; smoke from fire over scene;
Boy, on stake, seen through smoke. Elliott and
Baroni rush to stake. Medford faces savages.

The natives, astonished by the sudden appear-
ance of the whites, abruptly halt in their
dance, stand motionless, stare. Their chant
dies away. For a moment, there is complete
silence. Then, the witch doctor recovers,
advances toward Medford with a threatening
gesture.

                    Medford (quickly - in dialect)
(We want the white boy. You cannot kill him.)

                    Witch Doctor (fiercely - in dialect)
(White boy is cause of plague. He must be sacrificed.)

A murmur of approval comes from savages.

As was the case in all Tarzan movies, the climax involves a battle between Tarzan and the natives. He has already killed a lion, a charging rhino and other smaller game, now it is on to the Negroes or, in this case, the natives. In each movie the scene is always the same. It is not enough for the natives simply to be dispatched; they must appear clumsy and oafish. Tarzan doesn't defeat the warriors of a great African nation. Instead he conquers a group of buffoons barely capable of throwing a spear. In the script I examined, afterwards they were eaten by alligators.

Tarzan #3
Change   378-X5
6/27/41
                                                                114

378-X5   LONG SHOT - CANOES DOWNSTREAM (AS SEEN
              BY TARZAN) (ALL THE CANOES HE HAVE)

              The savages are paddling wildly, their canoes
              bristling with spears.

378-X6   CLOSE SHOT - TARZAN

              He gives his call.

378-X7   WIDER ANGLE - THE CANOES NEAR TARZAN

              The savages are stunned a moment at Tarzan's
              sudden appearance and call. Several savages
              recover, hurl spears which fall short. The
              chief orders the canoes to drive toward Tarzan.
              They paddle wildly.

378-X8   FULL SHOT - ELEPHANTS GRAZING - (STOCK)

              Tarzan's call arouses them. They lumber off.

378-X8A   MED. CLOSE SHOT - BULI

              She hears Tarzan's call, heads into jungle.

378-X8B   ANOTHER ANGLE - JUNGLE

              Two small elephants graze. Buli charges in,
              trumpets. They join Buli, races off.

378-X9 -
378-X12   OUT.

378-X12A   CLOSE SHOT - O'DOUL AND TUMBO

              Tarzan's call OVER SCENE.

              They ride log downstream, on their bellies. At
              sound of Tarzan's call O'Doul excitedly stands
              up on log.

                        O'Doul (cries out)
              I'm comin', Mr. Tarzan! I'm on me way!

              As he cries he loses his balance, tips log.
              Tumbo and he are spilled into river.

378-X13   OUT.

119A

386X10H3   MED. CLOSE SHOT - CANOES

Chief shouts orders. A dozen natives leap into
water with drawn knives, submerge.

386X10H4   CLOSE SHOT - JANE

Her face is taut, strained.

386X10H5   CLOSE SHOT - TARZAN - UNDERWATER

He grapples natives who attack him, disposes
of two.

386X10H6   MED. SHOT - BOY SWIMMING

He nears scene of battle. He looks off, sub-
merges.

386X10H7   MED. SHOT - UNDERWATER

Tarzan disposes of two more natives as last
two attack him. Boy swims into b.g. Tarzan
is finishing off last two natives when a third
pops up, attacks him from rear. Boy swims up,
grabs native by hair. Tarzan turns and
finishes him off.

Tarzan and Boy swim swiftly away.

386X11   MED. SHOT - FLEET

Savages in uproar now. Jane's canoe is
suddenly capsized. All are spilled into water.

386X12   CLOSE SHOT - JANE

helpless, bound, she flounders in water.

386X13-
386X14   OUT

386X15   WIDER ANGLE - RIVER AT CANOES

Elephants attack. Natives now mill about in
complete panic.

```
Tarzan
No.3                                                              119B
Chg.          386X16        UNDERWATER SHOT - TARZAN AND BOY
7-1-41
                            Tarzan swims to Jane, draws her down, cut her
                            bonds.  Boy helps.  They swim off underwater.


              386X17        WIDE ANGLE - RIVER - FLASH OF GENERAL MELEE


              386X17A       A CANOE - MED. CLOSE SHOT

                            An elephant swims toward canoe.  Two natives in
                            canoe raise spears.  Elephant disappears under
                            water.


              386X17B       ANOTHER ANGLE - SAME CANOE

                            Canoe rises in water - elephant's back under-
                            neath it, canoe is tumbled from elephant's back
                            into water.


              386X17C       MED. SHOT - NATIVES IN WATER

                            Crocodiles seize them, drag them down into water.


              386X17D       MED. SHOT - THE THREE SMALL ELEPHANTS - SWIMMING
                            TOGETHER

                            They butt canoe, smashing it, and sending
                            natives spilling into water.

              386X18-       OUT
              386X22

              386X23        MED. CLOSE SHOT - O'DOUL AND TUMBO

                            in battle now.  Back on log, O'Doul stands,
                            balancing himself precariously.  Log moves
                            swiftly down toward a small canoe, manned by
                            two savages who stand with spears poised ready
                            for O'Doul.

                            One savage lets his spear go.  O'Doul ducks,
                            escaping spear but almost tumbling into water.
                            He recovers, brandishes his club in a new rage.

                                          O'Doul
                        Spear throwers, are ya!
                                   (snort)
                        Humph! - me gran'father used to use sticks like
                        them to pick his teeth with!          CONTINUED:
```

So today, as was the case then, who wanted to be African, especially if you grew up African American? To question America's motives would be un-American and to question

Tarzan was to question America. To question America would involve accusing the country of my birth with destroying the continent of my ancestors. It would involve accusing the United States of genocide for selling weapons to both sides in Africa, and then sitting idly by as they killed each other off. That would mean Tarzan was not just stupid, but evil.

In the moral argument about Africa there are no winners, only losers. Sadly, fifty years later, the ghosts of Africa's dead demand answers. They want to know how a generation of African Americans watched while millions who looked like them, ate like them and danced like them…died. They want to know whether we cared.

Tarzan is still swinging from tree to tree but many of the Africans, who were alive when he splashed into theaters, are dead. They died from the guns America sold them and from the diseases America and the rest of the world could have cured. They died because the medicines that would have saved their lives were either too expensive or never made their way to the various villages and cities. They died because small children, with big guns, stopped aid trucks from reaching their intended destination. They died because the roads that men like Lumumba and Nkrumah and others wanted to build, were never built. There are three thousand miles of roads in the entire nation of the Congo. It is one of richest nations in the world when it comes to natural resources and minerals. There are seventy thousand miles of roads in the state of Virginia alone.

How they died, is now there for the entire world to see. Tarzan, you see, had nothing to do with it. The CIA did.

Tarzan of the Jungle (3)

Chapter Five

Thou Shall Not Kill

Richard Helms ordered (me) to destroy all records of the tests he had run... of specific poisons, to be used in killing Lumumba...

CIA Scientist Dr. Sidney Gottlieb testifying in 1975
concerning illegal activities by the CIA

America prides itself as a nation of laws. We also believe that God is on our side no matter what...so much so; we make sure God's name is on our courts, our congress and on our money. In God we Trust. That is why as many as half of all Americans go to church each and every Sunday praying to the same God...during segregated services. They pray in black churches and in white churches and Hispanic and Asian churches, each and every week. Sunday at eleven o'clock has been called the most segregated hour in America. We confess our sins and then go about our everyday lives committing them over and over again. We kill in the name of God. We covet in the name of God and we certainly bear false witness when it suits our needs. We are one nation and many races, under God...deeply divided.

The most sacred of the Ten Commandments is 'Thou Shalt Not Kill." Most Americans can still hear the thunderous voice of Charlton Heston saying so in the movie version of the day God handed down his laws, 'The Ten Commandments.' Ironically, that same Charlton Heston went on to head the NRA, or National Rifle Association. Their motto differs from the Ten Commandments in the sense that they maintain how you are killed matters more than who does the killing. 'Guns don't kill people'. According to the NRA, 'people do'. It is much easier than trying to explain the fact that guns are responsible for most of the killing we will discuss in this book.

Despite our solemn pledge that we will not kill we do, and, some argue, better than any nation in history, especially in Africa, where we kill without consequence. On this, the record is clear, and dates back more than four decades. In 1961, John F. Kennedy, who described himself as a friend of Africa, had to deal with an embarrassing moment early on in his administration. It was discovered that bombs falling on Angola had 'Made in America' stamped on them.

The response was to caution the Portuguese, our allies, against using our bombs against their enemies in Africa. Already the water in Africa was being muddied.

August 20, 1961

NATIONAL SECURITY ACTION MEMORANDUM NO. 77

TO: Secretary of State
       Secretary of Defense

(SUBJECT: Use of American Made Arms in Angola)

I understand that we have cautioned the Portuguese
government against the use of American equipment in Portugal.
I also understand that a recent story in a London newspaper
reported the finding of a "Made in America" mark on part of
a bomb dropped on an Angolan village. This is going to present problems to us both in Angola and in Portugal. Have we
considered (1) whether we can be successful in persuading the
Portuguese of this, or (2) whether this will have an adverse
effect upon the use of the Azores base. I wonder if we should
perhaps content ourselves with a public statement in regard
to the matter.

/s/ John F. Kennedy

Information Copy to:

    The Director, USIA

                                        cc: Mr. Belk
                                             Mrs. Lincoln
                                             Mr. Bundy's file
                                             Mr. Bromley Smith
                                             NSC Files

But what happens when there is concrete proof America actually authorized the pulling of the trigger. In 1975 Americans learned that the President of the United States authorized the assassination of an African leader, and didn't blink an eye. There was outrage among reporters, but no trials. No investigations were ever launched and no one was ever charged. The man responsible died decades later a free man, on the eve of his grand jury testimony, and America never flinched. He died a national hero. I know. I was the last journalist to interview him.

His code name was *"Joe from Paris."* The man he targeted for assassination was the sovereign leader of an emerging nation. He had a name, Patrice Lumumba of the Congo. He had a wife and a small child. The American President who ordered his assassination was Dwight David Eisenhower. Like the others, Eisenhower died never having to explain his actions. Neither did *"Joe from Paris,"* the man that Eisenhower sent to do *'the deed.'* That is the man I met.

'Joe from Paris's' real name was Dr. Sidney Gottlieb. He was the head of the CIA's Technical Services Division, or TSD. They were the spies featured in the movies who came up with the neat gadgets…trick pens, and knives in shoes and the like. In 1960, *"Joe from Paris"* was dispatched to the Congo to poison Patrice Lumumba's toothpaste. Unlike a dime store spy novel, this was real. A real spy from a real country, our country, had been sent to kill the foreign leader of another. There was one other problem. It didn't work.

Evidently Sidney Gottlieb couldn't get close enough to Patrice Lumumba to carry out the assassination. Perhaps it had to do with the fact that he was white…in the Congo. When efforts failed, cables indicated Gottlieb requested a high powered rifle, a gun! That's where the trail gets murky.

Clearly, however, the CIA feared Lumumba enough to want him dead and a short time later, he was.

Dr. Sidney Gottlieb/former CIA Scientist
Joe from Paris"

As the following document taken from the CIA's own files reveals, the Agency feared Lumumba each and every time he opened his mouth. It was Lumumba's ability to rally those around him that made him so dangerous.

Despite hundreds of pages of documents to the contrary the CIA says they didn't do it, they didn't actually pull the trigger. In truth the agency never admits so, even when it is clear it did. Instead the Agency continues to blame anti-

Lumumba forces in the Congo, most of which were on the CIA's payroll.

The Belgians, who had a sordid history of mass murder and mutilation in the Congo, say they didn't do it either, and pointed an indicting finger in the direction of those same rebels. In the end, however, Lumumba was killed. Both sides were complicit and both sides got away with killing Lumumba because, to put it mildly, no one cared. (In 2002 Belgium apologized for its role in Lumumba's assassination...but details are still are lacking). (4)

Lumumba's badly beaten body was burned beyond recognition in a vat of sulfuric acid. He died three days before the inauguration of President John F. Kennedy. There are reports that the assassination was hidden from the incoming administration for fear President-elect Kennedy would try to stop it. There are also reports that when John F. Kennedy learned of Lumumba's assassination he buried his head in his hands and wept. Neither report has been proven, few even cared.

Fifty years after the death of Patrice Lumumba no one knows why the US wanted him dead. Worst still few, if any, ever asked. Aside from Tarzan, Americans know little about The Congo, or Patrice Lumumba, or the fact that *we*, the United States, sent a man to assassinate Africa's equivalent of George Washington, or Thomas Jefferson, or Benjamin Franklin.

Lumumba was elected riding a wave of post colonial optimism that Africa's long nightmare had ended, and the shackles of slavery and colonialism had finally been broken. His story, however, remains largely untold. Sadly Africans don't write about Lumumba the way we write about Washington, or Jefferson, or Adams, because, fifty years later, they still don't know the truth. The one nation capable of providing that truth feels no inclination to do so. There are no 'Truth and Reconciliation Hearings' in America. Instead our sins remain buried in the thousands of pages of unread documents inside the nation's archives. Instead the signal that is given over and over again by our acquiescence is that: *"It is okay to kill Africans!"*

If you challenge that assertion or find it insulting you need only to sit through any movie that is set in Africa, about Africa, or references Africa. Sit in any theater and hear that line uttered over and over again. *"It's okay to kill. It's only Africa!"* Be it a film about blood diamonds, or corrupt pharmaceutical corporations gone awry, death in Africa, from Patrice Lumumba on down, has become acceptable. How else can you explain the deaths, the disease and the endless starvation? How else can you explain the fact that so many Africans die from diseases that have been cured for decades? How else can you explain the fact that so many Africans starve when American farmers are paid *not to grow* the crops that might save their lives.

The death of Patrice Lumumba is more than just a political assassination. Lumumba's death represents the end of a spectrum. If it is okay to kill the leader then killing the subjects must be okay as well. If no one investigates the death of the president then who will investigate the deaths of the masses? Africans die each and every day, their bodies tossed into shallow graves, unknown to the rest of the world. There are no 'Amber Alerts' for missing African children. They just die. Unlike other atrocities they do not even merit the dignity of a number.

It took the deaths of 6 million Jews before the world said *'never again'*. In Africa, the bodies are still being counted.

That is why the Ten Commandments work every-where...except Africa. *Thou shalt not kill....except in Africa. It is okay to kill Africans!"*

Patrice Lumumba (5)

Patrice Lumumba (5)

Chapter Six

Anatomy Of An Assassination

*"Assassination is an extreme measure not
normally used in clandestine operations. It should be assumed
that it will never be ordered or authorized by any U.S. Headquarters...No assassination instructions should ever be
written or recorded."*

From the CIA's Assassination manual

We should not kid ourselves. People have been assassinated in
Africa and our government; the government of the United
States pulled the trigger. It doesn't matter if we actually did
"the deed," dead is dead. A mother will no longer come home
to her children. The children will grow up orphaned and abused
in internment camps across Africa. A father suddenly disap-
pears leaving behind a child who wastes his or her life searching for answers. A powerful black man will feel powerless
because his government could not protect him, while white
governments flourished. Mothers, fathers, sisters, brothers,
aunts, uncles, cousins all are no more. Family units are broken
never to be repaired. We sent the "Joe from Paris's" to Africa
with the poison and, when that didn't work, we sent the guns.
When that didn't work we sent in the troops and, when that
didn't work, we watched as the Africans killed themselves.
Still, despite all of that, there are those who foolishly believe
that Africa should bear the brunt of the blame for what happened to Africa. Perhaps the following piece of information
might sway you.

Chapter Seven

PB Success

*Operation PBSUCCESS ... included in that
document cache, a paper entitled,
A Study of Assassination.*

The CIA's Assassination manual

Operation PBSUCCESS is proof that the CIA not only wanted
to kill political leaders but went so far as to print and publish
an 'Assassination Manual' explaining how it should all be
done. PBSUCCESS was authorized by President Dwight
David Eisenhower. Eisenhower is the same president that
signed off on the assassination of Patrice Lumumba by sending
'Joe from Paris' to the Congo. Keep in mind as you read these
accounts, Richard Nixon was Eisenhower's Vice President and
knew everything.

Eisenhower spent $2.7 million on 'psychological war-
fare and political action' and on 'subversion.' The target of
Operation PBSUCCESS was Guatemala's president, Arbenz. A
man the CIA believed held court over a "Banana Republic."
According to published reports, the option of assassination was
still being considered up to and until the day that Arbenz
resigned on June 27th, 1954. In the case of Arbenz, he got
away. He and his top aides were able to flee the country after
the CIA helped install its man, Castillo Armas. But what
happened next will seem vaguely familiar to those who have
studied the case of the collapse of Africa

In the days and weeks that followed hundreds of Gua-
temalans were rounded up and killed. According to human

rights observers as many as 100,000 civilians were murdered. That pattern will emerge over and over again in this book. First the elite are killed. The doctors, lawyers, politicians, artists and educators die first. They are the ones who would write the newspaper editorials, rally the nation and lead the underground. They are always killed first. When they die dissent dies with them. When the masses die there is no one left to protest, just to run and hope to survive. That pattern continues to this day. The question that needs to be asked is whether there is blood on America's hands as so many have argued. On that point the record leaves little doubt.

A study of Assassination

If the assassin is to die with the subject, the act will be called "lost." If the assassin is to escape, the adjective will be "safe." It should be noted that no compromises should exist here. The assassin must not fall alive into enemy hands."

From the CIA assassination manual

In 1997, the CIA released 1400 of an estimated 100,000 pages of secret documents outlining Operation PBSUCCESS. Included in that document cache, a paper entitled, 'A Study of Assassination', and the agency's own 'Assassination Manual.' The manual is a how to guide to killing and leaves little to the imagination. We begin with the agency's definition of assassination. "It is here used to describe the planned killing of a person who is not under the legal jurisdiction of the killer, who is not physically in the hands of the killer, who has been selected by a resistance organization for death, and who has been selected by a resistance organization for death, and whose death provides positive advantages to that organization."

The manual also makes it clear that the reason the world knows little about who the agency has targeted for assassination is because that, quite simply, that would be stupid. "Assassination is an extreme measure not normally used in clandestine operations. It should be assumed that it will never be ordered or authorized by any U.S. Headquarters, though the latter may in rare instances agree to its execution by members of an associated foreign service. This reticence is partly due to the necessity for committing communications to paper. No assassination instructions should ever be written or recorded."

PBSUCCESS also provides rare insight into the importance of Dr. Sidney Gottlieb, or "Joe from Paris," the man the agency sent to assassinate Patrice Lumumba of the Congo. The fact that Gottlieb was allowed to live, points out how important he was. It also points out how important Patrice Lumumba was to President Eisenhower and the CIA. He was so crucial that they would send one of their top guys to the Congo to kill him. This is what the assassination manual had to say about whether the assassin would live or die. "Assassinations in which the subject is unaware will be termed "simple"; those where the subject is aware but unguarded will be termed "chase"; those where the victim is guarded will be termed "guarded."

If the assassin is to die with the subject, the act will be called "lost." If the assassin is to escape, the adjective will be "safe." "It should be noted that no compromises should exist here. The assassin must not fall alive into enemy hands."

Now that we know the Agency ordered assassinations, and made sure it would never get caught, the only question that remains, is, how they did it. There the document reveals there was an endless series of scenarios and plans to carry out the Agencies deadliest "deeds." Everything from causing an "accidental fall" from a tall building, to killing a person with "bare hands," to the more traditional, "guns and explosives." The document contains diagrams and provides details as to which weapons work best.

PLANNING

When the decision to assassinate has been reached, the tactics of the operation must be planned, based upon an estimate of the situation similar to that used in military operations.

The preliminary estimate will reveal gaps in information and possibly indicate a need for special equipment which must be procured or constructed. When all necessary data has been collected, an effective tactical plan can be prepared. All planning must be mental; no papers should ever contain evidence of the operation.

In resistance situations, assassination may be used as a counter-reprisal. Since this requires advertising to be effective, the resistance organization must be in a position to warn high officials publicly that their lives will be the price of reprisal action against innocent people. Such a threat is of no value unless it can be carried out, so it may be necessary to plan the assassination of various responsible officers of the oppressive regime and hold such plans in readiness to be used only if provoked by excessive brutality. Such plans must be modified frequently to meet changes in the tactical situation.

TECHNIQUES

The essential point of assassination is the death of the subject. A human being may be killed in many ways but sureness is often overlooked by those who may be emotionally unstrung by the seriousness of this act they intend to commit. The specific technique employed will depend upon a large number of variables, but should be constant in one point: Death must be absolutely certain. The attempt on Hitler's life failed because the conspiracy did not give this matter proper attention.

Techniques may be considered as follows:

1. Manual.

It is possible to kill a man with the bare hands, but very few are skillful enough to do it well. Even a highly trained Judo expert will hesitate to risk killing by hand unless he has absolutely no alternative. However, the simplest local tools are often much the most efficient means of assassination. A hammer, axe, wrench, screw driver, fire poker, kitchen knife, lamp stand, or anything hard, heavy and handy will suffice. A length of rope or wire or a belt will do if the assassin is strong and agile. All such improvised weapons have the important advantage of availability and apparent innocence. The obviously lethal machine gun failed to kill Trotsky where an item of sporting goods succeeded.

In all safe cases where the assassin may be subject to search, either before or after the act, specialized weapons should not be used. Even in the lost case, the assassin may accidentally be searched before the act and should not carry an incriminating device if any sort of lethal weapon can be improvised at or near the site. If the assassin normally carries weapons because of the nature of his job, it may still be desirable to improvise and implement at the scene to avoid disclosure of his identity.

2. Accidents.

For secret assassination, either simple or chase, the contrived accident is the most effective technique. When successfully executed, it causes little excitement and is only casually investigated.

The most efficient accident, in simple assassination, is a fall of 75 feet or more onto a hard surface. Elevator shafts, stair wells, unscreened windows and bridges will serve. Bridge falls into water are not reliable. In simple cases a private meeting with the subject may be arranged at a properly-cased location. The act may be executed by sudden, vigorous [excised] of the ankles, tipping the subject over the edge. If the assassin immediately sets up an outcry, playing the "horrified witness", no alibi or surreptitious withdrawal is necessary. In chase cases it will usually be necessary to stun or drug the subject before dropping him. Care is required to insure that no wound or condition not attributable to the fall is discernible after death.

Falls into the sea or swiftly flowing rivers may suffice if the subject cannot swim. It will be more reliable if the assassin can arrange to attempt rescue, as he can thus be sure of the subject's death and at the same time establish a workable alibi.

If the subject's personal habits make it feasible, alcohol may be used [2 words excised] to prepare him for a contrived accident of any kind.

Falls before trains or subway cars are usually effective, but require exact timing and can seldom be free from unexpected observation.

Automobile accidents are a less satisfactory means of assassination. If the subject is deliberately run down, very exact timing is necessary and investigation is likely to be thorough. If the subject's car is tampered with, reliability is very lo w. The subject may be stunned or drugged and then placed in the car, but this is only reliable when the car can be run off a high cliff or into deep water without observation.

Arson can cause accidental death if the subject is drugged and left in a burning building. Reliability is not satisfactory unless the building is isolated and highly combustible.

3. Drugs.

In all types of assassination except terroristic, drugs can be very effective. If the assassin is trained as a doctor or nurse and the subject is under medical care, this is an easy and rare method. An overdose of morphine administered as a sedative will cause death without disturbance and is difficult to detect. The size of the dose will depend upon whether the subject has been using narcotics regularly. If not, two grains will suffice.

If the subject drinks heavily, morphine or a similar narcotic can be injected at the passing out stage, and the cause of death will often be held to be acute alcoholism.

Specific poisons, such as arsenic or strychine, are effective but their possession or procurement is incriminating, and accurate dosage is problematical. Poison was used unsuccessfully in the assassination of Rasputin and Kolohan, though the latte r case is more accurately described as a murder.

4. Edge Weapons

Any locally obtained edge device may be successfully employed. A certain minimum of anatomical knowledge is needed for reliability.

Puncture wounds of the body cavity may not be reliable unless the heart is reached. The heart is protected by the rib cage and is not always easy to locate.

Abdominal wounds were once nearly always mortal, but modern medical treatment has made this no longer true.

Absolute reliability is obtained by severing the spinal cord in the cervical region. This can be done with the point of a knife or a light blow of an axe or hatchet.

Another reliable method is the severing of both jugular and carotid blood vessels on both sides of the windpipe.

If the subject has been rendered unconscious by other wounds or drugs, either of the above methods can be used to insure death.

5. Blunt Weapons

As with edge weapons, blunt weapons require some anatomical knowledge for effective use. Their main advantage is their universal availability. A hammer may be picked up almost anywhere in the world. Baseball and [illeg] bats are very widely distributed. Even a rock or a heavy stick will do, and nothing resembling a weapon need be procured, carried or subsequently disposed of.

Blows should be directed to the temple, the area just below and behind the ear, and the lower, rear portion of the skull. Of course, if the blow is very heavy, any portion of the upper skull will do. The lower frontal portion of the head, from the eyes to the throat, can withstand enormous blows without fatal consequences.

6. Firearms

Firearms are often used in assassination, often very ineffectively. The assassin usually has insufficient technical knowledge of the limitations of weapons, and expects more range, accuracy and killing power than can be provided with reliability. Since certainty of death is the major requirement, firearms should be used which can provide destructive power at least 100% in excess of that thought to be necessary, and ranges should be half that considered practical for the weapon.

Firearms have other drawbacks. Their possession is often incriminating. They may be difficult to obtain. They require a degree of experience from the user. They are [illeg]. Their [illeg] is consistently over-rated.

However, there are many cases in which firearms are probably more efficient than any other means. These cases usually involve distance between the assassin and the subject, or comparative physical weakness of the assassin, as with a woman.

(a) The precision rifle. In guarded assassination, a good hunting or target rifle should always be considered as a possibility. Absolute reliability can nearly always be achieved at a distance of one hundred yards. In ideal circumstances, t he range may be extended to 250 yards. The rifle should be a well made bolt or falling block action type, handling a powerful long-range cartridge. The .300 F.A.B. Magnum is probably the best cartridge readily available. Other excellent calibers are. 375 M.[illeg]. Magnum, .270 Winchester, .30 - 106 p.s., 8 x 60 MM Magnum, 9.3 x

62 kk and others of this type. These are preferable to ordinary military calibers, since ammunition available for them is usually of the expanding bullet type, whereas most ammunition for military rifles is full jacketed and hence not sufficiently lethal. Military ammunition should not be altered by filing or drilling bullets, as this will adversely affect accuracy.

The rifle may be of the "bull gun" variety, with extra heavy barrel and set triggers, but in any case should be capable of maximum precision. Ideally, the weapon should be able to group in one inch at one hundred yards, but 21/2" groups are adequate. The sight should be telescopic, not only for accuracy, but because such a sight is much better in dim light or near darkness. As long as the bare outline of the target is discernable, a telescope sight will work, even if the rifle and shooter are in total darkness.

An expanding, hunting bullet of such calibers as described above will produce extravagant laceration and shock at short or mid-range. If a man is struck just once in the body cavity, his death is almost entirely certain.

Public figures or guarded officials may be killed with great reliability and some safety if a firing point can be established prior to an official occasion. The propaganda value of this system may be very high.

(b) The machine gun.

Machine guns may be used in most cases where the precision rifle is applicable. Usually, this will require the subversion of a unit of an official guard at a ceremony, though a skillful and determined team might conceivably dispose of a loyal gun crow without commotion and take over the gun at the critical time.

The area fire capacity of the machine gun should not be used to search out a concealed subject. This was tried with predictable lack of success on Trotsky. The automatic feature of the machine gun should rather be used to increase reliability by placing a 5 second burst on the subject. Even with full jacket ammunition, this will be absolute lethal is the burst pattern is no larger than a man. This can be accomplished at about 150 yards. In ideal circumstances, a properly padded and targeted ma chine gun can do it at 850 yards. The major difficulty is placing the first burst exactly on the target, as most machine gunners are trained to spot their fire on target by observation of strike. This will not do in assassination as the subject will not wait.

(c) The Submachine Gun.

This weapon, known as the "machine-pistol" by the Russians and Germans and "machine-carbine" by the British, is occasionally useful in assassination. Unlike the rifle and machine gun, this is a short range weapon and since it fires pistol ammunition, much less powerful. To be reliable, it should deliver at least 5 rounds into the subject's chest, though the .45 caliber U.S. weapons have a much larger margin of killing efficiency than the 9 mm European arms.

The assassination range of the sub-machine gun is point blank. While accurate single rounds can be delivered by sub-machine gunners at 50 yards or more, this is not certain enough for assassination. Under ordinary circumstances, the 5MG should be used as a fully automatic weapon. In the hands of a capable gunner, a high cyclic rate is a distinct advantage, as speed of execution is most desirable, particularly in the case of multiple subjects.

The sub-machine gun is especially adapted to indoor work when more than one subject is to be assassinated. An effective technique has been devised for the use of a pair of sub-machine gunners, by which a room containing as many as a dozen subjects can be "purifico" in about twenty seconds with little or no risk to the gunners. It is illustrated below.

While the U.S. sub-machine guns fire the most lethal cartridges, the higher cyclic rate of some foreign weapons enable the gunner to cover a target quicker with acceptable pattern density. The Bergmann Model 1934 is particularly good in this way. The Danish Madman? SMG has a moderately good cyclic rate and is admirably compact and concealable. The Russian SHG's have a good cyclic rate, but are handicapped by a small, light protective which requires more kits for equivalent killing effect.

(d) The Shotgun.

A large bore shotgun is a most effective killing instrument as long as the range is kept under ten yards. It should normally be used only on single targets as it cannot sustain fire successfully. The barrel may be "sawed" off for convenience, but this is not a significant factor in its killing performance. Its optimum range is just out of reach of the subject. 00 buckshot is considered the best shot size for a twelve gage gun, but anything from single balls to bird shot will do if the range is right. The assassin should aim for the solar plexus as the shot pattern is small at close range and can easily [illeg] the head.

(e) The Pistol.

While the handgun is quite inefficient as a weapon of assassination, it is often used, partly because it is readily available and can be concealed on the person, and partly because its limitations are not widely appreciated. While many well known assassinations have been carried out with pistols (Lincoln, Harding, Ghandi), such attempts fail as often as they succeed, (Truman, Roosevelt, Churchill).

If a pistol is used, it should be as powerful as possible and fired from just beyond reach. The pistol and the shotgun are used in similar tactical situations, except that the shotgun is much more lethal and the pistol is much more easily concealed.

In the hands of an expert, a powerful pistol is quite deadly, but such experts are rare and not usually available for assassination missions.

.45 Colt, .44 Special, .455 Kly, .45 A.S.[illeg] (U.S. Service) and .357 Magnum are all efficient calibers. Less powerful rounds can suffice but are less reliable. Sub-power cartridges such as the .32s and .25s should be avoided.

In all cases, the subject should be hit solidly at least three times for complete reliability.

(f) Silent Firearms

The sound of the explosion of the proponent in a fire-arm can be effectively silenced by appropriate attachments. However, the sound of the projective passing through the air cannot, since this sound is generated outside the weapon. In cases w here the velocity of the bullet greatly exceeds that of sound, the noise so generated is much louder than that of the explosion. Since all powerful rifles have muzzle velocities of over 2000 feet per second, they cannot be silenced.

Pistol bullets, on the other hand, usually travel slower than sound and the sound of their flight is negligible. Therefore, pistols, submachine guns and any sort of improvised carbine or rifle which will take a low velocity cartridge can be silenced. The user should not forget that the sound of the operation of a repeating action is considerable, and that the sound of bullet strike, particularly in bone is quite loud.

Silent firearms are only occasionally useful to the assassin, though they have been widely publicized in this connection. Because permissible velocity is low, effective precision range is held to about 100 yards with rifle or carbine type weapons, while with pistols, silent or otherwise, are most efficient just beyond arms length. The silent feature attempts to provide a degree of safety to the assassin, but mere possession of a silent firearm is likely to create enough hazards to counter the advantage of its silence. The silent pistol combines the disadvantages of any pistol with the added one of its obviously clandestine purpose.

A telescopically sighted, closed-action carbine shooting a low velocity bullet of great weight, and built for accuracy, could be very useful to an assassin in certain situations. At the time of writing, no such weapon is known to exist.

7. Explosives.

Bombs and demolition charges of various sorts have been used frequently in assassination. Such devices, in terroristic and open assassination, can provide safety and overcome guard barriers, but it is curious that bombs have often been the implement of lost assassinations.

The major factor which affects reliability is the use of explosives for assassination. The charge must be very large and the detonation must be controlled exactly as to time by the assassin who can observe the subject. A small or moderate explosive charge is highly unreliable as a cause of death, and

time delay or booby-trap devices are extremely prone to kill the
wrong man. In addition to the moral aspects of indiscriminate
killing, the death of casual bystanders can often produce public
reactions unfavorable to the cause for which the assassination
is carried out.

Bombs or grenades should never be thrown at a subject.
While this will always cause a commotion and may even result
in the subject's death, it is sloppy, unreliable, and bad propaganda. The charge must be too small and the assassin is never
sure of: (1) reaching his attack position, (2) placing the charge
close enough to the target and (3) firing the charge at the right
time.

Placing the charge surreptitiously in advance permits a
charge of proper size to be employed, but requires accurate
prediction of the subject's movements.

Ten pounds of high explosive should normally be regarded as a minimum, and this is explosive of fragmentation
material. The latter can consist of any hard, [illeg] material as
long as the fragments are large enough. Metal or rock fragments should be walnut-size rather than pen-size. If solid plates
are used, to be ruptured by the explosion, cast iron, 1" thick,
gives excellent fragmentation. Military or commercial high
explosives are practical for use in assassination. Homemade or
improvised explosives should be avoided. While possibly
powerful, they tend to be dangerous and unreliable. Anti-
personnel explosive missiles are excellent, provided the
assassin has sufficient technical knowledge to fuse them
properly. 81 or 82 mm mortar shells, or the 120 mm mortar
shell, are particularly good. Anti-personnel shells for 85, 88,
90, 100 and 105 mm guns and howitzers are both large enough
to be completely reliable and small enough to be carried by one
man.

The charge should be so placed that the subject is not
ever six feet from it at the moment of detonation.

A large, shaped charge with the [illeg] filled with iron fragments (such as 1" nuts and bolts) will fire a highly lethal shotgun-type [illeg] to 50 yards. This reaction has not been thoroughly tested, however, and an exact replica of the proposed device should be fired in advance to determine exact range, pattern-size, and penetration of fragments. Fragments should penetrate at least 1" of seasoned pine or equivalent for minimum reliability. Any firing device may be used which permits exact control by the assassin. An ordinary commercial or military explorer is efficient, as long as it is rigged for instantaneous action with no time fuse in the system. The wise [illeg] electric target can serve as the triggering device and provide exact timing from as far away as the assassin can reliably hit the target. This will avoid the disadvantages of commercial high explosives are practical for use in assassination. Homemade or improvised explosives should be avoided. While possibly powerful, they tend to be dangerous and unreliable. Anti-personnel explosive missiles are excellent, provided the assassin has sufficient technical knowledge to fuse them properly. 81 or 82 mm mortar shells, or the 120 mm mortar shell, are particularly good. Anti-personnel shells for 85, 88, 90, 100 and 105 mm guns and howitzers are both large enough to be completely reliable and small enough to be carried by one man.

The charge should be so placed that the subject is not ever six feet from it at the moment of detonation.

A large, shaped charge with the [illeg] filled with iron fragments (such as 1" nuts and bolts) will fire a highly lethal shotgun-type [illeg] to 50 yards. This reaction has not been thoroughly tested, however, and an exact replica of the proposed device should be fired in advance to determine exact range, pattern-size, and penetration of fragments. Fragments should penetrate at least 1" of seasoned pine or equivalent for minimum reliability.

Any firing device may be used which permits exact control by the assassin. An ordinary commercial or military explorer is efficient, as long as it is rigged for instantaneous action with no time fuse in the system.

The wise [illeg] electric target can serve as the triggering device and provide exact timing from as far away as the assassin can reliably hit the target. This will avid the disadvantages of stringing wire between the proposed positions of the assassin and the subject, and also permit the assassin to fire the charge from a variety of possible positions.

The radio switch can be [illeg] to fire [illeg], though its reliability is somewhat lower and its procurement may not be easy.

CONFERENCE ROOM TECHNIQUE

1.

(1) Enters room quickly but quietly
(2) Stands in doorway 2.

2.

(1) Opens fire on first subject to react. Swings across group toward center of mass. Times burst to empty magazine at end of swing.
(2) Covers group to prevent individual dangerous reactions, if necessary, fires individual bursts of 3 rounds.

3.

(2) Finishes burst. Commands"Shift." Drops back thru [sic] door. Replaces empty magazine. Covers corridor.
(1) On command "shift", opens fire on opposite side of target, swings one burst across group.

4.

(1) Finishes burst. Commands "shift". Drops back thru [sic] door. Replaces magazine. Covers corridor.
(2) On command, "shift", re-enters room. Covers group: kills survivors with two-round bursts. Leaves propaganda.

5.

(2) Leaves room. Commands "GO". Covers rear with nearly full magazine.
(1) On command "GO", leads withdrawal, covering front with full magazine.

6.
CONFERENCE ROOM TECHNIQUE

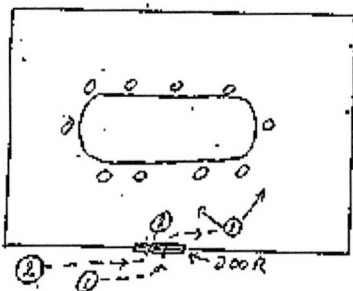

(1) Enters room quickly but quietly

(2) Stands in doorway

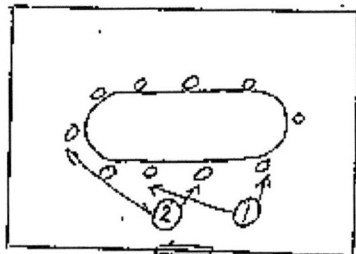

(2) Opens fire on first subject to react. Swings across group toward center of mass. Times burst to empty magazine at end of swing.

(1) Covers group to prevent individual dangerous reactions, if necessary, fires individual bursts of 3 rounds.

3.

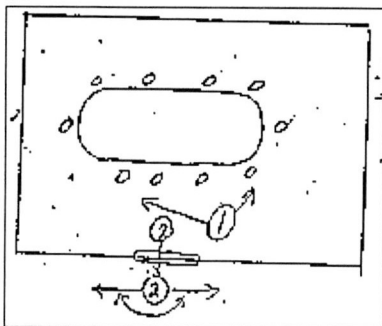

4.

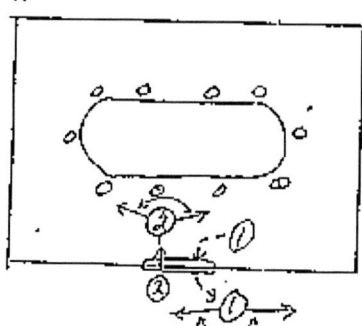

(2) Finishes burst. Commands"Shift." Drops back thru [sic] door. Replaces empty magazine. Covers corridor.

(1) On command "shift", opens fire on opposite side of target, swings one burst across group.

(1) Finishes burst. Commands "shift". Drops back thru [sic] door. Replaces magazine. Covers corridor.

(2) On command, "shift", re-enters room. Covers group: kills survivors with two-round bursts. Leaves propaganda.

5.

6.

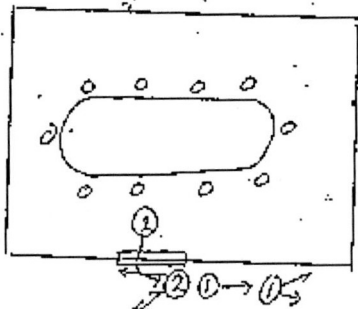

(2) Leaves room. Commands "GO". Covers rear with nearly full magazine.

(1) On command "GO", leads withdrawal, covering front with full magazine.

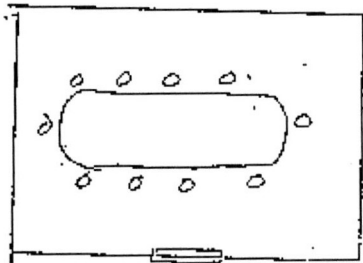

Actual Documents from CIA assassination manual

A STUDY OF ASSASSINATION

DEFINITION

Assassination is a term thought to be derived from "Hashish", a drug similar to marijuana, said to have been used by Hassan-Dan-Sabah to induce motivation in his followers, who were assigned to carry out political and other murders, usually at the cost of their lives.

It is here used to describe the planned killing of a person who is not under the legal jurisdiction of the killer, who is not physically in the hands of the killer, who has been selected by a resistance organization for death, and whose death provides positive advantages to that organization.

EMPLOYMENT

Assassination is an extreme measure not normally used in clandestine operations. It should be assumed that it will never be ordered or authorized by any U. S. Headquarters, though the latter may in rare instances agree to its execution by members of an associated foreign service. This reticence is partly due to the necessity for committing communications to paper. No assassination instructions should ever be written or recorded. Consequently, the decision to employ this technique must nearly always be reached in the field, at the area where the act will take place. Decision and instructions should be confined to an absolute minimum of persons. Ideally, only one person will be involved. No report may be made, but usually the act will be properly covered by normal news services, whose output is available to all concerned.

JUSTIFICATION

Murder is not morally justifiable. Self-defense may be argued if the victim had knowledge which may destroy the resistance organization if divulged. Assassination of persons responsible for atrocities or reprisals may be regarded as just punishment. Killing a political leader whose burgeoning career is a clear and present danger to the cause of freedom may be held necessary.

But assassination can seldom be employed with a clear conscience. Persons who are morally squeamish should not attempt it.

CLASSIFICATIONS

The techniques employed will vary according to whether the subject is unaware of his danger, aware but unguarded, or guarded. They will also be affected by whether or not the assassin is to be killed with the subject hereafter. assassinations in which the subject is unaware will be termed "simple"; those where the subject is aware but unguarded will be termed "chase"; those where the victim is guarded will be termed "guarded."

If the assassin is to die with the subject, the act will be called "lost." If the assassin is to escape, the adjective will be "safe." It should be noted that no compromise should exist here. The assassin must not fall alive into enemy hands.

A further type division is caused by the need to conceal the fact that the subject was actually the victim of assassination, rather than an accident or natural causes. If such concealment is desirable the operation will be called "secret"; if concealment is immaterial, the act will be called "open"; while if the assassination requires publicity to be effective it will be termed "terroristic."

Following these definitions, the assassination of Julius Caesar was safe, simple, and terroristic, while that of Huey Long was lost, guarded and open. Obviously, successful secret assassinations are not recorded as assassination at all. Chanda of Thailand and Augustus, Caesar may have been the victims of safe, guarded and secret assassination. These assassinations usually involve clandestine agents or members of criminal organizations.

THE ASSASSIN

In safe assassinations, the assassin needs the usual qualities of a clandestine agent. He should be determined, courageous, intelligent, resourceful, and physically active. If special equipment is to be used, such as firearms or drugs, it is clear that he must have outstanding skill with such equipment.

Except in terroristic assassinations, it is desirable that the assassin be a transient in the area. He should have an absolute minimum of contact with the rest of the organization, and his instructions should be given orally by one person only. His safe evacuation after the act is absolutely essential, but here again contact should be as limited as possible. It is preferable that the person issuing instructions also conduct any withdrawal or covering action which may be necessary.

In lost assassination, the assassin must be a fanatic of some sort. Politics, religion, and revenge are about the only feasible motives. Since a fanatic is unstable psychologically, he must be handled with extreme care. He must not know the identities of the other members of the organization, for although it is intended that he die in the act, something may go wrong. While the Assassin of Trotsky has never revealed any significant information, it was unsound to depend on this when the act was planned.

PLANNING

When the decision to assassinate has been reached, the tactics of the operation must be planned, based upon an estimate of the situation similar to that used in military operations. The preliminary estimate will reveal gaps in information and possibly indicate a need for special equipment which must be procured or constructed. When all necessary data has been collected, an effective tactical plan can be prepared. All planning must be mental; no papers should ever contain evidence of the operation.

In resistance situations, assassination may be used as a counter-reprisal. Since this requires advertising to be effective, the resistance organization must be in a position to warn high officials publicly that their lives will be the price of reprisal action against innocent people. Such a threat is of no value unless it can be carried out, so it may be necessary to plan the assassination of various responsible officers of the oppressive regime and hold such plans in readiness to be used only if provoked by excessive brutality. Such plans must be modified frequently to meet changes in the tactical situation.

TECHNIQUES

The essential point of assassination is the death of the subject. A human being may be killed in many ways but sureness is often overlooked by those who may be emotionally unstrung by the seriousness of this act they intend to commit. The specific technique employed will depend upon a large number of variables, but should be constant in one point: Death must be absolutely certain. The attempt on Hitler's life failed because the conspiracy did not give this matter proper attention.

Techniques may be considered as follows:

PLANNING

When the decision to assassinate has been reached, the tactics of the operation must be planned, based upon an estimate of the situation similar to that used in military operations. The preliminary estimate will reveal gaps in information and possibly indicate a need for special equipment which must be procured or constructed. When all necessary data has been collected, an effective tactical plan can be prepared. All planning must be mental; no papers should ever contain evidence of the operation.

In resistance situations, assassination may be used as a counter-reprisal. Since this requires advertising to be effective, the resistance organization must be in a position to warn high officials publicly that their lives will be the price of reprisal action against innocent people. Such a threat is of no value unless it can be carried out, so it may be necessary to plan the assassination of various responsible officers of the oppressive regime and hold such plans in readiness to be used only if provoked by excessive brutality. Such plans must be modified frequently to meet changes in the tactical situation.

TECHNIQUES

The essential point of assassination is the death of the subject. A human being may be killed in many ways but sureness is often overlooked by those who may be emotionally unstrung by the seriousness of this act they intend to commit. The specific technique employed will depend upon a large number of variables, but should be constant in one point: Death must be absolutely certain. The attempt on Hitler's life failed because the conspiracy did not give this matter proper attention.

Techniques may be considered as follows:

- 4 -

1. Manual.

It is possible to kill a man with the bare hands, but very few are skillful enough to do it well. Even a highly trained Judo expert will hesitate to risk killing by hand unless he has absolutely no alternative. However, the simplest local tools are often much the most efficient means of assassination. A hammer, axe, wrench, screw driver, fire poker, kitchen knife, lamp stand, or anything hard, heavy and handy will suffice. A length of rope or wire or a belt will do if the assassin is strong and agile. All such improvised weapons have the important advantage of availability and apparent innocence. The obviously lethal machine gun failed to kill Trotsky where an item of sporting goods succeeded.

In all safe cases where the assassin may be subject to search, either before or after the act, specialized weapons should not be used. Even in the last cases, the assassin may accidentally be searched before the act and should not carry an incriminating device if any sort of lethal weapon can be improvised at or near the site. If the assassin normally carries weapons because of the nature of his job, it may still be desirable to improvise and implement at the scene to avoid disclosure of his identity.

If the subject's personal habits make it feasible, alcohol may be used ~~very successfully~~ to prepare him for a contrived accident of any kind.

Falls before trains or subway cars are usually effective, but require exact timing and can seldom be free from unexpected observation.

Automobile accidents are a less satisfactory means of assassination. If the subject is deliberately run down, very exact timing is necessary and investigation is likely to be thorough. If the subject's car is tampered with, reliability is very low. The subject may be stunned or drugged and then placed in the car, but this is only reliable when the car can be run off a high cliff or into deep water without observation.

Arson can cause accidental death if the subject is drugged and left in a burning building. Reliability is not satisfactory unless the building is isolated and highly combustible.

3. Drugs.

In all types of assassination except terroristic, drugs can be very effective. If the assassin is trained as a doctor or nurse and the subject is under medical care, this is an easy and sure method. An overdose of morphine administered as a sedative will cause death without disturbance and is difficult to detect. The size of the dose will depend upon whether the subject has been using narcotics regularly. If not, two grains will suffice.

If the subject drinks heavily, morphine or a similar narcotic can be injected at the passing out stage, and the cause of death will often be held to be acute alcoholism.

Specific poisons, such as arsenic or strychnine, are effective but their possession or procurement is incriminating, and accurate dosage is problematical. Poison was used unsuccessfully in the assassinations of Rasputin and Holohan, though the latter case is more accurately described as a murder.

4.   **Edge Weapons**

Any locally obtained edge device may be successfully employed.
A certain minimum of anatomical knowledge is needed for reliability.

Puncture wounds of the body cavity may not be reliable unless
the heart is reached. The heart is protected by the rib cage and is
not always easy to locate.

A x d al wounds were once nearly always mortal, but modern
medical treatment has made this no longer true.

Absolute reliability is obtained by severing the spinal cord
in the cervical region. This can be done with the point of a knife or
a light blow of an axe or hatchet.

Another reliable method is the severing of both jugular and
carotid blood vessels on both sides of the windpipe.

If the subject has been rendered unconscious by other wounds
or drugs, either of the above methods can be used to insure death.

5.   Blunt Weapons

As with edge weapons, blunt weapons require some anatomical
knowledge for effective use. Their main advantage is their universal
availability. A k t ar may be picked up almost anywhere in the world.
Baseball and cricket bats are very widely distributed. Even a rock
or a heavy stick will do, and nothing resembling a weapon need be
procured, carried or subsequently disposed of.

Blows should be directed to the temple, the area just below
and behind the ear, and the lower, rear portion of the skull. Of
course, if the blow is very heavy, any portion of the upper skull will
do. The lower frontal portion of the head, from the eyes to the throat,
can withstand enormous blows without fatal consequences.

6.   Firearms

Firearms are often used in assassination, often very
ineffectively. The assassin usually has insufficient technical
knowledge of the limitations of weapons, and expects more range,
accuracy and killing power than can be provided with reliability.
Since certainty of death is the major requirement, firearms should be
used which can provide destructive power at least 100% in excess of
that thought to be necessary, and ranges should be half that considered practical for the weapon.

Firearms have other drawbacks. Their possession is often
incriminating. They may be difficult to obtain. They require a
degree of experience from the user. They are noisy. Their
lethality is consistently over-rated.

However, there are many cases in which firearms are probably
more efficient than any other means. These cases usually involve
distance between the assassin and the subject, or comparative physical
weakness of the assassin, as with a woman.

(a) The precision rifle. In guarded assassination, a
good hunting or target rifle should always be considered as
a possibility. Absolute reliability can nearly always be
achieved at a distance of one hundred yards. In ideal
circumstances, the range may be extended to 250 yards.
The rifle should be a well made bolt or falling block
action type, handling a powerful long-range cartridge. The
.300 F.N. Magnum is probably the best cartridge readily
available. Other excellent calibers are .375 H.&H. Magnum,
.270 Winchester, .30 - '06 r.*., 8 X 60 MM Magnum, 9.3 X

- 10 -

62 mm and others of this type. These are preferable to ordinary military calibers, since ammunition available for them is usually of the expanding bullet type, whereas most ammunition for military rifles is full jacketed and hence not sufficiently lethal. Military ammunition should not be altered by filing or drilling bullets, as this will adversely affect accuracy.

The rifle may be of the "bull gun" variety, with extra heavy barrel and set triggers, but in any case should be capable of maximum precision. Ideally, the weapon should be able to group in one inch at one hundred yards, but 2½" groups are adequate. The sight should be telescopic, not only for accuracy, but because such a sight is much better in dim light or near darkness. As long as the bare outline of the target is discernable, a telescope sight will work, even if the rifle and shooter are in total darkness.

An expanding, hunting bullet of such calibers as described above will produce extravagant laceration and shock at short or mid-ranges. If a man is struck just once in the body cavity, his death is almost entirely certain.

Public figures or guarded officials may be killed with great reliability and some safety if a firing point can be established prior to an official occasion. The propaganda value of this system may be very high.

(b) The machine gun.

Machine guns may be used in most cases where the precision rifle is applicable. Usually, this will require

-11-

the subversion of a unit of an official guard at a ceremony, though a skillful and determined team might conceivably dispose of a loyal gun crew without commotion and take over the gun at the critical time.

The area fire capacity of the machine gun should not be used to search out a concealed subject. This was tried with predictable lack of success on Trotsky. The automatic feature of the machine gun should rather be used to increase reliability y placing a 5 second burst on the subject. Even with full jacket ammunition, this will be absolutely lethal if the burst pattern is no larger than a man. This can be accomplished at about 150 yards. In ideal circumstances, a properly bedded and targeted machine gun can do it at 850 yards. The major difficulty is placing the first burst exactly on the target, as most machine gunners are trained to spot their fire on target by observation of strike. This will not do in assassination as the subject will not wait.

(c) The Submachine Gun.

This weapon, known as the "machine-pistol" by the Russians and Germans and "machine-carbine" by the British, is occasionally useful in assassination. Unlike the rifle and machine gun, this is a short range weapon and since it fires pistol ammunition, much less powerful. To be reliable, it should deliver at least 5 rounds into the subject's chest, though the .45 caliber U.S. weapons have a much larger margin of killing efficiency than the 9 mm European arms.

The assassination range of the submachine gun is point

12

blank. While accurate single rounds can be delivered
by submachine gunners at 50 yards or more, this is
not certain enough for assassination. Under ordinary
circumstances, the SMG should be used as a fully
automatic weapon. In the hands of a capable gunner, a
high cyclic rate is a distinct advantage, as speed of
execution is most desirable, particularly in the case
of multiple subjects.

The sub-machine gun is especially adapted to indoor
work when more than one subject is to be assassinated.
An effective technique has been devised for the use of
a pair of submachine gunners, by which a room containing
as many as a dozen subjects can be "purified" in about
twenty seconds with little or no risk to the gunners.
It is illustrated below.

Figs. 1 - 5.

While the U.S. sub-machine guns fire the most lethal
cartridge, the higher cyclic rate of some foreign
weapons enable the gunner to cover a target quicker with
acceptable pattern density. The Bergmann Model 1934 is
particularly good in this way. The Danish Madsen SMG
has a moderately good cyclic rate and is admirably compact
and concealable. The Russian SMG's have a good cyclic
rate, but are handicapped by a small, light protective
which requires more hits for equivalent killing effect.

(d) The Shotgun.

A large bore shotgun is a most effective

- 11 -

killing instrument as long as the range is kept under ten yards. It should normally be used only on single targets as it cannot sustain fire successfully. The barrel may be "sawed-off" for convenience, but this is not a significant factor in its killing performance. Its optimum range is just out of reach of the subject. OO buckshot is considered the best shot size for a twelve gage gun, but anything from single balls to bird shot will do if the range is right. The assassin should aim for the solar plexus as the shot pattern is small at close range and can easily miss the head.

-(c) The Pistol

While the handgun is quite inefficient as a weapon of assassination, it is often used, partly because it is readily available and can be concealed on the person, and partly because its limitations are not widely appreciated. While many well known assassinations have been carried out with pistols (Lincoln, Harding, Ghandi), such attempts fail as often as they succeed (Truman, Roosevelt, Churchill).

If a pistol is used, it should be as powerful as possible and fired from just beyond reach. The pistol and the shotgun are used in similar tactical situations, except that the shotgun is much more lethal and the pistol is much more easily concealed.

In the hands of an expert, a powerful pistol is quite deadly, but such experts are rare and not usually available for assassination missions.

.45 Colt, .44 Special, .455 Kly, .45 A.C.P. (U.S. Service) and .357 Magnum are all efficient calibers. Less powerful

rounds can suffice but are less reliable. Sub-power
cartridges such as the .32s and .25s should be avoided.

In all cases, the subject should be hit solidly at
least three times for complete reliability.

(f) Silent Firearms

The sound of the explosion of the propenant in
a firearm can be effectively silenced by appropriate
attachments. However, the sound of the projectile passing
through the air cannot, since this sound is generated
outside the weapon. In cases where the velocity of the
bullet greatly exceeds that of sound, the noise so generated
is much louder than that of the explosion. Since all
powerful rifles have muzzle velocities of over 2000 feet
per second, they cannot be silenced.

Pistol bullets, on the other hand, usually travel
slower than sound and the sound of their flight is negligible.
Therefore, pistols, submachine guns and any sort of improvised
carbine or rifle which will take a low velocity cartridge can
be silenced. The user should not forget that the sound of
the operation of a repeating action is considerable, and
that the sound of bullet strike, particularly in bone, is
quite loud.

Silent firearms are only occasionally useful to the
assassin, though they have been widely publicised in this
connection. Because permissible velocity is low, effective
precision range is held to about 100 yards with rifle or
carbine type weapons, while with pistols, silent or otherwise,

are most efficient just beyond arms length. The silent
feature attempts to provide a degree of safety to the
assassin, but mere possession of a silent firearm is
likely to create enough hazard to counter the advantage
of its silence. The silent pistol combines the disadvantages
of any pistol with the added one of its obviously clandestine
purpose.

A historically sighted, closed-action carbine shooting
a low velocity bullet of great weight, and built for accuracy,
could be very useful to an assassin in certain situations.
At the time of writing, no such weapon is known to exist.

7. Explosives.

Bombs and demolition charges of various sorts have
been used frequently in assassination. Such devices, in terroristic
and open assassination, can provide safety and overcome guard barriers,
but it is curious that bombs have often been the implement of lost
assassinations.

The major factor which affects reliability is the use of explosives
for assassination. The charge must be very large and the detonation
must be controlled exactly as to time by the assassin who can observe
the subject. A small or moderate explosive charge is highly unreliable
as a cause of death, and time delay or booby-trap devices are extremely
prone to kill the wrong man. In addition to the moral aspects of
indiscriminate killing, the death of casual bystanders can often
produce public reactions unfavorable to the cause for which the
assassination is carried out.

Bombs or grenades should never be thrown at a subject. While this

...always causes a commotion and may even result in the subject's death, it is clumsy, unreliable, and bad propaganda. The charge must be too small and the assassin is never sure of: (1) reaching his attack position, (2) placing the charge close enough to the target and (3) firing the charge at the right time.

Placing the charge surreptitiously in advance permits a charge of proper size to be employed, but requires accurate prediction of the subject's movements.

Ten pounds of high explosive should normally be regarded as a minimum, and this is exclusive of fragmentation material. The latter can consist of any hard, tough material as long as the fragments are large enough. Metal or rock fragments should be walnut-size rather than pea-size. If solid plates are used, to be ruptured by the explosion, cast iron, 1" thick, gives excellent fragmentation. Military or commercial high explosives are practical for use in assassination. Homemade or improvised explosives should be avoided. While possibly powerful, they tend to be dangerous and unreliable. Anti-personnel explosive missiles are excellent, provided the assassin has sufficient technical knowledge to fuse them properly. 81 or 82 mm mortar shells, or the 120 mm mortar shell, are particularly good. Anti-personnel shells for 85, 88, 90, 100 and 105 mm guns and howitzers are both large enough to be completely reliable and small enough to be carried by one man.

The charge should be so placed that the subject is not ever six feet from it at the moment of detonation.

A large, shaped charge with the cone filled with iron fragments (such as 1" nuts and bolts) will fire a highly lethal shotgun-type

- 17 -

...to 50 yards. This reaction has not been thoroughly tested, however, and an exact replica of the proposed device should be fired in advance to determine exact range, pattern-size, and penetration of fragments. Fragments should penetrate at least 1" of seasoned pine or equivalent for minimum reliability.

Any firing device may be used which permits exact control by the assassin. An ordinary commercial or military exploder is efficient, as long as it is rigged for instantaneous action with no time fuse in the system.

The wire screen electric target can serve as the triggering device and provide exact timing from as far away as the assassin can reliably hit the target. This will avoid the disadvantages of stringing wire between the proposed positions of the assassin and the subject, and also permit the assassin to fire the charge from a variety of possible positions.

The radio switch can be used to fire a charge, though its reliability is somewhat lower and its procurement may not be easy.

(There may be presented brief outlines, with critical evaluations of the following assassinations and attempts:

Marat	Hedrich
Lincoln	Hitler
Harding	Roosevelt
Grand Duke Sergei	Truman
Pirhvie	Mussolini
Archduke Francis Ferdinand	Benes
Rasputin	Aung Sang

Madero   Kasmara

Kirov   Abdullah

Huey Long   Ghandi

Alexander of Yugoslvia

Trotsky

Conference Room Technique

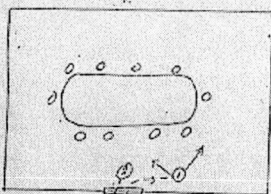

1.

② — ⑦ - - - Door

① Enters Room Quickly But Quietly

② Stands in Doorway

2.

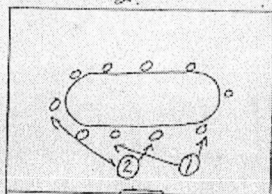

② Opens fire on first Subject to React. Swings Across Group Toward Center of Mass. Times Burst to Empty Magazine at end of Swing

① Covers Group to prevent Individual Dangerous Reactions, if necessary, fires individual Bursts of 3 rounds.

3.

② Finishes Burst. Commands "Shift." Drops Back Thru Door. Replaces Empty Magazine. Covers Corridor.

① On Command "Shift" Opens fire on Opposite Side of Target. Swings one Burst Across Group

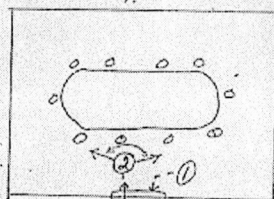

4.

① Finishes Burst. Commands Shift. Drops Back Thru Door. Replaces Magazine. Covers Corridor.

② On Command "Shift" Re-enters room. Covers group. Kills Survivors with Two-Round Bursts. Leaves Propaganda.

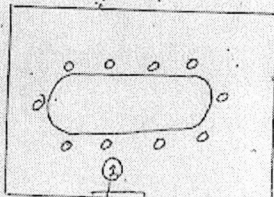

5.

② Leaves Room. Commands "Go." Covers Rear with nearly full Magazine

① On Command "Go", Leads Withdrawal. Covering front with full magazine.

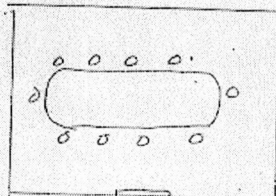

6.

Actual Documents from CIA assassination manual

To wrap it all up in a nice neat package, the manual explains why assassination is necessary.

JUSTIFICATION

Murder is not morally justifiable. Self-defense may be argued if the victim has knowledge which may destroy the resistance organization if divulged. Assassination of persons responsible for atrocities or reprisals may be regarded as just punishment. Killing a political leader whose burgeoning career is a clear and present danger to the cause of freedom may be held necessary.

But assassination can seldom be employed with a clear conscience. Persons who are morally squeamish should not attempt it.

Chapter Eight

The Cover Up

The decision to employ this technique must nearly always be reached in the field, at the area where the act will take place.

<hr>

CIA Assassination Manual

<hr>

Sadly, in the case of Patrice Lumumba of the Congo, the truth may have died with Dr. Sidney Gottlieb. One of the gray areas in Lumumba's assassination has always been whether the "hit" order came directly from President Eisenhower himself, or subordinates. On that the manual is clear:

EMPLOYMENT

Consequently, the decision to employ this technique must nearly always be reached in the field, at the area where the act will take place. Decision and instructions should be confined to an absolute minimum of persons. Ideally, only one person will be involved. No report may be made, but usually the act will be properly covered by normal news services, whose output is available to all concerned.

Guns do kill. US made guns in the hands of CIA agents across the world by order of U.S. Presidents have killed. Perhaps, even more importantly, those who pulled the trigger got away with it.

Consider this; between 1950 and 1975 The United States gave 312,000 M1 rifles to Turkey, 236,000 to South Korea, another 200,000 to France, 220,000 to South Vietnam, 186,000 to Greece, 165,000 to Iran which then turned against us. 150,000 guns went to Pakistan, with another 73,000 headed to Norway, 70,000 to Denmark, 60,000 to Israel, and another 110,000 to be divided equally between Venezuela and Indonesia. Guns don't kill people but people with guns certainly have made their case that guns do kill.

Chapter Nine

Face to Face with Joe from Paris

*'I left the CIA 20 years ago...
I don't want to talk about that, that is behind me."
Excerpt from interview with Dr. Sidney Gottlieb, the CIA
Scientist sent to assassinate*

Patrice Lumumba
Culpepper, Virginia ca. 1986

The woman answering the door looked like she was more at home baking cookies for her grandchildren than living with a man some call a serial killer, while others, a national hero. She is kind where he is callous, and warm where he is cold. She summons him to the room and he dispatches her in much the same manner a bull swats a fly. This is how my meeting with one of the most important figures in the life and death of the Congo began. This is what happened the day I came face to face with Dr. Sidney Gottlieb.

Dr. Gottlieb rounds the corner in a Greek fisherman's cap and wool coat. A few streaks of silver hair peak from underneath the hat. He is tan, but not too tan. It appears as if he has come in from outside through a back door. He looks as if the farm is far more than just a setting for our meeting, but instead his new occupation. Gottlieb is pleasant in our greeting, but it is clear from the look he shoots back toward the grandmother who should be baking cookies, he is not really that happy to see me.

"Dr. Gottlieb," I say by way of introduction. There is a momentary pause. He shakes my hand and offers a look that says he would be happier anywhere else but here. Realizing there will be little time for small talk, I begin my line of inquiry. "I'd like to talk to you about the program?" Again he pauses.

The program was the CIA's dirtiest little secret. The code name was MK Ultra. In reality, MK Ultra allowed the agency to get away with murder and much much more. MK Ultra was the CIA's secret search for the 'Manchurian Candidate," an assassin who could be hypnotized into carrying out the most gruesome of assignments all in the name of national security. MK Ultra was the agency's search for the perfect killing machine, and Africa was Dr. Gottlieb's playground. He went there frequently looking for mushrooms that might poison and diseases that could be spread.

As part of MK Ultra, the CIA, and Dr. Gottlieb secretly drugged thousands of unsuspecting civilians, spayed cancer causing chemicals in bus stations and trains stations in cities like Washington D.C., San Francisco California, Minneapolis Minnesota, and carried out other experiments we still probably know little about. There was also a film that showed what happened when the drug was used on unsuspecting soldiers. They couldn't march in formation, fire a weapon or for that matter complete simplest of tasks. It would be comical if it were not all true. It was also 'the Agency' that introduced LSD into the underground culture of San Francisco's hippies.

At the height of the Cold War, Dr. Gottlieb and his cronies were searching for new ways to assassinate people, and covertly change the world. 'The Agency' referred to those assassination plots, its dirtiest little secrets, as 'The Family Jewels." Dr. Sidney Gottlieb was keeper of the flame. You are about to meet one of his victims.

Chapter Ten

The Human Guinea Pig

"They used to bring in these cages," he told me. Inside the cages were monkeys that had been given the drugs he was about to get. One day he said, the monkeys showed no signs of life.

Eddie Flowers

Eddie Flowers was one of the agency's human guinea pigs. Physically, Flowers closely resembled basketball great 'Earl the Pearl' Monroe. Emotionally, he remained scarred because of what the government did to him. When we met in the early 90's, he stood just shy of six feet, was dark skinned and wore glasses. He was a handsome man on the outside but inside he was living with the type of demons only the CIA can produce. "The CIA," he says, 'murdered his soul."

Eddie Flowers was in prison when Dr. Gottlieb and the others were hard at work. It is possible they never met, but Gottlieb left an indelible mark on the life of Eddie Flowers. A former heroin addict, Flowers entered prison as a young man intending to do his time and start over. He left, addicted to a new drug, one he had never heard of before. No one ever told him what the drug was, he suspected it was LSD.

"They used to bring in these cages," he told me. Inside the cages were monkeys that had been given the drugs he was about to get. One day he said, the monkeys showed no signs of life. "They were no more good," I remember him telling me. That is when you can see him silently reliving the hell the CIA put him through. He knew he was next.

It was years before he learned what it was the government gave him. By then it was too late. In 1975, when financial records of Dr, Gottlieb's experiments were exposed, reporters descended on Eddie Flowers vowing to help him right the government's wrongs. No one could. The fire that consumed most of the records also consumed the truth. The damage, however, went far beyond the actual drugs themselves. Families were destroyed in the process too.

In the years he was in prison, Flower's lost contact with his son. Instead of the monkeys, it was Eddie Flowers who was "no more good." After years of trying to figure out why he was used as a human guinea pig, he gave up. He gave up on the government, and the reporters like me who vowed to get to the bottom of Eddie Flower's nightmare. He was too small, and the government too big. In the seventies it was the war in Vietnam that stole away reporter's attention; in the 90's, the first Gulf War, and in the new millennium, the War in Iraq. First, Eddie Flowers disappeared from the headlines, then the search engines until slowly but surely no one cared anymore. Eddie Flowers died the worst possible death. He died in plain sight and his obituary bore it out.

Eddie Flowers's obit said nothing about the CIA, or its intrusion into his life. It only pointed out that he spent the last years of his life as a substance abuse counselor. In the case of Eddie Flowers, 'the Agency' succeeded in getting away with another murder. They murdered his soul. Another sordid chapter in the life of the CIA came and went, and like Patrice Lumumba and the millions in the Congo, and millions more across Africa, no one bothered to point a finger of blame anywhere near Washington. Instead, Flowers died broken by a government that never believed he deserved to be fixed. He could only take solace in knowing he was not alone. There was also Dr. Frank Olson.

Chapter Eleven

Dr. Frank Olson

"It was a riddle, inside an enigma, inside a lie."

Alice Olson, Frank Olson's widow

Dr. Frank Olson, worked with Dr. Gottlieb at the CIA. I met Eric Olson, his son, in the mid 90's working on the same story that led me to Eddie Flowers. Highly educated, Eric Olson and his family made headlines in 1975 when those same reporters learned that the CIA secretly spiked Frank Olson's, drink with LSD, before they said, he committed suicide. The documents supporting the allegations were released as part of the Church Committee Hearings. At the time, Alice Olson, Dr. Frank Olson's widow told me, "It was a riddle, inside an enigma, inside a lie." She was talking about the layer upon layer upon layer of CIA constructed lies surrounding her husband's death. She died never knowing how close to the truth she was. The truth would take decades to be revealed and even now, we still don't know all of the details.

What we do know is this; Frank Olson was in charge of the CIA's newly developing program designed to experiment with Anthrax and other deadly pathogens. He was an insider's insider. Dr. Olson, had he not suffered a crisis of consciousness, would have gone down in history as another "hero" just like Dr. Gottlieb. Instead, he found out the way what happens to insiders who decide they want to take the agency to task for its activities. (6)

Published reports in 1975 painted a picture of a scientist who was given LSD, without his knowledge, in a hotel across from Madison Square Gardens in New York City. Moments later, he plunged through a window to his death several stories below. Those reports made it look as if Dr. Olson was a scientist who decided to experiment with LSD, himself. It was textbook CIA. Remember it was the Agency's manual that stated a fall from a high place was the best way to get away with murder. The manual even suggested making it look like a suicide. In truth, the death of Dr. Frank Olson was a lie, to cover up an even bigger lie.

An autopsy would later reveal Dr. Frank Olson was murdered. The CIA got away with killing a man, by staging his suicide. The man in the center of the controversy was the same man who would play a role in the death of Eddie Flowers and Patrice Lumumba in the Congo, Dr. Sidney Gottlieb. What's worse, Dr. Frank Olson was white, which goes to show that the agency held no bias when it came to murder. Africans, African Americans, third world dictators, and traitors were all viewed through the same lens.

In June of 1994, following a series of high profile investigations I conducted in Washington, the body of Dr. Frank Olson was exhumed. Professor James Starrs, a noted forensic pathologist at George Washington University led the post exhumation examination. It took weeks before he would reach his conclusion, but once he did, it sent shockwaves through the world of spooks and spies. Dr. Frank Olson, Dr. Starrs concluded, was murdered before he was sent crashing through that New York City hotel window. Let me repeat that. Dr. Frank Olson, contrary to published reports in the 70's did not kill himself, but instead was killed before he allegedly committed suicide.

Professor Starrs concluded that Olson was struck in the head by a heavy object, and rendered unconscious before being tossed from the hotel's window. The only way he could have committed suicide is if he did so 'sleepwalking!' That left only one conclusion. Dr Frank Olson was killed because he knew too much. Suddenly the man in the Greek fisherman's hat was on every reporter's radar. (7)

Soon all eyes were on Dr. Sidney Gottlieb for reasons other than the assassination of Patrice Lumumba. The truth is, Lumumba, throughout all of this controversy was a side-bar...just another African leader. The Lumumba assassination often appears as a single line in the larger question of who killed Dr. Frank Olson? Who killed this white CIA scientist? Oh, and by the way...the articles written about Dr. Frank Olson also mention in a line or two...the life of an African leader was also snuffed out. Sometimes Patrice Lumumba is mentioned by name, sometimes he is not.

This time, Dr. Gottlieb was wanted for questioning in connection with the murder of an American citizen. He was wanted in connection with his role in the death of Eric Olson's father, Dr. Frank Olson. No one walked away satisfied. 'The agency', perhaps, made sure of it.

Whatever he knew, about Patrice Lumumba, Dr. Frank Olson, and countless others whose lives he ruined, the world will never know. Dr. Sidney Gottlieb, the little man in the Greek fisherman's hat, took it to the grave with him. He died Just days before he was to testify before a New York grand jury looking into charges of murder. He died; it should be pointed out, a national hero.

The New York Times, in Gottlieb's obit, said nothing about Lumumba, or the Congo, or the millions of deaths that took place inside the Congo in the years following Lumumba's assassination. It made no mention of the fact that Gottlieb, an American, had been sent to Africa to assassinate the George Washington of an emerging African nation. There was not mention of 'Joe from Paris.' Instead, Dr. Sidney Gottlieb was eulogized as a cold war hero. The article made no mention of murder, but instead referred to a grandfatherly figure that spent his later years running a commune in the suburbs of Washington, folk dancing and fighting lawsuits. (8)

The last words I remember Gottlieb telling me, were simple, "I don't want to talk about that!" He uttered those words as defiantly as he lived his life. Why after all, should I, a black reporter, merit any special treatment when he had been sent to assassinate the leader of a country of people who looked like me? When I explored just how repentant he was, the old agency operative came out. 'I left the CIA 20 years ago…I don't want to talk about that part of my life…that is behind me." With that, our conversation was over and the secrets he would take to his grave escaped another close call.

A decade later, Dr. Sidney Gottlieb was found dead at the age of 80.

As for the Congo, the killing there continued. History has proven that the events set into motion on the day of my birth back in 1957, continue to haunt the country to this day. The rape and murder of the Congo that Dr. Sidney Gottlieb and his colleagues participated in never stopped. Like the story of Patrice Lumumba and Eddie Flowers, and Dr. Frank Olson, reporters just got tired of searching for the truth. Even when the truth came about the Congo and Patrice Lumumba, and Dr. Gottlieb, no one cared. Most reporters had already moved on. 'The Agency' won.

On June 26, 2007 the CIA released hundreds of pages of documents it referred to as "The Family Jewels," or the documents that revealed the CIA's dirty tricks around the globe. Included in that collection were the documents naming Dr. Sidney Gottlieb, and his plot to assassinate Patrice Lumumba. Reporters paid them little attention. It was, after all, old news.

In the Congo, Dr. Death got away with murder. The question is…why?

MORI DocID: 1451843

14 February 1972

MEMORANDUM FOR THE RECORD:

In November 1962 Mr. [   ] advised Mr. Lyman Kirkpatrick that he had, at one time, been directed by Mr. Richard Bissell to assume responsibility for a project involving the assassination of Patrice Lumumba, then Premier, Republic of Congo. According to [   ] poison was to have been the vehicle as he made reference to having been instructed to see Dr. Sidney Gottlieb in order procure the appropriate vehicle.

00464

14 February 1972

MEMORANDUM FOR THE RECORD:

In November 1962 Mr. [   ] advised Mr. Lyman Kirkpatrick that he had, at one time, been directed by Mr. Richard Bissell to assume responsibility for a project involving the assassination of Patrice Lumumba, then Premier, Republic of Congo. According to [   ] poison was to have been the vehicle as he made reference to having been instructed to see Dr. Sidney Gottlieb in order procure the appropriate vehicle.

00464

(9)

Chapter Twelve

The White Hand!

Africa had another name for the coups that destroyed their continent, "The White Hand!" Getting away with murder… in Africa!

In Africa, it is called 'The White Hand.' Many Africans believe the majority of the coup d'états that have left their governments in ruins were caused by 'white people.' The common euphemism for the CIA led coups is 'The White Hand.' In Liberia, the wife of President William Tolbert, who was slain in a bloody coup, wrote that 'The White Hand' was responsible for his death. Aside from a few well timed documents, such as the CIA's 'Family Jewels' documents that were released in the summer of 2007, there is little proof of any foreign involvement white or otherwise. When documents are released, the names of those responsible remain blacked out until long after they are dead. It is policy.

Sometimes, however, the agency slips. Sometimes, something that was supposed to be hidden forever, surfaces. In this case it is a film that had been long hidden away from public view. The film leaves little doubt; 'The White Hand' was at work in Africa, and, in the case of the Congo, with deadly results.

There are more than three billion textual records housed in the National Archives and Records Administration in College Park, Maryland, and at any given time, fewer than twenty million have ever been read. There are also hundreds of thousands of films, so the chances of historians stumbling upon the one document or film that tells the story, are slim. That is how our government hides its secrets. It hides them in plain sight!

That is why, for years, the true story of what happened inside the Congo has never been told. Few were looking, and those who were, couldn't find what they were looking for. Such is the case of a single film in record group 306.

The film is black and white and grainy, but if a picture is worth a thousand words, this one could re-write the history of the Congo, in the days following the death of Patrice Lumumba. The world was told, and the U.S. was telling the story, that rebels loyal to Lumumba had seized and were killing white missionaries in Stanleyville and other cities across the Congo. It was the world's worst nightmare...armed Africans killing and possibly raping innocent white women. The horrors to a white America, weaned on Tarzan, were almost unimaginable.

The Africans, however, were telling a different story, but they were black, and few, outside of Africa, were listening. Sadly, 'The White Hand' was at work again.

The ensuing diplomatic frenzy resulted in one of the largest rescue missions ever mounted. After all, as Roger Morris, the former National Security Council member during administration of President Lyndon Johnson put it, "Johnson was concerned about the possibility of armed black men seizing and killing innocent white women."

The truth is, racism may have played a role in one of the biggest cover-ups in history ... a cover-up involving the massacre of innocent African civilians by armed white solders. How else do you explain a film that shows white soldiers killing black Africans at will? It is a film that was recorded by an American citizen, an American photographer with American equipment, and covered up by the United States Government. It is a film that was bought and paid for with U.S. taxpayer dollars. It was code named," Operation Red Dragon."

Chapter Thirteen

Operation Red Dragon

When Africans kill Africans, the world stands aside. A few Hollywood celebrities raise their voices but when they disappear so does the issue from the world's headlines. But, when Africans kill whites, the world springs into action...

Patrice Lumumba, the Congo's first democratically elected president, was already dead. His assassination sparked international and national outrage. The Congolese were told that he died at the hands of his own people. It was, they were told, another example of African upon African violence. Lumumba's death, and the ensuing power struggle, plunged the Congo into chaos. Forces loyal to Patrice Lumumba were waging a bloody war against forces backed by U.S. and European interests.

The rebels had passion; they were the revolutionaries. But the U.S.-backed forces had guns and an endless supply of money. They also had one other thing; a massive public relations machine that the rest of the world believed. Still the rebels fought on. In a different time they would have been called freedom fighters. Instead, they were cast as the enemies of an emerging democracy, our democracy.

Between January and August of 1964, rebels had seized five of the nation's twenty-one provinces, and another five were on the verge of collapse. A total collapse of the government forces was inevitable. The man suffering the most defeats was Joseph Mobuto, Lumumba's former friend, turned Brutus. Mobuto, with U.S. backing, was head of the Army National Congolese, or ANC, and the army's Chief of Staff.

Mobuto was also a CIA puppet. That meant Mobuto's defeat, in a very real sense, was a U.S. defeat. That simply could not be allowed to happen!

The situation reached a crescendo on September 5, 1964. The day I turned nine years old! The revolutionary government announced that it had seized almost half of the Congo, which was then named Zaire, holding 7 out of 21 local capitals. Rebel forces complained to other African leaders that foreign forces were to blame for the ensuing carnage, but no one outside of Africa was listening. That's when the word went out that this predominantly African conflict had taken on a deadly new twist.

When Africans kill Africans, the world stands aside. A few Hollywood celebrities raise their voices but when they disappear, the issues usually disappear from the world's headlines. But, when Africans kill whites, the world springs into action. Reports surfaced that as part of their uprising, the rebels decided to hold 'white hostages' to strengthen their bargaining positions.

The Congolese have long argued that from this point on, historians got it wrong. They maintain, Mobuto, fearing a defeat at the hands of the rebels, did the one thing he knew would guarantee western intervention. Congolese elders told their sons and daughters that Mobuto ordered his secret police to begin the systematic massacre of whites in the areas of the Congo believed to be under rebel control. Mobuto's mindset, they argued, was that the western world wouldn't stand by and watch 'white people' dying at the hands of blacks in the jungle. Apparently it worked. In later chapters you will see how American presidents first ask how many whites occupy an African country before deciding a course of action.

Those white hostages proved just how far two governments, the U.S. and Belgium, would go to save the lives of any white people being held hostage in Africa. "Operation Dragon

Rouge or Red Dragon" a top secret, multi-national, rescue mission was launched in the days leading up to Thanksgiving.
November 17, 1964.

It was a Tuesday evening, and crews were told to report to the operations room on the Margarite where the airplanes had been stationed. Each crewmember was instructed to bring their rig and be ready to take off. Once in the air, navigators were given plain manila envelopes and told not to open those envelopes until the planes reached an altitude of 2,000 feet. Once in the air, the crew members learned they were headed to Klinebrogel, which was a Belgian military outpost on the outskirts of Brussels. They were not told why.

Once in Klinebrogel, the pilots met their crew and learned of their next destination. The crew would include hundreds of specially trained Belgian paratroopers. The destination was the Ascension islands in the South Atlantic. Again, according to accounts of those who participated, little, if any, detail was given. Eighteen hours after the rescue mission began the troops arrived and were instructed to await their next orders.

Back in Washington, and in Belgium, frantic negotiations with the African rebels were underway and not going well. The leader of the rebels warned that any foreign intervention would result in the hostages being killed. One week before thanksgiving, all hopes of any negotiated settlement had faded and "Operation Dragon Rouge" was underway.
November 23, 1964.

Five C-130 transport planes took off carrying 64 Belgian Red Berets in full metal jacket. Behind those five planes, a Herk transport plane, that had been reconfigured as a hospital ship. Dropping to treetop altitudes and following the Congo River, the planes loaded with paratroopers made their way toward the city of Stanleyville. Seconds later, another 310 Belgium Solders were on their way to what was to become the most historic rescue mission of its time.

By day's end, more than 2,000 people had been airlifted out of the city. Already, champagne corks were being popped in Washington, and Africans were complaining of a cover-up. The mission was far from over. What happened next would never be reported.

Chapter Fourteen

Operation Dragon Noire
(Operation Black Dragon)

King Baudouin welcomed the Belgian paratroopers upon their return and gave their two American commanders the Order of Leopold II, one of the nation's greatest honors.

The next day, still reveling in the glory of Operation Dragon Rouge, a separate mission was launched code named, "Operation Dragon Noire, or Operation Black Dragon!" "Dragon Noire" was a cleanup mission of sorts aimed at rescuing hostages being held in a town about 225 miles northwest of Stanleyville, Paulis. Paulis gained international fame when the world became glued to the story of an American missionary who had been beaten to death after being tortured by the Congo's rebels. Not surprisingly the missionary was white.

The Belgium soldiers, the world was told, acted heroically in "Dragon Noire," just as they did in "Dragon Rouge." They went to Africa, risked their lives, and saved the whites who were being threatened with death. They were heroes.

Both missions went down in history as two of the most successful rescue missions ever launched. When it was all over, the U.S. forces and their Belgian counterparts had flown 4,000 miles to rescue the whites being held hostage in the jungles of Africa. There is little or no mention of how many Africans died during the rescue mission, or for that matter, who killed who? Instead, it seemed that once the white hostages were saved, no one cared. Since that day, 10 million Congolese have died from endless conflicts, most of which involve U.S. supplied arms…more people than died in all of World War II.

Each of the U.S. crewmembers involved in "Operations Dragon Rouge and Noir" received the MacKay trophy for the most meritorious flight of the year by the United States Air force. Each crewmember was given the Air Medal, which they proudly pinned on their chests; the leader of the mission was given the Distinguished Flying Cross. But while the Americans were hailed as heroes, the Belgians were being given the keys to the city. King Baudouin welcomed the Belgian paratroopers upon their return and gave their two American commanders the Order of Leopold II, one of the nation's greatest honors. Afterwards, the Americans were taken on a tour of the city.

The problem is, there is one other group that traveled with soldiers, a film crew assigned to record the history making adventure. The film group was part of the United States Information Agency or USIA. They were there to record every detail of the mission, from launch to return. This is the true story of the massacre they ignored. After all, the victims were African.

Chapter Fifteen

The Cover-up

"For the remainder of the afternoon it was open season on Simba's in Stanleyville"

Article written on Rescue Mission to Stanleyville

The rescue mission to Stanleyville was carried out with the cameras of the world in tow. Most were still, or print photographers brought in at the last minute to take the photos that would cause the world to react in horror at how the savages in Africa had taken the lives of whites, some of them missionaries. One historian did briefly mention what happened next, but even then, it was with the qualification that any atrocities committed on the part of the U.S., or its allies, were to be expected.

He wrote, "The sight of the bloodshed left the Belgians angered, as would be the white mercenaries who came into the city a few hours later, spearheading a ground assault from the east. For the remainder of the afternoon, it was open season on Simba's in Stanleyville as the rebels paid in blood for their folly"

"Open season" it seems involved opening fire on innocent civilians as well. A volley of bullets tore through the bodies of innocent civilians, fired by some of the same Belgium soldiers that were later hailed as heroes. And it was all captured on film, but the world saw none of it! It was all part of the cover-up.

To highlight the mission, the United States Agency for International Development or USIA, produced a documentary that aired around the world. Because of the agency's mission statement, it was never shown in the United States. By law, the U.S would have to wait 25 years before the film could be shown here, and by then few, if anyone, cared. History had been hidden once more, in plain sight.

"Rescue Mission to Stanleyville" as it was called, had the makings of a Hollywood blockbuster. It showcased heroic soldiers who risked their lives to save the lives of innocent white people who had been held hostages by savage rebels in the jungles of Africa. It was a script lifted from a Tarzan movie complete with an African American narrator telling the story. It was pure propaganda for the rest of the world, telling how the United States came to the rescue of whites in African working alongside the 'legitimate' government of the Congo. That government was headed by the CIA's puppet, Joseph Mobuto.

With a stern face, the African American narrator described how the Congo had suffered through "tumultuous years" following the death of Patrice Lumumba. The narrator never mentioned the role of the U.S. in his assassination. There was no mention in the film of Dr. Sidney Gottlieb, or "Joe from Paris," nor was any mention made of the Eisenhower administration ordering Lumumba's death. All of that information was still classified, stamped Top Secret in government papers.

Nor was there any mention of the fact Lumumba's assassination had been discussed at the highest levels of the United States government. Instead, the narrator made it appear as if the Congo had suddenly collapsed into chaos without any explanation, and that the whites who were there to bring order, suddenly found themselves caught in the crossfire. Those Africans, it seemed, had just started killing each other. The world was told, and something needed to be done. The natives were restless, and order had to be restored.

Scenes from Operation Red Dragon

Photographers take pictures of bodies shot by white soldiers; these scenes were not included in any historical films

None of the images you have just seen made their way past the editing room floor. The movie, produced by the government, instead told a completely different story. One scene in particular stands out. As the cameras zoomed in for a close-up, an elderly white woman who could have been anyone's grandmother, makes her way to a transport looking as if she had survived the worst nightmare of her life. There she was, with her silvery white hair, disheveled, and a blanket over her shoulders. She had been saved from the clutches of the black savages in the Congo. There was even a note in the film's textual records that they were to play up any rebel atrocities. It was hard not to cheer for the rescuing soldiers.

"There were massacres," the grim toned announcer stated matter-of-factly. Forty plus years later, the truth about the mission can be told. It was all a lie. This is what really happened in Stanleyville that day. This is what was on the film that the USIA chose not to share with the rest of the world.

Chapter Sixteen

The Thirty Seconds Hidden From History

When the bullets find their target each body rises upwards from the impact of the explosion and then crumples downward

Description of what happens when white soldier fires on unarmed blacks

This is what the world never saw. It is roughly thirty seconds of atrocities and war crimes all committed on camera. No faces were blurred; no effort was made to hide the fact that the atrocities were taking place. The mere fact that the film exists is proof the crimes were committed. It is also proof of the cover-up.

The soldier in the film, tall, white, wearing the beret of the Belgium forces and smoking a cigarette, raises his rifle shoulder level before firing the first shot into the pile of wounded bodies. The bodies on the ground are black. The two soldiers firing the shots from their American made weapons were white. There are no guns near the victims nor do they appear to be wearing military style clothing. If they were rebels, they had clearly surrendered, but they appear to be civilians. There are eight in all, each on the ground, apparently wounded. The soldier then raises the gun again and fires, striking another body.

When the bullets find their target, each body rises upwards from the impact of the explosion and then crumples downward. The camera does not blink and rolls during the entire episode. Four bodies in all are filmed being fired on. A spray of blood and an end to the heaving signals another round has been dispatched.   One person has his head completely blown away. The victims are black. They are men, women, and most appear to be little more than children. Thirty seconds later, they are dead. There is no more movement in the bodies. The breathing that appeared a few frames earlier has ended. No one seems to care.

Operation Red Dragon

Soldier reloads and prepares to take aim as part of Operation Red Dragon.
These scenes were not included in any historical films

Chapter Seventeen

The Photographers

*The white hand' came and killed and raped while the world
watched and did nothing.*

Poly Mutumbo, reacting to the photographs

The film jumps as if it has been edited inside the camera.
Almost out of nowhere, the other still photographers arrive.
They, too, casually take the pictures of the victims as if nothing
has happened. The soldier with the gun, still smoking his
cigarette, can be seen in the foreground. There is no rush seen
by the other photographers to ask what had just occurred.
There is no visible outrage. There is only the pile of bodies,
black bodies, being photographed by white people with cameras, standing next to a white man with a gun. None of those
pictures made it into the finished product that was shown to the
world. The African American narrator never described these
scenes. They were left intentionally on the cutting room floor.

The image of a young black man shackled nude to a
stretcher never made the final cut either. The cast on his foot
made it clear he could not escape even if he wanted to. There
he sits clutching what appears to be a bible or some other book,
praying to the God the missionaries said would save him. They
never told him the devil could be white.

Moments later the camera jumps again as if another edit
has been made. The boy on the stretcher is being moved.
Instead of being afforded a modicum of privacy inside the area
where he is being held, his naked shackled body is taken by
two more white soldiers outside for all the world to see. He is

still clutching his bible. He is still nude; there is no attempt to place a blanket over his body. He is exposed.

What makes the images so outrageous is the fact that four decades after those images were recorded, the world reacted with horror at similar photos taken elsewhere, in Iraq. Soldiers at the Abu Ghraib prison in Iraq were photographed with prisoners in similar compromising positions. Several, like the man in the Congo film, were nude. In Iraq, unlike in Africa, there were no images of prisoners being shot. That only appears to have happened in Africa. Heads rolled as a result of what happened inside Abu Ghraib. In Africa, the bodies are still being counted, and the cover-up continues.

The outrage is just now starting to register in the African community.

Poly Mutumbo lives in the suburbs of Washington, D.C. Inside a Starbucks restaurant, he saw firsthand the evidence of the stories he was told as a little boy. He saw the footage of the massacre in Stanleyville, the massacre of blacks. He was not surprised. Instead, in a thick accent still belonging to his native land, he described how his father told him exactly what unfolded on the film. He said the elderly of the Congo had long since spoke of how 'the white hand' came and killed and raped while the world watched and did nothing. Mutumbo says what happened on the film was never a secret inside the Congo, only among whites in the U.S. He says, his father and others maintained, just like the photographers in the film, the world simply chose not to listen.

The white hand in Africa had done the deed, and someone in Washington decided to cover it up. As history watched, soldiers there to save lives, claimed lives. Someone got away with murder. Someone took the pictures and decided to say nothing. Someone hid the film inside the archives. No one seemed to care. After all, this was Africa.

Operation Red Dragon

Soldier prepares to fire on wounded civilians
These scenes were not included in any historical films
Operation Red Dragon

Photographers take pictures of bodies as part of Operation Red Dragon (Note civilian clothes)
These scenes were not included in any historical films

Operation Red Dragon

Soldier prepares to fire on wounded victims Operation Red Dragon outtakes
These scenes were not included in any historical

Chapter Eighteen

Coup D'états

Coup d'état: a sudden decisive exercise of force in politics; especially: the violent overthrow or alteration of an existing government by a small group

In Africa, the weapons of mass destruction are the Coup d'états, the violent overthrows of seemingly stable governments that have become commonplace. So commonplace, no one questions them anymore.

It seems tragic to simplify but here's how it works. Somehow, suddenly, African leaders find themselves face to face with a gun barrel, and forced to make an unpleasant choice, leave, or die! Between 1960 and 1974, according to statistics, there were 9 coups and 17 conflicts in Africa. Coups that took place coincidently enough, in countries that had natural resources the Western county wanted. The Congo had uranium the United States needed to build the two 'A' bombs that were dropped over Hiroshima and Nagasaki. Liberia had the rubber that was needed for tires on cars and trucks in WWII. Namibia had diamonds, and uranium and zinc. Other nations had cocoa and coffee. Others were needed for their strategic locations, such as fly over rights, and refueling rights, so we could spy on the Soviets during the cold war. All, however, were inhabited by Africans, and in the eyes of the White House, as you have just read, that meant the decision whether to launch a coup was economic, not humanitarian.

In the end history shows it mattered little how many Africans died in the name of keeping our lights on. It only mattered that we got what they had.

Randall Robinson, the former head of TransAfrica and the man credited with leading the effort to get Nelson Mandela released from prison, maintains that the United States is responsible for the coups in Angola, the Congo, Liberia, Sierra Leone, and just about every West African nation that has seen its government collapse.

Roger Morris says that number is even greater. "I would have to say that every coup d'état that takes place in post colonial Africa from about 1956-57 right up to, and including the first years of the twenty-first century, as far as we know…and the evidence is fragmentary and rudimentary, but it's enough…as far as we know, I would say all but perhaps two or three, and we're talking dozens here, all but perhaps two or three were really truly independent of the United States."

When I pointed out to Morris that if that were true, it meant that the U.S. Government committed cold blooded murder in the name of "we want what you have," his answer let little room for argument.

"Of course! Of course."

Morris says he sees little difference between the simple coups we launched or sanctioned, and the more sophisticated CIA launched coups involving men like '*Joe from Paris*'.

"Now, involvement can be everything from, wherein the old days, if you supplied a hundred guys with small automatic weapons and a couple of trucks filled with gas, you had yourself an invasion force that could overthrow a sitting government in some small African state." Morris goes onto say that coups took on many different faces. "It can be the infusion of money; it can be arms; it can be the manipulation of the market. 'The Agency', (CIA) is very good at that. The manipulations of commodities markets can have a devastating effect on the vitality of an African government."

In the upcoming chapters you will see how the CIA coups were conducted and how evidence of atrocities was covered up. You will see how coups caused the collapse of entire countries, and how the puppets that the United States and its allies installed as a result of those coups, killed their populations by the thousands. You will also see, in writing, how the United States secretly drafted policies during the Nixon years that made it all possible. You will see how our definition of national security changed to fit our needs, usually based on lies. You will see how it evolved from winning World War II, to a communist threat in Africa that never really materialized. (9)

Coups in Africa were so commonplace, that just about every African leader who was a target of a coup, knew they were targets. They also knew who had targeted them. In the case of Patrice Lumumba in the Congo, his assassination was planned even as U.S. leaders invited him to our shores for dinner. The plot is contained in a document entitled, Assassination planning and the plots.

III. ASSASSINATION PLANNING AND THE PLOTS

A. CONGO

1. INTRODUCTION

The Committee has received solid evidence of a plot to assassinate Patrice Lumumba. Strong hostility to Lumumba, voiced at the very highest levels of government may have been intended to initiate an assassination operation; at the least it engendered such an operation. The evidence indicates that it is likely that President Eisenhower's expression of strong concern about Lumumba at a meeting of the National Security Council on August 18, 1960, was taken by Allen Dulles as authority to assassinate Lumumba.[1] There is, however, testimony by Eisenhower Administration officials, and ambiguity and lack of clarity in the records of high-level policy meetings, which tends to contradict the evidence that the President intended an assassination effort against Lumumba.

The week after the August 18 NSC meeting, a presidential advisor reminded the Special Group of the "necessity for very straight-forward action" against Lumumba and prompted a decision not to rule out consideration of "any particular kind of activity which might contribute to getting rid of Lumumba." The following day, Dulles cabled a CIA Station Officer in Leopoldville, Republic of the Congo,[2] that "in high quarters" the "removal" of Lumumba was "an urgent and prime objective." Shorty thereafter the CIA's clandestine service formulated a plot to assassinate Lumumba. The plot proceeded to the point that lethal substances and instruments specifically intended for use in an assassination were delivered by the CIA to the Congo Station. There is no evidence that these instruments of assassination were actually used against Lumumba.

A thread of historical background is necessary to weave these broad questions together with the documents and testimony received by the Committee.

In the summer of 1960, there was great concern at the highest levels in the United States government about the role of Patrice Lumumba in the Congo. Lumumba, who served briefly as Premier of the newly independent nation, was viewed with alarm by United States policymakers because of what they perceived as his magnetic public appeal and his leanings toward the Soviet Union.

Under the leadership of Lumumba and the new President, Joseph Kasavubu, the Congo declared its independence from Belgium on June 30, 1960.[3] In the turbulent month that followed, Lumumba

---

[1] Indeed, one NSC staff member present at the August 18 meeting, believed that he witnessed a presidential order to assassinate Lumumba.

[2] Since the period in which the events under examination occurred, the names of many geographical units and governmental institutions have changed. For instance, the nation formerly known as the Republic of the Congo is now the Republic of Zaire and the present capital city, Kinshasa, was known then as Leopoldville. For the sake of clarity in dealing with many of the documents involved in this section, the names used in this report are those which applied in the early 1960's.

[3] For detailed reporting of the events in the Congo during this period, see the New York Times, especially July 7, 1960, 7:3; July 14, 1960, 1:1; July 16, 1960, 1:1 and 3:2; July 28, 1960, 3:7; September 3, 1960, 3:2; September 6, 1960, 1:8; December 3, 1960, 1:8; January 18, 1961, 3:1; February 14, 1961, 1:1.

Others, like Kwame Nkrumah of Ghana, knew they were targets for overthrow and believed their positions on 'improving and empowering Africa' were the reason. Nkrumah studied the non-violent philosophies of Gandhi at the University of Pennsylvania. It was his dream that there would be a united Africa that would be a coalition of separate countries acting as one giant trading block. Nkrumah's plans for Africa were much the same as the modern day European Union. That made him dangerous, and Nkrumah knew it.

After an attempted coup the CIA sent a telegram assessing Nkrumah's mental health. Not surprisingly the CIA found the attempted bombing left him rattled.

"President Nkrumah," the CIA wrote, "seems to have been affected more mentally than physically from the bomb attack."

For his part, Nkrumah blamed the "imperialists" stating, "They would be delighted to see me dead,"

NLK 01-099-6-2

TELEGRAM INFORMATION REPORT TELEGRAM

CENTRAL INTELLIGENCE AGENCY

This material contains information affecting the National Defense of the United States within the meaning of the Espionage Laws, Title 18, U.S.C. Secs. 793 and 794, the transmission or revelation of which in any manner to an unauthorized person is prohibited by law.

CONFIDENTIAL

CLASSIFICATION — DISSEMINATION CONTROLS

NO FOREIGN DISSEM

COUNTRY	GHANA	REPORT NO.	TDCS -3/521,163
SUBJECT	APPRAISAL OF NKRUMAH'S MENTAL STATE	DATE DISTR.	31 AUGUST 1962
		PRECEDENCE	ROUTINE
DATE OF INFO.		REFERENCES	IN 14970
PLACE & DATE ACQ.		EO 12958 3.4(b)(1)>25Yrs (C)	
APPRAISAL		FIELD REPORT NO.	

THIS IS UNEVALUATED INFORMATION. SOURCE GRADINGS ARE DEFINITIVE. APPRAISAL OF CONTENT IS TENTATIVE.

SOURCE

EO 12958 3.4(b)(1)>25Yrs (C)

1. PRESIDENT KWAME NKRUMAH APPEARS, FROM A CONVERSATION WITH HIM HELD SINCE THE KULUNGUGU ATTEMPT ON HIS LIFE, TO HAVE BEEN AFFECTED MUCH MORE MENTALLY THAN PHYSICALLY BY THE BOMB ATTACK.

EO 12958 3.4(b)(1)>25Y (C)

2. HE SEEMED UNREASONABLY BITTER IN HIS DENUNCIATION OF THE "IMPERIALISTS" WHOM HE SAID WERE RESPONSIBLE FOR THE ATTEMPT TO ASSASSINATE HIM. NORMALLY, HE IS AMENABLE TO JOSHING ON THE SUBJECT OF HIS ATTITUDE TOWARD "IMPERIALISTS." HE WAS NOT THIS TIME. WHEN IT WAS SUGGESTED TO HIM THAT THE BRITISH CERTAINLY COULD NOT WANT HIM OUT OF THE WAY, HE SNAPPED

BRANDT
DUNGAN
HAYSEN
KILDUFF
PETERSEN
SCHLESINGER
TAYLOR
BELK
FORRESTAL
JOHNSON
KEIN
MYER
ASKIN
SAUNDERS

CONFIDENTIAL

CLASSIFICATION — DISSEMINATION CONTROLS

NO FOREIGN DISSEM

STATE	ARMY/ACSI	NAVY	AIR	JCS	SECDEF	NSA	NIC	USIA	OCI	ONE	OCR	OER	OO	DIA	EXO

TELEGRAM INFORMATION REPORT TELEGRAM

CLASSIFICATION — DISSEMINATION CONTROLS		IN 14970
~~CONFIDENTIAL~~ (When Filled In) ~~NO FOREIGN DISSEM~~	TDCS -3/521,163	PAGE 2

BACK THAT "THEY WOULD BE DELIGHTED TO SEE ME DEAD."

    3. WHEN DISCUSSING THE EXPULSION FROM GHANA OF THE ANGLICAN

BISHOP, RICHARD ROSEVEARE, HE BECAME ALMOST VITRIOLIC IN REJECTING

A SUGGESTION THAT THE BISHOP HAD ONLY BEEN DOING HIS DUTY AS A

MINISTER.

    4. FIELD DISSEM STATE.

E0 12958 3.4(b)(1)>25Yrs
(C)

END OF MESSAGE

Kwame Nkrumah with Dr. Martin Luther King (10)

Whether men like Nkrumah were paranoid, or whether they had legitimate fears, the bottom line is, shortly after their fears, their governments were overthrown. In the case of Kwame Nkrumah, he was overthrown while overseas trying to broker a deal between the U.S. and the Viet Cong.

So why did we do it?

The NSC's Morris says, "Greed!" He continues, "Why do we do them? Well of course it's always defined as being in the national interest at a given moment. It may be to avert this instability that we're talking about, it may be to protect a base for over flight privilege that we have, or an American business interest that we have in a country. We were deeply involved in Liberia because of Firestone...deeply involved in Rhodesia because of Union Carbide...deeply involved in Rwanda and Burundi and looking the other way...because of Folgers coffee." It quickly becomes clear that Morris has a natural resource to match every coup.

History has shown that CIA-led coups in Africa betrayed any spirit of what America stands for. Torture was common, for no apparent reason. Men were brutally killed in ways that defied any convention, Geneva or otherwise. The CIA sent Dr. Gottlieb to poison Patrice Lumumba's toothpaste. When that didn't work he was tortured. In the end Lumumba's badly beaten body was found tortured, and burned almost beyond recognition, in a vat of sulfuric acid. There are other examples.

The body of Haile Selassie, the Emperor of Ethiopia, has never been found. There are reports he was dismembered and buried inside a restroom wall. William Tolbert of Liberia was disemboweled. Tolbert was a Baptist minister. The man who overthrew him was castrated and had his ear cut off. Samuel Doe found out quickly that in Africa it is not good to be the king. Students study the fact that Nelson Mandela was imprisoned for 28 years before being released from prison, but rarely ask why he was placed there in the first place.

John Stockwell, the CIA's station chief in Angola, writes in his book that the United States is responsible for the deaths of 1.5 million people because of its actions in just one country. The library on U.S. led coups in Africa is so vast that the bibliography, alone, would represent a separate book. No one disputes our role in the collapse of these governments, and conversely, few look back to view the results.

Instead, we type away at our laptops, sip our coffee, converse on our cell phones, and act as if Africa's demise has nothing to do with our quest for its endless supply of natural resources. There has, however, been a terrible human price paid for our greed. We did, to Africa, what we never would consider doing to France, or Britain, or Germany. Africa's blood is on the hands of almost every US Corporation and president who has ordered an armed invasion of a sovereign African country.

In the case of Patrice Lumumba, the Congo never recovered. By last count, as many as ten million people died in
the ensuing wars and instability. But history has shown that the
coups were far more deadly than even their planners realized.
Africa lost a generation of leaders during those coups. It lost
bold men of vision who dreamed of an African continent that
would rival Europe and Asia. Some were felled by assassin's
bullets, most suffered worse. The entire leadership of a continent was systematically destroyed by those who sought its
natural resources. Little attention was paid to the consequences.
No, instead, if anything, a world bent on greed saw the potential for wealth, paying little attention to the human prices
extracting that wealth would take. History will show that the
men who replaced the slave owners created their own global
slave trade, with Africa at its core, and got rich in the process.

Chapter Nineteen

Coup D'états in Africa since 1960

"Coups come and go and whether the agency was involved or not is not a matter for congressional investigation...nobody pays any attention..." "The vast majority, we either knew about... sanctioned... engineered...or participated in."

Roger Morris National Security Council/Johnson
and Nixon Administrations

So just how many coup d'états were there in Africa? The sad fact is, no one knows for sure. There were rebellions that were put down and never reported by the "Tinhorn dictators," and future coups that have been drawn up during CIA planning sessions that have yet to be launched.

According to the NSC's Roger Morris, "the benefit almost always is financial in some way. And I don't mean nakedly commercial. It may mean that you're protecting an interest like Firestone, or like Folgers, or American property owned in these places. But financial interest could also be a friendly government purchasing American arms from the pentagon, and those American arms as you know are not made on the other side of the Potomac. They're made by the military industrial complex in the United States, so there are a lot of people profiting from these merchants of death are who are not limited to those who cut the deals. So this is a seamless web of interests that are served with a friendly government in Africa."

There is also, according to Morris and other sources, a more frightening development that is occurring in Africa.

Global, multi-national companies with deep pockets and vast resources, much of it blood money, who have hired their own paramilitary forces. Those forces made up of former U.S. Special Forces soldiers and retired agency men, launch their own coups. Contrary to popular belief, instability in Africa is good for business. An unstable government can't raise taxes, support workers rights or negotiate strong deals in the national interest.

Paramilitary forces that act outside the law can squash any attempts at a free press, national or international and operate outside the borders of the Geneva Convention. Those forces can torture their enemies, and act outside known rules of military engagement. This is perhaps the most thorough list of coups that have taken place on the African continent since 1960. It should be noted that while this book was being considered by publishers, another coup occurred.

•1960: Military coup in Democratic Republic of the Congo.

•1960: Failed military coup against Haile Selassie I in Ethiopia

•1963: Military coup in Togo.

•1965: Military coup in Democratic Republic of the Congo.

•1966: Military coup in Ghana.

•1965–1966: Military coup in Central African Republic.

•1966: Military coup in Upper Volta (now Burkina Faso).

•1966: Military coup in Nigeria leading to end of first republic. Major-General J.T.U Aguiyi-Ironsi becomes Head of State.

•1967: Attempted military coup ("Guitar-boy") in Ghana

•1967: Military coup in Nigeria. Yakubu Gowon comes to power.

•1969: Colonel Qadhafi overthrows monarchy in Libya.

•1969: Military coup in Somalia.

•1969: Military Coup in the Sudan.

•1971: Military coup in Uganda led by Idi Amin.

•1972: Colonel Ignatius Kutu Acheampong led a coup d'état to overthrow the democratically elected government of the Progress Party and its leader Dr. Kofi Busia on 13 January 1972.[Ghana]

•1974: Military coup in Ethiopia by the communist junta led by General Aman Andom and Mengistu Haile Mariam.

•1975: Military coup in Nigeria overthrows Yakubu Gowon. Murtala Ramat Mohammed comes to power.

•1975: Military coup in Chad overthrows and kills President François Tombalbaye.

•1976: Failed coup attempt in Nigeria. Murtala Ramat Mohammed killed but Olusegun Obasanjo escapes assassination and becomes head of state.

•1980: Military coup in Liberia, led by Master Sergeant Samuel K. Doe, overthrows government led by President William R. Tolbert, ending 102 years of continuous rule by the True Whig Party.

•1980: Military coup in Guinea Bissau.

•1980: Successful coup in Suriname by military officers led by Dési Bouterse that resulted in military rule until 1988.

•1981: Failed coup in The Gambia led by Kukoi Sanyang; suppressed by Dawda Jawara with the assistance of Senegalese troops

•1981: Failed coup in Suriname, led by Wilfred Hawker

•1981: 31 December Flt. lt. Jerry John Rawlings stages a second successful military coup in Ghana overthrowing Dr. Hilla Limann's constitutional government.

•1981: Failed coup in Seychelles led by Mike Hoare.

•1982: Failed coup in Kenya by some members of the Kenya Air Force.

•1982: Failed coup in Suriname, led by Surendre Rambocus.

•1983: Military palace coup in Nigeria. Second republic president Shagari overthrown; Muhammadu Buhari takes power.

•1984: Cameroonian Palace Guard Revolt

•1984: Maaouya Ould Sid'Ahmed Taya raise to power in Mauritania after a coup that overthrow the president Mohamed Khouna Ould Haidalla.

•   1985: Military coup in Uganda led by Bazilio Olara-Okello and Tito Okello.

•1985: Military coup in Nigeria. Ibrahim Babangida replaces Muhammadu Buhari.

•1987: Bloodless Palace coup in Tunisia led by Prime Minister General Zine El Abidine Ben Ali overthrow President Habib Bourguiba.

•1990: Failed coup attempt in Nigeria led by Col. Gideon Orkar.

•1992: Military coup in Algeria cancels elections and forces President to resign.

•1994 : Military coup in The Gambia.

•1999: Military coup in Côte d'Ivoire (Ivory Coast).

•2002: Military coup in Central African Republic.

•2003: Attempted coup in Mauritania.

•2003: Military coup in Guinea-Bissau.

•2004: Attempted coup in the Democratic Republic of Congo.

•2004: Failed coup d'état in Chad against President Idriss Déby.

•2004: Second attempted coup in the Democratic Republic of Congo (June).

•2004: Attempted coup in Equatorial Guinea.

•2005: Coup in Togo legalized by parliamentary vote but unrecognized by international community.

•2005: A military coup in Mauritania overthrows President Maaouya Ould Sid'Ahmed Taya. A new government is set up by a group of military officers headed by Ely Ould Mohamed Vall. The group formed the Military Council for Justice and Democracy to act as the governing council of the country.

•2006: The United Front for Democratic Change allegedly attemptes to instigate a military coup in Chad to overthrow President Idriss Déby.

•2006: The Malagasy Popular Armed Forces allegedly attempt a military coup in Madagascar against President Marc Ravalomanana.

•2006: The military of Côte d'Ivoire claims to foil a coup attempt targeting President Laurent Gbagbo.

•2008: A military coup in Mauritania involving the seizure of the president, prime minister, and interior minister after the sacking of several military officials and a political crisis in which 48 MPs walked off the job and a vote of no confidence in cabinet.

Chapter Twenty

The 'White Hand' Inside the White House

"Those that vote for abortion vote for it because they think that those aborted are the little black bastards!"

Richard Nixon, 37th President of the United States

Richard Nixon was the 37th President of the United States. He was also a bigot. Despite that, there is little, if anything to suggest that those around him ever sought to speak out against his attacks on the *other* America. The America he so frequently chose to ignore, the Jews, blacks and Hispanics. Many of those groups voted for Nixon, and yet you wouldn't know it from his speeches. Instead his record of rhetoric reflects a man who saw the world in 'black and white.'

My film, Apocalypse Africa, Made in America, begins with a simple question. It asks, *"Can racism kill a continent?"* It then shows what Africa looks like from space, the picture I featured in the opening chapters of this book. The United States and Europe are awash in lights. Africa is dark. It seems that *'The Dark Continent'*, moniker became a self fulfilling prophecy for Africa. Perhaps better than any U.S. President, Richard Nixon knew the rest of the developing world needed Africa's vast natural resources to keep its lights on, to survive. The reason may be more troubling than the results.

Why does Africa look different than China, when the CIA suggested it (China) was worse off at the turn of the century? Why are people from India talking about their country producing a new generation of millionaires and a burgeoning middle class? Is it that Africans can't produce? Or is there something else?

There is an 800lb Gorilla in the middle of the room when it comes to Africa, one that defies all logic. That 800lb Gorilla is bigotry. The film asks what would happen to a continent of color is the most powerful man in the world was a bigot?

Can racism kill a continent? Some would argue it already has. I asked Roger Morris, the former head of African Affairs in the National Security Council during the Lyndon Johnson and Richard Nixon years, if Africa were a continent of white people, would things be different? It took less than a second for him to respond.

"No! Different ballgame, different world, different cultural attachments, everything would be different," Morris argues.

Sadly, in the case of Africa, bigotry did play a role. The truth on this issue sits right in front of our eyes, but we choose to see what we want see. It is contained in thousands of pages of declassified government memos, outlining speeches were American presidents ask who is black and who is white before deciding a course of action in an African country. It is there in thousands of once Top Secret documents, recordings, and it is there in the files and films of the National Archives. America's bigotry inside the Oval office is hidden in plain sight, daring us to look at our own societal dirty laundry. Racism not only killed Africa, it continues to do so each and every day and we ignore it.

Chapter Twenty-One

The Nixon Tapes

"I'm not saying that Blacks cannot govern. I am saying they have a hell of a time."

Richard Nixon on Africa, October 7th, 1971

On February 16th, 1971 President Richard M. Nixon installed a series of secret microphones and other recording devices inside the Oval Office. There are hundreds of hours of audio tapes in which Nixon comes off as a bigot. He is recorded referring to blacks as *"niggers"* and Africans *"as just out of the trees with spears!"* Nixon on the tapes hates blacks, Jews, and just about every other ethnic group. Despite that, when the tapes were released, few, if any, historians asked, what impact did Nixon's attitudes have on that continent of color? What would happen to Africa if the President of the United States, just happened to be a bigot? What would happen to Africa, if the most powerful man in the world, hated all things black?

One of the recordings involves the two men most able to help, or hurt Africa, Richard M. Nixon, and Daniel Patrick Moynihan, who at the time represented U.S. interests in the United Nations. (11) It was recorded on October 7th, 1971. On the tape, Nixon begins the conversation by condemning each and every African leader. Moynihan could have, and should have objected. He did not. Instead like many who listened to Nixon's rants, he either agreed…or laughed.

October 7th, 1971

Nixon: I'm not saying that Blacks cannot govern. I am saying they have a hell of a time.
Daniel P. Moynihan: Mm-hmm.

Richard Nixon on the Italians, French and Spanish

Nixon: Now let's look at that. The Italians aren't any good at government. The Spanish aren't any good at government.
Moynihan: Yeah.

Nixon: the French have had a hell of a time and they're half Latin. And all of Latin America's not any good at government. They either go to one extreme or the other. It's either a family, well, three extremes: family oligarchy, or a dictatorship, or a dictatorship on the right or one on the left.

Richard Nixon on Black countries"

(Notice how countries involving people of color are identified by race and not nationality)

Looking at the Black countries . . . of course, there are only two old ones – Haiti is an old one, and Liberia is a very old one. Ethiopia is a very old one, but they have a hell of a time running the place.
Moynihan: It's a pretty miserable world.

Richard Nixon on Asia

Nixon: Now, now, now, you look at Asia, and you can say, well what about out there? You don't have democracies. Of course you don't, except Japan – where we impose it, and the Philippines – and it's a hell of a mess. But on the other hand, Thailand, with its oligarchy, has the right kind of a

*government for Thailand. And we have to say too that Iran
with the benevolent Shah . . .*
    Moynihan: [Interrupting] – works pretty well?
    *Nixon: . . . with the benevolent Shah, that's the right
thing for those folks.*
    Moynihan: Yeah.

"The Africans just can't run things!"

    *Nixon: I think. ….this whole black-white deal is gon-
na come out the fact that. . . Asians are capable of governing
themselves, one way or another. That we and the Caucasians
have learned it after slaughtering each other in religious
wars and other wars for many, many years, including a
couple in the last…this century. The Latins do it in a miserable way, but*
    *they do it…. But the Africans just can't run things.
Now that's a very, very fundamental point in the international scene. See my point?*
    *Moynihan: Oh boy, you sure see it around this place!
[Moynihan is at the United Nations]*
    *Nixon: Well, of course you do, you see them – You
know, I have mixed feelings…I receive their ambassadors,
they change all the time, and I've had in the past… I love
'em, they're so kind, and so nice…and they're children!*
    Moynihan: Yeah.
    Nixon: Children…

Athletics isn't a bad achievement!

    *Moynihan: [Laughing] Yeah…and they always want
something like children…*
    *Nixon: Oh god yes, they why…well what can you
do…But what I meant is it is so childlike…the childlike faith,*

and this and that...And of course a lot of them are crooks but
we have crooks too! Anyway, what I am getting at is, I think
you've got in the field of business; you've got the field of
education, and so forth and so on. But there are many other
areas, as you've well pointed out, where they can beat the hell
out of us. Now – and they should be proud of those! Athletics
isn't a bad achievement!
    Moynihan: Not at all!
    Nixon: And you look at the World Series, for God's
sake, what would either of these teams done without – what
would Pittsburg be without . . .? heh, heh . . .
    Moynihan: Yeah...sure...
    Nixon: A hell of a lot of blacks! And, and music... the
dance! Now - and these things, are they to be therefore just
pissed upon, hell no, they're important! And also, also, in
certain areas – poetry, et cetera. They have a free and easy
style, that creates – that adds enormously to our culture. But
on the other hand, when you to some of the more, shall we
say, some of the more profound, rigid disciplines, basically...
They have a hell of a time makin' it.
    [Conversation continues, irrelevant]

Roger Morris maintains Nixon *was* a bigot and that history blew it. He says, "you've got to remember this is a small
town southern California bigot at heart...[q] You think he is a
bigot...[a] oh absolutely this is a kid who grew up in a Quaker
town that was known for it's hypocrisy...he grows up in a
fundamentally prejudiced family and he never really outgrows
that." Sadly for Nixon, and Africa, Morris goes further. "He's
a terrible bigot in terms of American domestic politics. He's
anti Semitic and he's certainly racist and carries with it all the
classic stereotypes of the American middle class. The Italians
are crooked. The Irish are volatile and drunk. The Jews are out
to cheat you and the blacks are indolent and can't be trusted

and so forth...it's an old set of prejudices!" He was hardly the type of guy you want leading foreign policy of the most powerful nation on earth.

Bigoted leaders either create or endorse bigoted Policy

Nixon was also Vice President during the Eisenhower Administration and knew of the assassination plans for Patrice Lumumba, and other plans to destabilize the continent. He never mentions those facts anywhere in the audio tapes. He makes no mention of any U.S. blame for the collapse of the Africa continent. Instead he acts throughout the recordings, as if Africa is to blame for all of the coup d'états and other CIA led incursions into Africa that destabilized the governments of millions of Africans. Africa, according to Richard Nixon, was to blame for Africa's problems. Like the people who manufacture guns, and ignore the consequence of their devices, the United States, according to Richard M. Nixon didn't destroy Africa, Africans did.

Richard M. Nixon was not only a bigot, he and some of the other members of his cabinet, despite their impressive resumes, were culturally stupid.

Roger Morris witnessed the bigotry I found on the tapes, first hand.

"When I would come into the White House to staff meetings Al Haig and Kissinger would beat the table like this, (Morris then beats the table like a drummer) Tom Toms, because my clients were these ...these savages who had just come out of a Tarzan movie." Incredulously I ask the obvious, "This was the white house! This was the seat of American power and majesty in the world...yes...yes!"

Morris says the bigotry inside the White House was so bad, it literally made him sick to his stomach, "I wanted to scream, and eventually I quit. I found it repugnant and awful. I found it shocking. "

The problem is, others didn't find it quite so shocking and stayed behind, not even daring to challenge a president that so willfully insulted one in twelve Americans. Among them, Donald Rumsfeld, who later went onto become Defense Secretary for President George W. Bush, and subsequently led the ill-fated war in Iraq.

When Nixon referred to blacks as "niggers," Rumsfeld could be heard on one of the tapes laughing, even though it was on that same tape that Nixon referred to Africans as, "just out of the trees with spears." Perhaps Donald Rumsfeld felt the same way about the people of Iraq when he pushed for that country's invasion. After all, Iraq, like Africa was another country of color. And Iraq, like Africa, had something the United States wanted, oil.

Richard Nixon and Donald Rumsfeld
Nixon: Black Americans are as good as black Africans, most of them are basically just out of the trees...now my point is that if we say that they say, Well by god, well, ah, even the southern say, "well our niggers is better than their niggers, hell that's the way they talk."
Donald Rumsfeld: That's right."
Nixon: "I can hear 'em."
Donald Rumsfeld: "I know."
Richard Nixon: "It's like when our black athletes, I mean in the Olympics are running against the other black athletes, the southerners may not like the blacks but he's for that black athlete."
Donald Rumsfeld: "That's right."
Richard Nixon: "Right?"
Donald Rumsfeld: "That's for sure."
Richard Nixon: "Well, enough of that."
(Note this is the version posted on the University of Virginia historical website) (12)

Roger Morris says bigotry inside the Nixon White House, was common, "I was in meetings, privately with other members of the government…with Henry Kissinger…with members of his staff he let his hair down … it was common to talk about niggers and about putting something in it in a statement in a message for the Congress, something for the jigs…he was fond of saying."

Richard Nixon was not alone.

According to the minutes of the National Security Council, during a June 27th meeting in which the situation in Angola was being discussed, one of the first questions then President Gerald Ford asked, was, "what are the *white areas* within the borders of Angola?" He then goes on to ask, "What is the *white population*?" He was told that out of a population of between 5-7 million people, only three to four hundred thousand were white. And if that is not insult enough to Africa, he asks, "Are there many educated blacks?" Clearly in the mind of Gerald Ford there was a difference between whites and blacks in Africa, when it came to deciding decisions of war, or arms sales. It appears he even delineated between educated and non educated blacks.

The President: Bill [to Colby], will you brief us on Angola and related problems.

Mr. Colby: Yes, sir. [Briefed - as attached.]

The President: Cabinda was a part of the Portuguese territories? [This was in reference to a point in Mr. Colby's brief as he described Cabinda.]

Mr. Colby: Yes, sir.

The President: What are the white areas within the borders of Angola?

Mr. Colby: These are essentially tribal, not military areas. These are additional tribes and I just chose [pointing on the chart] to mention those three. They have different languages and are different socially.

The President: Did the Portuguese do much in combatting illiteracy? Are there many educated blacks?

Mr. Colby: The Portuguese were not forceful in this area. The literacy rate is between 10-15 percent.

Secretary Kissinger: Mr. President, until the coup, the Portuguese had no intention of leaving their territories in Africa and didn't organize them for independence.

Secretary Schlesinger: Most of the educated classes are in Luanda and support the MPLA.

The President: What is the white population?

Mr. Colby: Three to four hundred thousand.

The President: Out of a total population of how many?

Mr. Colby: About 5.7 million.

Roger Morris maintains he never worked for a President who in some way, shape or form, wasn't a bigot. That, he says, is the ultimate problem with how we deal with Africa. "I think it's fair to say that, and I don't know the subsequent American politicians as well as these two...but I think it's fair to say both Johnson and Nixon (were bigots) Johnson, once when I was in his office, he had just seen a TV thing about starving babies in Biafra, called him up and said, we got to do more to get these starving nigger babies off my TV screen." Roger Morris says Johnson didn't consider himself to be a bigot, and explains that was how America saw Africa. Not unlike the little boys who beat their chests and imitated Tarzan, America's bigotry toward Africa is cultural. Latent racism that he maintains is deeply imbedded in the American psyche.

"Now it's just part of this depersonalization, it's part of this dehumanization of racism. They're different than we are and so therefore you can make the argument about inferiority and how they behave different and there you are. It's what I said earlier about racism being inseparable from the way American politicians see the world and see themselves." That according to Morris is why it is so easy for America's leaders to walk away from their TV sets when so much suffering in Africa occurs on their watch. "Inevitably, whether it's black or whether it is Asian, there's a sense that life matters less. (In those countries) That life is less valued. I mean my goodness, isn't life less valuable in Vietnam than it is in Chicago? Isn't life less valuable in the Congo than it is Whittier? This is a profound problem in American life."

Perhaps most frightening is what Morris says last on the subject of racism and bigotry inside the White House.

"We're not over it by any means!"

Chapter Twenty-Two

NSSM 200

*Global population as a threat to the national security of the
United States. The present world population growth is unique.
Rates of increase are much higher than in earlier centuries,
they are more widespread, and have a greater effect on economic life, social justice, and -- quite likely -- on public order
and political stability*

Source: NSSM 200 April 1974

In April of 1974, the developing world declared war on
the growing population of the third world, and the third world
never saw it coming. The declaration was contained in a Top
Secret document known as NSSM 200, or National Security
Study Memorandum 200. NSSM's, as they are called, are the
Top Secret studies ordered by U.S. presidents before the
official policies of the United States are changed. Most remain
classified to this day.

Roger Morris, was the former National Security Council member in the Johnson and Nixon administrations. He
described a NSSM this way; "a NSSM is initially the document
by which the President orders the bureaucracy to review a
given policy...and then it's known as the NSSM. The response
that comes back from these endless meetings comes back up as
a NSSM and becomes a NSDM, a National Security Decision
Memorandum based upon the NSSM."

Morris says, make no mistake about it, NSSM 200 was
sinister in its origins, "Population was always one of those

phantoms that lurked in the closet." He also says NSSM 200 was racist. "Oh my God the rest of the world which is mostly nonwhite is getting bigger and bigger, what are we going to do about it? NSSM 200 was just one of many exercises in which the bureaucracy comes up with a new rationalization to do what it wants to anyway."

What the Nixon administration wanted to do, was to make sure that there were fewer of them, than there were of us. The reason why was simple. We wanted to keep the lights on. Remember that photo in the beginning of the book. Remember that picture of Africa from space. The continent didn't get that way on its own. There had to be outside interference.

NSSM 200 declared the growing populations of the third world, a threat to the national security of the United States. In a nutshell, we feared that if those countries continued to grow unchecked, they might one day want the natural resources that, up until now, we had access to unfettered. We wanted them even though they were their natural resources.

Africa, according to the CIA, was the fastest growing continent on the planet. The combination of a young population and newly energized leaders, like Patrice Lumumba, Nelson Mandela and Kwame Nkrumah, threatened the stability of the status quo. NSSM 200 saw to it that that could not and would not happen.

NSSM 200 found its way to the desks of decision makers inside the CIA and the industrial military complex. Loosely translated, controlling the world's population fell upon the shoulders of the people whose specialties were 'guns, bombs and spies'. Africa and the rest of the developing world never stood a chance.

According to Roger Morris, "Anything that defines anything as strategic, a strategic material, and a strategic location automatically ups the ante and automatically brings the Pentagon in. The definition of a NSSM is that it is an interagency study and automatically at that table, no matter

what the administration does ... are all the fiefdoms of government. State, Defense, Treasury all automatically have seats
at the table."

Suddenly, the U. S. foreign aid, that had been a staple
of many African economies, had new strings attached. African
leaders that wanted our help, our money, had to do something
in return. They had to, according to NSSM 200, reduce their
populations. The devil, in this case, is in the details. The devil
involved how they were to do so.

UNCLASSIFIED
E.O. 12958, as amended, Sect 3.3
V(2)Reuben to Smith 4/04/2003
By ___ Date 02/03/__
                                NATIONAL SECURITY COUNCIL
                                  WASHINGTON, D.C. 20506

CONFIDENTIAL - GDS

                                                    April 24, 1974

National Security Study Memorandum 200

TO: The Secretary of Defense
               The Secretary of Agriculture
               The Director of Central Intelligence
               The Deputy Secretary of State
               Administrator, Agency for International Development

SUBJECT: Implications of Worldwide Population Growth for U.S.
               Security and Overseas Interests

The President has directed a study of the impact of world population growth
on U.S. security and overseas interests. The study should look forward
at least until the year 2000, and use several alternative reasonable pro-
jections of population growth.

In terms of each projection, the study should assess:

    -- the corresponding pace of development, especially in poorer
        countries;

    -- the demand for US exports, especially of food, and the trade pro-
        blems the US may face arising from competition for resources; and

    -- the likelihood that population growth or imbalances will produce
        disruptive foreign policies and international instability.

The study should focus on the international political and economic implications of population growth rather than its ecological, sociological or other
aspects.

The study should then offer possible courses of action for the United States
in dealing with population matters abroad, particularly in developing
countries, with special attention to these questions:

    -- What, if any, new initiatives by the United States are needed to
        focus international attention on the population problem?

        Can technological innovations or development reduce growth or
        ameliorate its effects?

CONFIDENTIAL - GDS

NSSM 200 Continues:

•By about 1830, world population reached 1 billion.
The second billion was added in about 100 years by 1930. The
third billion in 30 years by 1960. The fourth will be reached in
1975.
  •Between 1750-1800 less than 4 million were being
added, on the average, to the earth's population each year.
Between 1850-1900, it was close to 8 million. By 1950 it had
grown to 40 million. By 1975 it will be about 80 million

Source: NSSM 200

The pretext for NSSM 200 was simple. Imagine a
world where every African had two cars in every garage. Now
imagine what the cost of a gallon of gas might be, if that were
to happen. How much might we be paying at the pump if
hundreds of millions of other drivers were added to the equation. Now add in another factor. African nations like Nigeria,
Libya, Chad, Algeria, Liberia, and a host of others, had their
own oil. Oil that they might one day use for their own populations first, and oil wasn't the only natural resource Africa had
everything that the Western world coveted. Africa had uranium, cobalt, bauxite, coltan, iron ore, cocoa, coffee, rubber,
diamonds, and every other precious mineral conceivable.
  According to Roger Morris, "we were deeply involved
in Liberia because of Firestone, deeply involved in Rhodesia
because of Union Carbide, deeply involved in Rwanda and
Burundi and looking the other way because of Folgers coffee."
  Morris goes on to say that, "just because there wasn't
an American company there didn't mean that one day there
wouldn't be. We must not forget that underlying all of this that
this was a relatively underdeveloped continent. There weren't
very many African states that didn't have some kind of mineral

or other wealth that didn't stand to be exploited. Just because American

Companies or American investors weren't involved didn't mean that there wasn't some interest there."

Africa had the minerals to fuel our cars, build our bombs and bullets, construct our skyscrapers, and outfit the ring fingers of our fiancés and wives while we sipped our latte and dined on chocolate. Africa had everything that we wanted, and we were willing to do whatever it took to keep it…even if it meant facilitating abortions. NSSM 200 made it clear that if Africa's population were to be reduced, abortion was not only needed, it was necessary.

Abortion

1. Worldwide abortion practices certain facts about abortion need to be appreciated:

No country has reduced its population growth with-out resorting to abortion.

Thirty million pregnancies are estimated to be terminated annually by abortion throughout the world. The figure is a guess. More precise data indicate about 7 percent of the world's population live in countries where abortion is prohibited without exception and 12 percent in countries where abortion is permitted only to save the life of the pregnant woman. About 15 percent live under statutes authorizing abortion on broader medical grounds, that is, to avert a threat to the woman's health, rather than to her life, and sometimes on eugenic and/or juridical grounds (rape, etc.) as well. Countries where social factors may be taken into consideration to justify termination of pregnancy account for 22 percent of the world's population and those allowing for elective abortion for at least some categories of women, for 36 percent. No information is available for the remaining 8 percent; it would appear, however, that most of these people live in areas with restrictive abortion laws

Source: NSSM 200

There was, however, one major problem. Abortion was not only illegal in the United States but politically unpopular, especially among the same republicans who were behind NSSM 200. The problem for Africa and the rest of the developing world was that those same republicans didn't see abortion in Africa the same way they saw abortion in Arizona. Richard Nixon, for instance, was secretly recorded inside the Oval Office referring to aborted black fetuses as "The little black bastards!" The solution to the problem was simple. Rather than recommend abortions, the entire debate would be framed as research. Research, after all, was not only legal, it was all American.

A.I.D. funds may continue to be used for research relative to abortion since the Congress specifically chose not to include research among the prohibited activities.

A major effect of the amendment and policy determination is that A.I.D. will not be involved in further development or promotion of the Menstrual Regulation Kit. However, other donors or organizations may become interested in promoting with their own funds dissemination of this promising fertility control method. b. DHEW Pro-grams Section 1008 of the Family Planning Services and Population Research Act of 1970 (P.L. 91-572) states that "None of the funds appropriated under this title shall be used in programs where abortion is a method of family planning." DHEW has adhered strictly to the intent of Congress and does not support abortion research. Studies of the causes and consequences of abortion are permitted, however.

The Public Health Service Act Extension of 1973 (P.L. 93-45) contains the Church Amendment which establishes the right of health providers (both individuals and institutions) to refuse to perform an abortion if it conflicts with moral or religious principles. c. Proposed Legislation on Abortion Research There are numerous proposed Congressional amendments and bills which are more restrictive on abortion research than any of the pieces of legislation cited above.

It would be unwise to restrict abortion research for the following reasons:

1. The persistent and ubiquitous nature of abortion.
2. Widespread lack of safe abortion technique.
3. Restriction of research on abortifacient drugs and devices would:

a. Possibly eliminate further development of the IUD.

b. Prevent development of drugs which might have other beneficial uses. An example is methotrexate (R) which is now used to cure a hitherto fatal tumor of the uterus -- choriocarcinoma. This drug was first used as an abortifacient.

Source: NSSM 200

But abortion wasn't the only controversy squarely on the table. So was sterilization.

d. Sterilization of men and women has received widespread acceptance in several areas when a simple, quick, and safe procedure is readily available. Female sterilization has been improved by technical advances with laparoscopes, culdoscopes, and greatly simplifies abdominal surgical techniques. Further improvements by the use of tubal clips, transcervical approaches, and simpler techniques can be developed. For men several current techniques hold promise but require more refinement and evaluation.

Approx. Increased Cost $6 million annually.

Despite that, not even the Nixon White House was naive enough to believe that the world's leaders would stand by and permit abortion and sterilization in Africa and the rest of the developing world. So rather than target specific nations, they simply changed the definition of who was being targeted and framed the debate using clever euphemisms. Africa wasn't a target of NSSM 200, LDC's were.

Chapter Twenty-Three

LDC's

"Lesser Developed Countries"

Source: NSSM 200

The vernacular was to call the emerging world LDC's or lesser developed countries. A close examination reveals all those countries had one thing in common...they were countries of color. Those countries were targeted in various ways, but always the intent was the same. The end result was making sure there were fewer of their people lining up for the world's natural resources than in the United States and Europe.

Past experience suggests that easily available family planning services are a vital and effective element in reducing fertility rates in the LDCs.

Two main advances are required for providing safe and effective fertility control techniques in the developing countries: source:

NSSM 200

NSSM 200 had one, and only one, bottom line. That bottom line was to reduce competition for resources, by reducing the mouths at the world's table. Ultimately, it all boiled down to a form of economic apartheid, in which food supplies and other forms of foreign aid were suddenly tied to population control. Badly needed school construction projects, roads, dams and hospitals were suddenly on hold if the countries seeking foreign aid couldn't present plans to reduce their population.

When that didn't work...enter the army and bring in the guns.

NSSM 201
Increased arms sales to black Africa

"*I never knew a pentagon officer...whoever approached arms sales from a moral point of view." Roger Morris, from Apocalypse Africa, Made in America*

NSSM 201, written a day after NSSM 200, called for studying what would happen if the U.S. decided to increase arms sales to black Africa. Keep in mind, inside the State Department and other government agencies; Africa was divided along lines of color and influence. Those countries in Africa, run by predominantly white governments, frequently were referred to only as Africa. While sub-Saharan Africa was usually described as Black Africa. That blatant racism has never been rectified.

In the studies supporting NSSM 201, the authors warned increasing arms sales to black Africa would produce one of four results. Some argued there would be no change in Africa, and that African leaders would simply ignore calls for more military assistance in favor of building those hospitals, bridges and roads. Others, however, argued that doing so would destabilize the continent and lead to arms races. The end result was to increase arms sales to Africa, and the affect is not subject to debate. African leaders suddenly saw themselves as heads of their own military machines. The arms race in Africa was on, and Africa was never the same.

Roger Morris maintains, few, if any questioned the fact U.S. guns were killing people in Africa, in record numbers. It wasn't personal Morris maintains, just business. "I never knew a pentagon officer...whoever approached arms sales from a moral point of view. It was strictly national interest. Do we want influence with these people? Do we want to make money at the same time? Do we want our people to be there as a listening post, and if you sell weapons, do you need technical advisors? No, it's a very practical matter of influence." I then asked the question that begged to be asked, "so US guns don't kill people?...[a] well of course they do, but that's the price you pay for influence, and besides, you can rationalize a million ways...oh my god they're the ones who are doing the killing."

Few have ever questioned the relationship between NSSM 200 and NSSM 201, even though they were written a day apart and ordered by the same racist President, Richard M. Nixon. Few ever examined the tapes recorded inside the Oval Office, where Nixon referred to Africans as," just out of the trees with spears," and African men as "niggers." No one ever asked, what would happen to that continent of color if the president of the United States was a bigot. No one cared, after all, *"this was Africa!"*

Many believe what happened in NSSM 201, resulted in widespread genocide across the African continent, where the weapons of choice were U.S. supplied guns. African leaders, as a result of NSSM 201 were forced to choose between guns and butter. Badly needed resources to rebuild a continent still shackled by slavery and colonialism, were now being diverted to build bigger and better equipped armies. African leaders were told by arms dealers that they needed the weapons to protect their populations from other African leaders with guns. Arms dealers got rich while millions of Africans died. Africa's slow descent into hell was well underway. The question is, why?

(14)

NATIONAL SECURITY COUNCIL
WASHINGTON, D.C. 20506

SEGRET GDS   April 25, 1974

National Security Study Memorandum 201

TO: The Secretary of Defense
              The Deputy Secretary of State
              The Director of Central Intelligence

SUBJECT: Military Assistance and Arms Policy
              in Black Africa

The President has directed a study of United States policy for providing
military assistance and arms to the countries of Black Africa. Since
the United States can expect to receive requests for arms assistance
and training from a number of Black African states in the future, the
study should examine the policy options for responding to such requests,
in light of our economic, political and strategic interests.

The study first should describe current U.S. policy and its objectives
and evaluate our success in achieving these objectives. The study
then should examine and assess possible alternative U.S. policies
which would take into account such factors as:

   -- present or potential requests for new or more sophisticated
      categories of equipment or military assistance from Black
      African countries;

   -- potential requests from countries now embargoed in part
      or whole from United States Government military assistance.

   - reactions by other interested states, including potential arms
      suppliers who are commercial or political competitors of
      the United States;

      the effect of each alternative policy on African insurgencies;

   -- arms as a cause of rivalries between African countries or con-
      frontation in Africa between outside powers;

SEGRET GDS

SECRET GDS   -2-

-- criteria for grant, credit and sales including impact on
   social and economic development;

-- Congressional limitations on levels and kinds of aid; and,

-- impact on U. S. arms embargo policies in Southern Africa.

This study should be prepared by the NSC Interdepartmental Group for
Africa and submitted by May 24, 1974 for review by the NSC Senior Review
Group prior to consideration by the President.

Henry A. Kissinger

cc: Chairman, Joint Chiefs of Staff

Chapter Twenty-Four

The Smoking Gun?

I call it assisted genocide; we can no longer go into country with tanks and bombs and planes; that would be condemned by the world. Instead, we allow the people to kill themselves.

Brian Clowes, Human Life International

The definition of genocide is "The systematic and planned extermination of an entire national, racial, political or ethnic group. No one argues when the word genocide is used to describe Jews in World War II. It is only in Africa that so many have had problems for so long. Perhaps, it is because if what is happening in Africa does rise to the level of genocide, the world will look inward. The developed world will discover there is plenty of blame to go around. It is as simple as any street crime unfolding in any urban area. The person pulling the trigger is charged with murder as is the person who supplied the gun. That person is called an accessory, if that person knew the gun was going to be used in the commission of a crime. Despite that he National Rifle Association has made it clear that "guns don't kill people, people do."

In Africa, however, it is not that simple. In Africa, guns do kill, and millions have died simply because of the proliferation of weapons that have flooded the African continent since NSSM 201. But was it all innocent? Was it simply business-as-usual, or was there something else? If so, did what happened in Africa rise to the level of genocide?

Look up the word Genocide in any dictionary and it usually refers to the German, "final solution." The "final solution," was the German method of killing Jews during World War II. Certainly, there can be no doubt that what happened to the Jews was genocide. Hitler set out to destroy as many Jews as possible, using whatever means he could. When bullets proved to be too costly, Hitler turned to gas. As many as six million Jews died in what is now commonly known as the Jewish holocaust. In Africa...the bodies are still being counted while the world debates whether what is happening in Africa, is indeed genocide. One body has already made its decision. History!

Genocide has since been used to define the massacre of thousands of Hutus by Tutsis in Rwanda, and the ongoing conflict in Darfur. There is, however, a film that argues genocide began much earlier, in Africa! A single, previously undisclosed film raises serious questions about whether arms sales to Africa by countries such as the US, are purely economic in their mission. The film maintains that the origins of the word genocide date back to the earlier part of the twentieth century, forty years before the Jewish Holocaust. First let's examine just how many guns there are on the African continent.

It is no secret why so many African's die. They die because of guns. Guns do kill people. They kill them by the millions worldwide. The popular phrase, "guns don't kill people, people do," couldn't be further from the truth especially in Africa. Take away the guns and the millions of people who are dead and cold in the grave, would be walking and talking among us today. Nowhere is that more clear than in Africa, and the guns that are killing people there were supplied, in large part, by the United States and its allies.

In many parts of Africa, an AK-47 can be bought for $6, or even traded for a chicken. It is the weapon of choice in Africa, so common, no one ever asks where they come from.

The weapon has become so popular it is now part of the culture. For instance, a silhouette of an AK can be found on the Mozambican flag. Fighters in Angola, Namibia, South Africa and Zimbabwe even have songs about the gun.

Perhaps the most misleading point about an AK 47 is where they come from. Because the weapons were Russian made, many believe they were sold to Africans by Soviet bloc countries. That is and is not true.

According to John Stockwell, the former head of the CIA's Angola task force, "The CIA has the world's largest supplies of foreign made weapons." No one has ever asked the agency why it would keep such large stockpiles of guns not made in the U.S., but it doesn't take a genius to figure it out. Guns not only kill people, they are an effective form of genocide. In fact, historians will one day write, guns were an integral part of the worst genocide ever.

There is little doubt that what happened in Namibia rose to the level of genocide. There were death camps, numbering, and the systematic slaughter of thousands, perhaps as many as 100,000 Africans that were identified by their tribal names. Despite that, some debate whether what happened in Namibia was actually genocide. The Africans who died don't, and neither does a newly discovered United Nations documentary, that film.

These are the facts. In 1904, a German by the name of Lothar Von Trotha, ordered his troops to systematically slaughter members of the Nama and Herero tribes.

Simple cattle farmers, the members of both tribes were fighting to regain the rights to their land that the Germans had taken and handed to settlers. The settlers like the rest of those who came to rape Namibia, were interested in one thing and one thing only, Namibia's diamonds. White settlers were killed, and the Germans fought back. What happened next was hardly an example of equal and opposite reaction. Instead,

historians regard it as a massacre. Others say it was the
world's first recorded example of genocide.

14,000 well armed German troops handily defeated the
Nama and Herero tribes that totaled less than five thousand.
Those who were not killed fled to the desert. An order was
given to then kill all the men, women and children. There was
no mention of civilian versus military casualties, just mass
murder. Many of those targeted by the Germans starved to
death. Those who survived were rounded up and placed in
concentration camps where they were given numbers, and their
deaths recorded. Others were studied in medical experiments.

An internet article that was written about the massacre
reports that a man called Eugene Fischer, who was interested in
genetics, came to the camps to study them and carried out
medical experiments on them, as well. He decided that each
mixed-race child was physically and mentally inferior to its
German father (a conclusion for which there was and is no
respectable scientific foundation whatever) and wrote a book
promoting his ideas: 'The Principles of Human Heredity and
Race Hygiene'. Adolf Hitler read it while he was in prison in
1923, and cited it in his own infamous pursuit of 'racial purity'.
(15)

But the United Nations documentary goes one step further. It outlines how the Germans cleverly set out to begin the
systematic slaughter of both tribes in Africa. According to the
documentary, the Germans learned that guns could be used to
kill large numbers of their enemies, or "problems" as the
documentary put it, without *them* pulling the trigger. We
should also keep in mind why German needed to control 'the
natives'. Germany wanted Namibia's gold, diamonds, and
uranium, but the Africans, who were growing tired of being
treated like slaves, rebelled.

When the unruly Africans got out of hand, the documentary states," Bismarck," who was the German Emperor at
the time, dispatched a squad to clean up the "problem." It was

led by the father of a man who would later become the number two man in the Nazi Third Reich. His name was Goering.

"When two tribes were hostile to each other," the documentary states matter-of-factly, the German policy was to enter into protection agreements with both tribes, arm them, and influence the natives to kill each other for us." Us in this case meant the Germans.

What happened next is what historians frequently refer to as genocide, the decision to massacre tens of thousands of Herero and Nama tribesmen. Few historians cite the events leading up to the massacre, or what the documentary concludes.

"This is what the United Nations, in a latter day would call, genocide!"

Fast forward to 2004, 100 years after the massacre of the Herero and Nama peoples. Representatives of the German government traveled to Namibia to apologize for what they now admit *was* genocide. Despite that, no checks were written or reparations issued. The German's maintain that because they offered as much as 11 million dollars a year to Namibia in economic assistance, paying for the sins of their fathers is not necessary. The family of Lothar Von Trotha, however, saw things differently.

Von Trotha, is recorded as saying, "'All the Herero must leave the land. If they refuse, then I will force them to do it with the big guns. Any Herero found within German borders, with or without a gun, will be shot. No prisoners will be taken. This is my decision for the Herero people'."

In a documentary that ran on the British Broadcasting Corporation, or the BBC, the family of Lothat von Trotha apologized. "We, the von Trotha family, are deeply ashamed of the terrible events that took place 100 years ago. Human rights were grossly abused at that time," Wolf-Thilo von Trotha said."

That brings us back to the guns and what was stated in the documentary about the massacre. Are guns used in Africa as a means to systematically destroy entire tribes and nations so we can have access to their natural resources? Have guns replaced the gas chambers and concentration camps of World War II to destroy entire civilizations? One group leading the battle to alleviate guns from the African continent says, 'what happened in Namibia was not the exception, but the rule'.

Brian Clowes is a researcher for Human Life International, a group based in the suburbs of Washington D.C. Clowes frequently travels to the African continent and has seen the problem up close. He has a term for what he sees.

"Assisted genocide, or assisted self genocide," he explains. "We can no longer go into a country with guns and bombs and tanks and planes...that would be condemned by the world." Instead, he says, "we allow the people to kill themselves. I call it assisted genocide, or assisted self genocide. We (the United States) are doing it to countries and continents around the world."

Clowes, who has also studied NSSM 200, believes that there is a direct correlation between Nixon's study and what is happening in Africa.

"We want these resources for ourselves," he reasons. "We see Africa as a threat." He continues, "because in twenty or thirty years the average African will be 30, while the average European will be 50, and the average person in the United States will be 47. So we see Africa as a direct and proximate threat."

Clowes says it all boils down to one thing, Africa's natural resources. "We want those resources for ourselves," he says.

Roger Morris, while not believing U.S action amounts to deliberate genocide, says there is no doubt that the U.S. by its action or lack thereof, supports genocidal policies. "I certainly think it's a holocaust. Genocide would have to be differentiated. You've got what amounts to genocidal neglect...in many of these societies, in terms of American policy. Genocide has come to mean a much more specific deliberate action by governments. We never did that; we were never about the extermination of a whole people. We were certainly about getting along with dictators we knew were about the extermination of their people, and we looked the other way at genocidal practices."

TransAfrica's Randall Robinson says it all boils down to one simple fact, "There is blood on America's hands in Africa," he says. He has been saying it for years.

Roger Morris goes one step further, "Oh I think it's arguable that we perhaps and I wouldn't to absolve the French and British, I think it's arguable that we are very much responsible by what we did or didn't do, for what I think is the greatest single continental disaster in the history of the planet. We're watching a continent die in front of our eyes here, and none of that was necessary … none of that, the poverty, none of the disease, none of the ignorance, none of the lack of

development, none of the tortuous history of these regimes.
This parade of tin horned dictators that came and went, none of
that was necessary, none of that was necessary to American
national security." Instead Morris says, it was all based on a lie,
"none of that was necessary to the waging of the cold war
against the soviets ... none of it. It's all a mindless and extra-
ordinarily selfish phenomena in American foreign policy."

Morris is even harsher as to why he thinks the United
States did what it did in Africa. "The blunt truth is that we
didn't give a damn about these people in American foreign
policy. They were targets of opportunity and they were
incredibly weak... incredibly malleable."

Today, no one knows exactly how many guns there are
in Africa. Estimates vary. The affect of all those guns on the
African continent is not, however, in dispute. In 1999, the Red
Cross estimated that in the Somali capital of Mogadishu, alone,
the city's 1.3 million residents possessed over a million guns --
among an estimated 550 million small arms in circulation
worldwide.

Guns in Africa *are* the weapons of mass destruction.
By some estimates as many as twenty million lives have been
lost in the various conflicts that have taken place across the
continent. Some say that number is far too low. Whatever the
argument, the number is more than three times the number of
people who died in the Jewish Holocaust. While this is not
meant to minimize what happened in Germany, not enough has
been done to recognize what happened, and continues to
happen in Africa.

Guns do kill people, and they have killed millions of
Africans. To quote the documentary, *"This is what the United
Nations now calls, genocide!"*

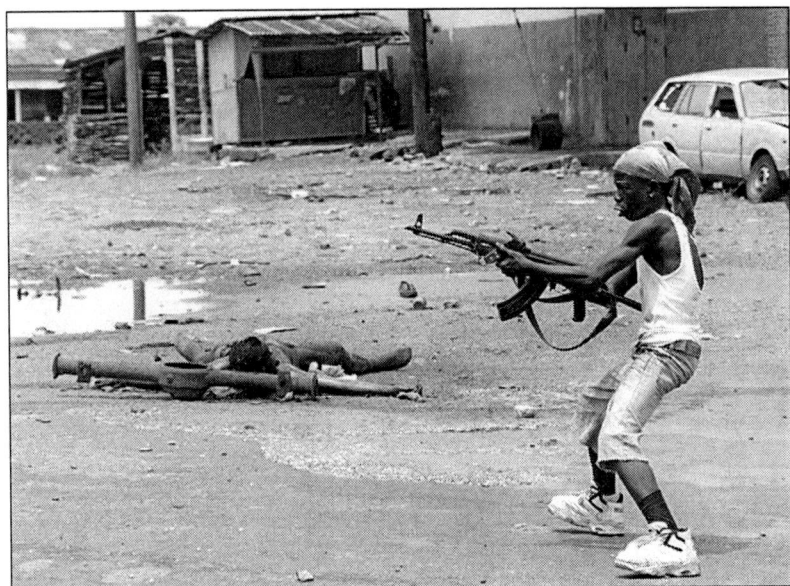

Chapter Twenty-Five

The Soviet Myth

"The pretext of soviet influence, the pretext that the Russians
were coming was never a principle
motive."

Roger Morris, NSC

In the post 9/11 world, we watched as an American president
lied about a threat to the national security of this country and
took our nation to war. That war was the invasion of Iraq. The
nation that was first told the war had to do with 9/11, the attack
on the World Trade Centers and Pentagon by Al Qaeda. We
were attacking those who attacked us. The President was
George W. Bush. It was his father who was the former head of
the CIA during the years when many of the coups and attacks
on Africa were planned. Donald Rumsfeld, Bush's Secretary
of Defense, was part of the Nixon Administration, as was Vice
President Dick Cheney. Brent Scowcroft, a Bush advisor,
signed off on NSSM 201. Henry Kissinger, the author of
NSSM 200, also is said to be one of George W. Bush's closest
advisors. Had America known more about NSSM 200, perhaps more people would have asked whether the invasion of
Iraq had more to do with its oil, than its politics.

Others would have questioned whether history had indeed repeated itself. It did. Like the war in Iraq, America was
told military action in Africa was necessary to protect Americans from a growing threat, communism! The communists, we
were told, were on the march in Africa. Imagine the horror.
The fear was an African continent, with all of those resources

in the hands of the communists. Imagine every African with Chairman Mao's Little Red Book, or looking like Lenin. That was the argument the CIA used to convince us that we had a strategic interest in Africa. It was all based on a lie, and the White House knew it.

As early as 1969, the CIA knew that Africans were more interested in rebuilding Africa than in communism or capitalism for that matter. Specialists argued, rightly so, that Africans found it difficult to trust white people. The same white people, who had enslaved them, were now talking about helping them rebuild that which slavery had destroyed. For Africans, the decision of who to trust boiled down to a matter of skin color. They didn't trust anyone white, those who spoke English, those who spoke Chinese, or those who spoke Russian, it mattered little. African leaders, the CIA found, didn't trust anyone white. It was bigotry in reverse.

S-E-C-R-E-T

CENTRAL INTELLIGENCE AGENCY

OFFICE OF NATIONAL ESTIMATES

13 March 1969

MEMORANDUM

SUBJECT: The Soviets and Black Africa: New Approaches
and the African Response

SUMMARY

The decline of prospects for Communist-oriented
radicalism in Africa has apparently led Moscow to some
shifts of emphasis in its approach to black Africa.
Moscow now seems unwilling to depend so heavily on such
allies as Nkrumah, and may have moved Africa somewhat
farther down on its order of priorities. New tactics
include a more extensive diplomatic presence and some
new aid and training overtures to the African military
elite. The new Soviet approach to Africa is more varied
than the old, but still contains inherent contradictions.
Though the USSR now portrays itself as a respectable and
friendly great power, it has not abandoned its cultivation
of assets for political subversion.

The African elite tends to view Soviet ideology as
irrelevant, and is still culturally attuned to the West.
Moreover, this elite, though eager for aid from the USSR
or any other source, is growing more nationalistic and
suspicious of foreigners. Even if new leftist leaders
emerge, as seems likely, we doubt that the Soviets will
find them easy to influence or control.

Excluded from automatic
downgrading and
declassification

S-E-C-R-E-T

I-21335/69

Attach 6

The problem is the document that reveals the lie, wasn't revealed itself until October of 1999, some thirty years after it was written. By then for Africa it was already too late. Most of the coups had been launched, and the damage was done. Brutal dictators like Idi Amin of Uganda, Samuel Doe of Liberia, Joseph Mobuto of the Congo and others, had been

installed as U.S. puppets to plunder their populations by the
thousands. All represented the front lines in the U.S. war
against communism.

Again Roger Morris, "The pretext of soviet influence,
the pretext that the Russians were coming, was never a principle motive." Instead, Morris argued, not surprisingly, it all
boiled down to money and power. "The motive was always
power, influence in a much more general way, a more friendly
government. It was often swayed by how effective the lobbying
efforts of the rebels were in a region. If they had friends, it
certainly was affected by the lobbying of American business
interests."

The bottom line according to Morris and others was
that for the Soviet lie to work in Africa, Americans had to be
ignorant. They had to continue to think that Africa was a land
of "savages straight from a Tarzan movie." As long as America
saw Tarzan, it could be argued, that the African leaders got
what they deserved. After all, they were Africans, we were
Tarzan.

Roger Morris says it all boils down to the bottom line.
"It's important to remember that this is the absolute lowest
priority in American foreign policy. So, therefore, you have
relatively greater freedom here to play games with the continent, to do outrageous things, or to act in an outrageous way
for fairly flimsily reasons than you do elsewhere. Not enough
attention was being paid here to make it risky to do so."

Does it matter that John Stockwell, the man the CIA
sent to do its dirty work in Angola, wrote a book blaming 'the
Agency', the CIA, for getting it wrong? Does it matter that he
also wrote we backed the wrong horse? It should, but for the
most part, it doesn't.

In a lecture he gave in October of 1987, Stockwell had
this to say. "I did 13 years in the CIA altogether. I sat on a
subcommittee of the NSC, so I was like a chief of staff, with
the GS-18s (like 3-star generals) Henry Kissinger, Bill Colby

(the CIA director), the GS-18s and the CIA, making the important decisions, and my job was to put it all together and make it happen and run it, an interesting place from which to watch a covert action being done." He goes onto say, "I found that the Senate Church committee has reported, in their study of covert actions, that the CIA ran several thousand covert actions since 1961, and that the heyday of covert action was before 1961; that we have run several hundred covert actions a year, and the CIA has been in business for a total of 37 years." Stockwell said that the watchdog system in place to make sure abuses did not occur, is broken, "What I found, quite frankly, was fat old men sleeping through sub-committee meetings of the NSC, in which we were making decisions that were killing people in Africa. I mean literally!" (16)

The truth is, Africa was divided up in much the same manner a group of greedy children sitting around a table would divide a pie. While it was being divided, 'those old fat men' as Stockwell put it were asleep at the switch. Each developing nation was seeking to take a larger piece than the other, and hide the deed once done. No single document points that out more than the minutes of a meeting that took place inside the Oval office with the Gerald Ford, President of the United States, representatives from the Peoples Republic of China, Secretary of State Henry Kissinger, Brent Scowcroft, a National Security advisor to the president, and George Bush, who at that time was the Chief Liaison Officer with the Chinese.

At that meeting, those present talked about making sure each got what they wanted out of Africa. The United States would help China with arms shipments to groups it supported, while the Chinese would help the United States with guerilla training.

White House Meeting Transcripts

"Kissinger: We can give them weapons...but what they need is guerilla training..."

The President: If you would like we can talk to Zambia with regards to Transshipment."

At one point, President Ford faces Vice Premier Teng and says the meeting has been

"beneficial and encouraging."

The response from Vice Premier Teng, **"We have said we have many things in common."**

"The President: will you move to the north...if we move to the south?"

Roger Morris says we could do so in Africa because no one was watching. "We were playing the Chinese against the soviets really from Kissinger's first overtures to them...which happened in 1971. This is triangle diplomacy." Morris says Africa was always outside of the triangle. "Africa is one of those places, again, because of the throw away nature of the continent, this is one of those places. This is a place that you can make the Chinese feel good because of that kind of collaboration. Because it was all twisting the tail of the bear ... but it's all so convoluted because the Chinese are in bed with the Cubans and the Cubans are cooperating with our enemies over there. But we were allied with the Chinese. This had been going on for some time."

The problem is the Africans were among the last to learn they had been betrayed.

China & the United States, 1960-1973

Doc.# 00398

NSA

THE WHITE HOUSE
WASHINGTON

SECRET/SENSITIVE

MEMORANDUM OF CONVERSATION

PARTICIPANTS:	Teng Hsiao-p'ing, Vice Premier of the People's Republic of China
	Ch'iao Kuan-hua, PRC Foreign Minister
	Wang Hai-jung, Vice Foreign Minister
	Huang Chen, Chief of the PRC Liaison Office in Washington
	Lin P'ing, Director, Department of American and Oceanic Affairs, Ministry of Foreign Affairs
	T'ang Wen-sheng, Deputy Director, Department of American and Oceanic Affairs, Ministry of Foreign Affairs
	Ting Yuan-hung, Director, United States Office, Department of American and Oceanic Affairs, Ministry of Foreign Affairs
	Chao Chi-hua, Deputy Director, United States Office, Department of American and Oceanic Affairs, Ministry of Foreign Affairs
	Tsien Ta-yung, Political Counselor, PRC Liaison Office in Washington
	Shih Yen-hua (Interpreter)
	Lien Cheng-pao (Notetaker)
	Sui Chu-mei (Notetaker)
	Gerald R. Ford, President of the United States of America
	Henry A. Kissinger, Secretary of State
	Brent Scowcroft, Assistant to the President for National Security Affairs
	George Bush, Chief of the United States Liaison Office in Peking
	Philip C. Habib, Assistant Secretary of State for East Asian and Pacific Affairs
	Winston Lord, Director, Policy Planning Staff, Department of State
	William H. Gleysteen, Deputy Assistant Secretary of State for East Asian and Pacific Affairs
	Richard H. Solomon, Senior Staff Member, National Security Council.
DATE AND TIME:	Wednesday, December 3, 1975
	9:25 a.m. - 11:55 a.m.

SECRET/SENSITIVE ·(XGDS) -

SECRET — XGDS (3)
CLASSIFIED BY: HENRY A. KISSINGER

SECRET/SENSITIVE   22

Vice Premier Teng: But you should give greater help in the north too. As far as I know, you have many ways to help. Also through third countries.

The President: We have and will.

Vice Premier Teng: Good.

Secretary Kissinger: We are working with France. They will send some equipment and training.

The President: I just approved before I left Washington $35 million more above what we have done before; and that [amount] is on its way as I understand it.

Vice Premier Teng: It is worth spending more money on that problem. Because that is a key position of strategic importance.

The President: Yes. They have an important port; and their natural resources are vital.

Vice Premier Teng: So should we call it a morning and continue our talks tomorrow? We spent two and a half hours making a round the world trip.

The President: It has been very beneficial and encouraging to work with you, Mr. Vice Premier, to be very frank, and to see how our interests are similar in many, many areas of the world.

Vice Premier Teng: We have said we have many things in common.

Secretary Kissinger: What should we say to the press?

Vice Premier Teng: We may say that we have continued significant discussions on a wide range of international issues.

Secretary Kissinger: All right.

Vice Premier Teng: We will see you tomorrow.

SECRET/SENSITIVE

SECRET/SENSITIVE   21

countries have begun to support Neto. I think through Zaire. If you can get South Africa out of Angola as soon as possible, or find some other means to replace South Africa on the southern front, this would be good. We are in no position to help except in the north through Zaire.

The President: We had nothing to do with the South African involvement, and we will take action to get South Africa out, provided a balance can be maintained for their not being in. In addition, if you would like, we can talk to Zambia with regard to transshipment.

Vice Premier Teng: I am afraid it is very difficult. Yesterday I said we could try with Mozambique, but we don't expect great results.

Secretary Kissinger: I talked with their Foreign Minister in New York. They feel very close to China.

Vice Premier Teng: Yes, we have good relations with Mozambique, but on this particular issue it is another matter, because Mozambique takes a very strong poistion on Zimbabwe -- Rhodesia -- and South Africa. I believe the better way is for you to help through the southern front, and I believe you will find the way.

There is one point which is evident. Since Nyerere would not permit transshipment through Tanzania, how could Zambia account to Tanzania if it accepted transshipment of weapons?

Secretary Kissinger: Can we talk to Kaunda and see what he thinks? We have some influence with him.

Vice Premier Teng: Please understand this with regard to African countries -- even the small ones; they are extremely sensitive on matters involving national pride. /Because of this/ we have not raised the suggestion with them, despite all our assistance to them -- as in Tanzania and Zambia in railway construction.

The President: You have been effective. Will you move in the north if we move in the south?

SECRET/SENSITIVE

SECRET/SENSITIVE   20

Vice Premier Teng: We have a good relationship with Zaire, but what we can help them with is only some light weapons.

Secretary Kissinger: We can give them weapons. What they need is training in guerrilla warfare. If you can give them light weapons it would help, but the major thing is training. Our specialty is not guerrilla warfare. (Laughter)

Vice Premier Teng: In the past we trained the three organizations — including Neto.

Secretary Kissinger: Like NATO! (Laughter)

Vice Premier Teng: And we helped to train the soldiers of FNLA for some time.

Secretary Kissinger: They needed it most.

Vice Premier Teng: And in the past, we assisted all three organizations, and more so to Neto. And the organization which we helped earliest was MPLA. With respect to UNITA — Savimbi — we supplied them with weapons by way of Tanzania, but they were not delivered.

The President: Both UNITA and FNLA need help particularly.

Vice Premier Teng: We have no way of transferring weapons into their hands.

Secretary Kissinger: Zambia or Zaire?

Vice Premier Teng: Zambia does not support Neto and the MPLA. If we asked them to allow our weapons to pass through their territory they wouldn't allow it.

Secretary Kissinger: Really?

Vice Premier Teng: Yes. As I mentioned to you just now, the primary problem is the involvement of South Africa. In those countries which

Authority NND 979520
By CA NARA Date 4/6/12

SECRET/SENSITIVE   19

The President: In my visit to Indonesia and the Philippines, I will make this very clear. We are vigorously opposed to it.

Secretary Kissinger: But it warrants attention that India has a treaty with the Soviet Union, and India wants to establish treaties with these countries.

Vice Premier Teng: We have seen that India is making efforts to sell the so-called collective security system of Asia, but to no avail. Their Vice President has made a round of trips to Southeast Asian countries especially for this purpose.

We have established diplomatic relations with a majority of the ASEAN countries. Indonesia does not have good relations with us, but we are in no hurry.

The President: When I am in Indonesia, we will speak very forcefully to them concerning this effort.

Vice Premier Teng: It seems not to be easy for the time being. The diplomatic relations between our two countries were suspended in 1965. And that [situation] also involves several million Chinese descendents. As far as China is concerned, we are willing to improve relations with Indonesia, but we have patience.

Finally, we may discuss the issue of Angola. Actually this issue was already discussed in Mr. President's conversation with Chairman Mao. We hope that through the work of the two sides we can both bring about a better situation there. The relatively complex problem is the involvement of South Africa. And I believe you are aware of the feelings of the black Africans toward South Africa.

Secretary Kissinger: We are prepared to push South Africa out as soon as an alternative military force can be created.

The President: We hope your Ambassador in Zaire can keep us fully informed. It would be helpful.

SECRET/SENSITIVE

Chapter Twenty-Six

Tinhorn Dictators

Tinhorn dictator: internationally insignificant dictator: a doctorial head of state who is regarded as insignificant in terms of global politics

Africa is full of 'Tinhorn dictators', puppets wearing military uniforms adorned with medals that mean nothing and titles they make up on their inauguration days. Most of them are there because the U.S. or one of its allies wants them there. It is their job to make sure that U.S. interests are kept above the interests of the Africans. That is, after all, what the U.S. means by "Strategic Interests." The problem is, in Africa those 'Tinhorn Dictators' we install also have the reputation of killing their populations by the thousands. Samuel Doe, Idi Amin, Mobuto Sese Seko and others were all in the pocket of the CIA. That alone should be problematic enough but in the vast majority of cases, and the records prove so, the United States not only knew they were propping up 'Tinhorn dictators', but also allowed the senseless slaughter of millions of Africans to continue in the process. The list of countries to which this applies is endless, including Rwanda, Liberia, Uganda, and the Congo.

Roger Morris maintains many of those 'Tinhorn dictators' were in the pocket of the U.S. government even though they were literally getting away with murder. "Certainly we have a hand in the tribal or communal killing that goes on, the civil wars that happen one way or another either through instigation, coup d'état, the arms trade or whatever. We're responsible for supporting in some way directly and indirectly, genocidal policies by a bunch of dictators like Idi Amin who we tolerated for years and years, not just tolerated, but aided and abetted."

That in itself is a bold statement, but is it true? Is it possible that the United States knew the people it supported were carrying out genocide, and ethnic cleansing, in many cases using the very weapons we sold them? And if the United States knew it, did it stop the flow of arms to the African continent, or boast them? On both issues the records are clear. Yes! Let he examine several examples where 'Tinhorn Dictators' were propped by the United States government in the name of national security. It is not a pretty sight.

Africa is full of 'Tinhorn dictators', puppets wearing military uniforms adorned with medals that mean nothing and titles they make up on their inauguration days. Most of them are there because the U.S. or one of its allies wants them there. It is their job to make sure that U.S. interests are kept above the interests of the Africans. That is, after all, what the U.S. means by "Strategic Interests." The problem is, in Africa those 'Tinhorn Dictators' we install also have the reputation of killing their populations by the thousands. Samuel Doe, Idi Amin, Mobuto Sese Seko and others were all in the pocket of the CIA. That alone should be problematic enough but in the vast majority of cases, and the records prove so, the United States not only knew they were propping up 'Tinhorn dictators', but also allowed the senseless slaughter of millions of Africans to continue in the process. The list of countries to which this applies is endless, including Rwanda, Liberia, Uganda, and the Congo.

Roger Morris maintains many of those 'Tinhorn dictators' were in the pocket of the U.S. government even though they were literally getting away with murder. "Certainly we have a hand in the tribal or communal killing that goes on, the civil wars that happen one way or another either through instigation, coup d'état, the arms trade or whatever. We're responsible for supporting in some way directly and indirectly, genocidal policies by a bunch of dictators like Idi Amin who we tolerated for years and years, not just tolerated, but aided and abetted."

Chapter Twenty-Seven

Idi Amin

The African bureau at the Department of State looked the other way at Idi Amin's excesses with his own people long before he became an international cause célèbre. "

Roger Morris/NSC Johnson and Nixon Administration

There are so many dictators vying to title of the worst African dictator ever, it was difficult to cull the list. But at the top of any list is the brutal dictator Idi Ami who by all accounts slaughtered as many as 300,000 Ugandans during his brutal reign of terror. Amin's bloody reign of terror even made Hollywood stand up and take notice. The movie, *'The Last King of Scotland,'* netted an Oscar for Forrest Whitaker, but did little for Uganda in the long run.

Roger Morris says make no mistake about it, Idi Ami was our guy. "Oh absolutely the African bureau at the Department of State looked the other way at Idi Amin's excesses with his own people long before he became an international cause célèbre."

In fact memos produced by the State Department regarding Idi Amin prove just that.

In a memo to the White House on November 1st, 1972, Henry Kissinger confirms the U.S. knew that Amin ws killing off the elite of Uganda. Keep in mind; those were the writers, poets, journalists and others who would stage the protest to his policies.

"General Idi Amin has been destroying the elite of all tribes not allied or belonging to his own grouping. The judiciary, top civil servants, academics..."

Kissinger goes on to write: **"There are no reliable estimates of deaths. They most probably number several thousand but not above 10,000 in a population of 10 million."**

As for the flow of U.S. military aid, or guns, to Uganda while the killing was taking place:

"US aid to Uganda is presently suspended although we have not stopped on-going technical assistance." That technical assistance in many cases means...guns or keeping in place the men and women who supply them.

The memorandum is stamped, **"The President has seen."** (17)

Still, as the bodies began to pile up, the debate continued, as did the flow of weapons into Uganda. The *madman* described in Henry Kissinger's 1972 memo, became *the man the United States believed it could do business with.* Idi Amin was well on his way to becoming another U.S. puppet. Another 'Tinhorn dictator' in the U.S.'s grasp.

Memo #1

**Department of state telegram: October 1, 1974.
Classified "Secret State"
Paragraph 3, "We are prepared to provide technical assistance..."**

Memo #2

Department of State Telegram: 3/5/71 "Now consider it desirable to continue forward movement toward normalization relations *in a low-key manner, avoiding public statements"*

Memo #3

Department of State Telegrapm:3/71
subject: US/Uganda Relations "We should
move...loan agreement forward, submitting it to GOU
(Government of the Uganda) if you have not already done
so and indicating USG (U.S. Government) readiness to sign,
again without publicity."

Memo #4

Department of State: Confidential:
 Subject: Normalization of relations with the New
Ugandan Government (Action Memorandum)

"Since the January 25 military coup in Uganda, we
have gradually expanded our working relationship with the
new government of General Idi Amin Dada."
"We further wish to instruct Ambassador Ferguson
to move an AID bilateral and a Development Loan Agreement forward for signature, two actions that will effectively
normalize our relations with the new government."

Memo #5

State department Telegram: Classified Confidential:
3/13/71 "We would hope signing could be accomplished *with little or no publicity"* 3.2 million people at
stake.

Five memos written to officials in the highest levels of
the United States government and five memos signaling that
the flow of arms into the West African nation would continue
despite the mounting death toll.

In July 1978, The American columnist Jack Anderson revealed that 10 of Amin's henchmen from the "Public Safety Unit" were trained at the International Police Academy in the exclusive Washington D.C. suburb of Georgetown. Anderson wrote, " The CIA-run academy was responsible for training police officers from all over the world until its closure in 1975."

According to *"The making of Idi Amin "* by Pat Hutton and Jonathan Bloch, in an article in a magazine entitled the New African in February of 2001, "The Americans and Israelis worked in very close co-operation in Uganda, particularly through their respective intelligence agencies the CIA and the Mossad. Throughout the late 1960s, Obote (Milton Obote, Uganda's president before Amin) was consolidating his personal power and introducing legislation that was to shake the colonial interests."

The article goes onto say, "A vital source of raw materials, Uganda was not about to be permitted to determine its own political development at the expense of the entrenched interests. Soon, plans were being laid by Britain in combination with Israel and America to remedy this situation." It is another blatant example of how Africans were allowed to die because someone, somewhere wanted its natural resources.

Overlooked, why Amin was choosen. He was according to one memo, *"the stupidest and the easiest to manipulate."*

Idi Amin (18)

Idi Amin

Chapter Twenty-Eight

Mobuto Sese Seko

"Mobutu embezzled over $5 billion USD from his country, ranking him as the third-most corrupt leader in world history and the most corrupt African leader ever"

Transparency International

Perhaps no African leader conjures up image of 'Tinhorn dictator' more than Mobuto Sese Seko the colorful leader of the Congo then renamed Zaire. When Patrice Lumumba rose to power, Mobuto was Secretary of State for Defense. Some accounts describe him as a "drunken wannabe" the type of person the CIA would find attractive, stupid and easy to manipulate. Before *his* bloody reign of terror would end, Mobuto would pillage the nation's treasury, stealing billions for his own personal wealth, and dash any hopes that the Congo had of being a truly independent country.

Mobuto was a key U.S. ally in the overthrow of Lumumba. Mobuto was Lumumba's Brutus, *and* Judas, selling him out for his own personal riches. He was also in the pocket of both the CIA and the Belgium government. By some estimates at the time of his death, Mobuto was worth between 3.5 and 5 billion dollars which he secreted away in Swiss Bank Accounts.

Mobuto took control of the Congo when Patrice Lumumba was captured in 1960 as part of the CIA's secret war on the country we discussed in prior chapters. Less than a year later, Lumumba was dead. Despite that, and an avalanche of evidence to the contrary, the U.S. State Department's own website still maintains that Lumumba died under "mysterious circumstances."

"Prime Minister Lumumba died under mysterious circumstances; and Col. Joseph Désiré Mobutu (later Mobutu Sese Seko) took over the government and ceded it again to President Kasavubu."

State Department Website: 9/14/2008

In 1965, with the Congo in turmoil, Mobuto seized control of the country entirely and declared himself President, with U.S. backing, for five years. Five years later he ran unelected and became president by electorate in 1970. (19)

There can be no doubt Mobuto had help. The above mentioned document states, **"We wish...give every possible support in eliminating Lumumba from any possibility...resuming governmental position."**

The next page asks if, **"anything can be done about this, through the U.N. or covertly?** Notice the last word, covertly!'

Other newly declassified internal documents reveal the depths the CIA went through to keep Mobuto in power including this one that states, "Now more important than ever to support those elements which can strengthen … fabric ... overall opposition to … Lumumba."

    Once in power, Mobuto was ruthless. Public execution in the Congo became commonplace. His Minister of Mines and Energy was tried in 1966 and hanged in front of a crowd of more than 50,000. Another Mobuto enemy was tortured to death. While still alive, his genitals were ripped off and his limbs cut off one by one. As if to add insult to injury, his eyes were also gouged out.

Despite that, Mobuto was our man. He was our puppet.

At the height of his power and arrogance Mobuto toured the Congo in a fleet of Mercedes-Benz automobiles. Cars that would be driven to his various palaces on the country's few roads. While Mobuto lavished luxury upon luxury upon himself his people starved. According to published reports. "Only the Special Presidential Division - on whom his physical safety depended - was paid adequately or regularly."

Unlike other 'Tinhorn dictators' propped up by the United States, Mobuto died in exile living out his years in Morocco a very, very, very wealthy man. Death to Mobuto came from prostate cancer, on September 7th, 1997.

Mobuto with Richard Nixon (20)

Chapter Twenty-Nine

Liberia America's Only Colony in Africa

"If the U.S. didn't know what was happening in Liberia, it couldn't have known what was happening anywhere."

William Tolbert, Son of Slain Liberian President

To fully understand the affect these 'Tinhorn dictators' had on their populations, it is necessary to take a closer look at how the world reacts when Africa dies. When those dictators rise to power, usually following a bloody coup, they are welcomed to Washington, wined and dined and then sent home with millions of dollars in U.S. foreign aid. More times than enough, that foreign aid is spent on the guns they use to kill their political enemies, all under the watchful eyes of the CIA and the U.S. Department of State.

Nowhere is the story more compelling than in the West African National of Liberia, where the ethnic cleansing that took place involved the killing of anyone with American blood flowing through their veins. No one knows the sense of betrayal and hopelessness more than Dr. Lincoln Brownell, a Baptist minister who lost his mother, father and 20 relatives in Liberia's bloody civil wars. For Brownell, his bloody descent into hell began on April 12th, 1980, the day Liberia's President William Tolbert, a Baptist minister himself, and the nation's other leaders were toppled in a bloody, and violent coup.

On that day, the members of his cabinet were lined up, stripped of their clothing, and shot execution style tied to poles, as a cheering mob looked on. The weapons of choice were

American made. In fact, according to CIA records of the time, putting down a coup would have been relatively simple. Liberia, according to those records had only one functioning naval ship, and a helicopter that was used mostly for civilian purposes. Despite that, the world watched while Liberia died. But, what makes Liberia so different is its origin. Liberia was America's only colony in Africa. It was founded by freed American slaves and funded by an act of the United States Congress. The first President of Liberia, Joseph Jenkins Roberts hailed from Petersburg, Virginia. Liberia was as American as apple pie, and slavery. Its betrayal was as American as racism.

Lincoln Brownell remembers April 12th, 1980 as if it were yesterday. It was supposed to be Liberia's shining moment in the sun. Instead, a celebration suddenly turned bloody. "We were rehearsing as Baptists with our 100 voice choirs, and we were on our way home when all of sudden we heard the shots. At first we thought it was firecrackers, and then a friend said, "No those are not firecrackers, those are gunshots." That is when we saw a lady, she was bleeding. She was bleeding profusely from her side. She had been shot."

Brownell and his fellow choir members were in shock. The violence that they had seen and heard about elsewhere in Africa had now hit Liberia, "She said there were police and soldiers shooting at each other and somehow a stray bullet hit her. So it was less than five minutes and we passed the capital and we were around the university and were next to the executive mansion and there were these shots...one basically hit the car."

Brownell and the others had never heard gunshots before. Contrary to popular belief, Brownell and others told me the African of their childhood was not filled with violence but endless days in hot schools and churches. Africa, he said, wanted to be all things American, while at the same time becoming all things African. Many of those who would lead the country hailed from some of the finest colleges and universities in the United States. They were men like Kwame Nkrumah of Ghana. One by one they were being targeted for assassination or overthrow and it all happened on Brownell's watch.

"Junior! Junior! Wake up...there's been a coup...there's been a coup in Liberia." Brownell says those words shattered any sense of the Africa he once knew. The tranquil moments with his mother and father, and his dreams of a better life for his yet unborn child had all changed. "I can still see her... (The woman they picked up in the taxi) she was bleeding and we were applying pressure to her side. I was kinda scared ... I was afraid for my family. I often times think about what happened to her, I think she may have made it, but there were a lot of people who didn't make it ... friends... family ... folks. "

Roger Morris says the U.S. watched it all, and did nothing. "We knew good and well what was happening and had happened." He says getting involved might have jeopardized those 'strategic interests' the U.S. so quickly mentions. "We have this long term strategic interest in Liberia, we had a listening post, and we had over flight rights which were important for various covert actions in Africa. We had refueling rights in Monrovia which were important for the navy and of course we had this huge Firestone (Firestone Tire and Rubber) presence all of which would automatically by our silence...our acquiescence." He sums it up by saying that the U.S. simply didn't care. "There was the assumption that we had owned every government up to that point and we would own every government from that point on."

Randall Robinson remembers a different Liberia. He remembers a country where a tailor promised a suit one day and delivered it the next. He remembers turmoil among the various working classes, but nothing that would rise to more than two decades of bloodshed and violence. He too has long suspected U.S. involvement. He says what the U.S. didn't do in Liberia speaks volumes. "If the U.S. didn't know what was happening in Liberia, it couldn't have known what was happening anywhere! It was impossible for the U.S. not to know, it is inconceivable that the U.S. did not know what had gone on, and what was going to go on in Africa!"

By June of that year the violence had grown so bad, that Dr. Lincoln Brownell's mother, a nurse, was spending most of her time tending to the wounded in the hospital where she worked. She died that month. Even though she was a nurse, the constant sight of death made her beg to die with dignity. A month later, his father was dead. Brownell will never forget his father's last words, "Stay home, he said stay home Junior."

That was the last time he talked to his father. Fearing to leave the house he never got the chance to say goodbye in person. It was a simple human dignity that is all too often denied in Africa.

Liberia's coup was led by an army sergeant with an eighth grade education by the name of Samuel Doe. Doe embodied the 'Tinhorn dictator.' He even looked dumb during his first news conference where he seemed to be intimidated by both reporters and their microphones.

"Will you continue the policies of the United States," an unidentified reporter asked?

A nervous Doe could be seen on camera barely muttering the words, "yes."

Randall Robinson says Samuel Doe was a pathetic excuse for a leader, "Doe had no chance, no chance, even if he were so inclined, even if he were of good heart."

What Doe was good at, however, was killing. Like many of those who seized power in Africa by a bullet, Doe spent no time in eliminating his enemies. The bloodbath that followed left little doubt who was in charge. It also should have triggered a U.S. response, after all, the people Doe targeted for execution were so called Americo-Liberians, or

Liberians who were the direct descendents of those freed American slaves. Doe, it seemed, had targeted all things American in Liberia, and America watched it all unfold. Killing in African slipped under the radar once more, even when the blood being spilled was American or in this case, African American.

For his part Samuel Doe did little to dash his low expectations. This man, this army sergeant, this mental midget offered no vision for the country he had just toppled. Perhaps it was because he was only the puppet. The true '*white hand*' would not be seen for decades.

Roger Morris says Samuel Doe was one of many U.S. puppets in Africa. "Any given Nigerian, Liberian, or Sierra Leonean, any given west African leader as in the case of Idi Amin practicing genocide is bound to be ours to begin with. I mean Doe was after all what was still regarded as protecting what are still American interests."

Samuel Doe, despite the trail of bodies he left behind, was given an all expense paid trip to Washington D.C. where he was wined and dined, and the guest of President Ronald Reagan. Reagan rolled out the red carpet and presented his new friend, this new conquering hero, to the world's press. Few who gathered bothered to ask 'The Gipper' why he rolled out the red carpet for a 'tinhorn dictator' who engaged in a policy of ethnic cleansing of American blood. Instead they smiled for the cameras and moved onto the business of America. No one knew then that two of the people Doe had executed on the shores of the Atlantic during his bloody rise to power, graduated from Howard University, a historical black university located just up the road from the White House.

Few if anyone, cared.

Ronald Reagan with Samuel Doe at the White House (21)

"Americans are abysmally ignorant of Africa," Randall Robinson says. "All they knew is that some Africans killed some other Africans on the shores, and here was Ronald Regan welcoming the man who had done the deed."

But Ronald Reagan went one step further. Samuel Doe left Washington with 500 million dollars. For Doe it was enough money to either rebuild or destroy a country. History proved he did the latter.

"Ronald Reagan gave Doe more money to carry out the senseless slaughter of Liberians than had ever been given in the entire 100 year history of Liberia," said William Tolbert III. Tolbert is the son of the Liberian president who was disemboweled during the Doe's bloody coup. Tolbert says his father knew there were "forces working against him, but that he didn't know when or where."

Chapter Thirty

The Reagan Cover-up

When Ronald Reagan met with Samuel Doe at the White House...all anyone saw was an American President and here was the man who had done the deed...

Randall Robinson/ Former President/ TransAfrica

So why did Ronald Reagan meet with Samuel Doe? Why would the leader of the world's greatest democracy meet face to face with a man who had engaged in a pattern of ethnic cleansing based on those with American blood? Why? Money! That is perhaps why the real reason for the meeting was 'classified' until long after Doe had left.

Eleven years after the meeting with Samuel K. Doe at the White House, the Reagan Library released the once top secret foreign policy paper that outlined the reasons behind the meeting with Doe. The document is remarkable in that it makes no mention of the fact that Doe was a mass murderer, or that the people being killed spilled American blood on African soil. Instead it talked about 'strategic interests,' and the age old myth that somehow a defeat in Africa meant a gain for the communists. No one questioned any of it because few if any cared.

UNCLASSIFIED
SYSTEM II
91015

THE WHITE HOUSE
WASHINGTON

UNCLASSIFIED
~~SECRET~~

September 2, 1983

National Security Decision
Directive 101

UNITED STATES STRATEGY TOWARDS LIBERIA (S)

Liberia is important to the United States as the site of a variety of valuable US facilities, military access rights, and private investment. Equally importantly, an unusual historical relationship has resulted in a domestic and international perception of Liberia as a special US responsibility. The objectives of the US strategy toward Liberia are:

-- To promote political and economic stability through the development of democratic institutions and free enterprise;

-- To preserve our facilities and access rights;

-- To avoid a major defeat or embarrassment for the United States through Liberian political or economic disintegration;

-- To prevent the development of Libyan, Soviet and other hostile influence. (S)

In order to achieve these objectives, the US will pursue a comprehensive and coordinated strategy which includes the following specific elements:

-- Use US influence and resources to support and guide the Liberian political process in a way that will improve its prospects for success, help maintain stability, protect US interests, and be publicly and privately defensible. This will include intensified dialogue with Head of State Doe and increased contact with all political actors to encourage the development of a moderate and viable political coalition that can be legitimized through the planned democratic process.

-- Provide adequate assistance to the Liberian transitional process through Project Democracy funding, the Human Rights Fund, USIA programs, appeals to foreign donors and private foundations, and ESF.

~~SECRET~~ UNCLASSIFIED
Declassify on: OADR

Declassified/Released on 5-17-91
under provisions of E.O. 12356
by S. Tilley, National Security Council
(F97-1055)

-- Be alert to the possibility of meddling by unfriendly foreign governments and take necessary counter measures.

-- Step up contact with the Army and the People's Redemption Council to improve discipline and professionalism and promote their backing for the political process.

In this regard, move ahead with the military housing construction program, seek to implement the report of the Security Assistance Assessment Team and either increase the size of the US Military Mission in Liberia or try to increase IMET to accomplish the same goals.

-- Maintain and expand as appropriate a public information campaign to sensitize Congress and the public to Liberia's importance and our unique special relationship. This will include promoting high level visits in both directions and establishing appropriate bodies to assist in carrying out our policies.

-- Promote economic stability and sound financial management by working with the highest levels of the Liberian government and providing economic advisors.

-- Develop a private sector strategy to strengthen the Liberian economy and encourage the US business community to take a greater interest in Liberia. Facilitate the provision of adequate US Government financing and investment guarantees in support of this.

-- Actively encourage the World Bank with other foreign donors to increase their constructive involvement in and support for Liberia, and work with the IMF and Government of Liberia to help develop a workable adjustment and stabilization program.

-- Continue to give sufficient priority in the budget process to maintaining assistance flows to meet our objectives in Liberia. Current levels are approximately $75 million a year.

-- Use of USG influence and resources to support and guide Liberia as soon as possible to a stable economic situation that is not dependent on extraordinary sources of external financing, including the IMF, debt relief, and large budgetary grants.

Ronald Reagan

The document spelled out Liberia's importance from a military standpoint, and even talked about increasing the U.S. military presence there. Unfortunately for those struggling to escape the ethnic cleansing and other violence in Liberia, or those who fled, the document made no mention of their suffering. Death in Africa once again somehow slipped under the radar.

In his book, *Veil, the Secret Wars of the CIA*, Washington Post investigative reporter Bob Woodward writes that even then, the secrets, and the CIA's involvement in Liberia didn't stop. Woodward says many of those close to Liberian leader Samuel K. Doe were also in the pocket of the CIA.

"The deputy chief of Doe's personal Guard, Lt. Col. Moses Flanzamaton, became a CIA agent and later, in 1985 attempted to seize power by leading a machine gun ambush on Doe's jeep. Doe was not injured, but Flanzamaton was captured, confessed to CIA ties and embroidered his tail to include CIA sponsorship of the assassination. It was white knuckles at Langley for days where top officials feared the agency would be accused unfairly of an assassination attempt. But Flanzamaton was executed a week after the coup attempt, and the agency's fears went unrealized."

From: Veil, the Secret Wars of the CIA, Bob Woodward

Chapter Thirty-One

Betrayal

The dogs were feasting on these mutilated bodies, the bodies were floating on the water and the dogs are hungry and they're trying to pull limbs and all that stuff."

Dr. Lincoln Brownell, lost mother, father and 20 relatives in Liberian Civil Wars

Lincoln Brownell says his little piece of paradise, was now no different than those other African nations he had heard of, "The dogs were feasting on these mutilated bodies, the bodies were floating on the water and the dogs are hungry and they're trying to pull limbs and all that stuff."

Ultimately, Samuel Doe fared no better than the other U.S. installed "Tinhorn dictators." He too was toppled in a bloody coup by an African leader who somehow managed to escape from an American prison, avoid authorities and a massive manhunt in New England, evade U.S. Customs and Border Patrol Agents who were looking for him, and wound up in Africa. Doe didn't last long after Charles Taylor came to town.

At the hands of an angry mob led by forces loyal to Charles Taylor, Doe was captured and paraded through the streets of Liberia naked, his ear and penis cut off. In Africa, you see, it's not good to be the king or the dictator for that matter. With Samuel Doe out of the way Liberia was now Charles Taylor's to pillage. As the world watched Charles Taylor ushered in a new form of terror, the era of "The Child

Soldier." Now U.S. guns were not only killing 'people' they were killing children, and, once again, the world watched.

Dr. Lincoln Brownell, meanwhile, was now down to less than 90 lbs. He and the others who fled the Baptist compound where they were seeking shelter were forced to live on rainwater, and rice. Occasionally they were lucky enough to catch a fish in a nearby river, and eat it. The roaming packs of wild dogs made death even less palatable. He remembers Charles Taylor's child soldiers.

"I'm looking through these windows and my eyes just locked on this teenager, about fourteen, fifteen, and he's wearing these torn up clothes and he's using this wild weed on his hair, and he carrying this AK with lots of ammunition across his chest. But what stunned me the most was not the gold chain he was wearing but the human skull that was hanging from it, and it was more like I just kind of froze."

Soon, not even the confines of a church offered much in the way of protection. A close call with another soldier forced Brownell to flee, and get caught. It was then; he came face to face with death for the third time. "He pushes my wife to the side and he loads the gun, and he shoots at me but the gun doesn't go off. And then he takes his gun and fires at me, and then he screams at me, and hits me again and this time it's like all of the blood in my body feels like it's going to come out of my mouth." The child soldier was not finished. Brownell, a man he never before had met, was still alive. "He points the gun again a second time and he says I don't want your dirty blood touching me, and he fires the gun again and the gun doesn't go off a third time. He loaded the gun and he fires at me and the gun doesn't go off." Brownell says it happened so fast he didn't have time to pray.

All the while Brownell and the others he fled with believed the U.S. was on its way. Sooner or later the country of their ancestor's origin would return and save them, protect them. He remembered as a child reading about the U.S. involvement in other foreign wars, and heard the older Liberians talk about how they helped the U.S. win World War II with their strategic assistance provided to the army, and Firestone's rubber. He knew the Americans were coming. He just knew it.

The Americans, however, never came. Fighting back the tears, Brownell describes the wait. "The United States is like a parent who never comes home, it's like a parent and a child, and the child loves the parent but the parent doesn't want that child."

These days Dr. Lincoln Brownell travels the country seeking souls for God. A Baptist minister himself he only talks about his experiences during the twenty years of Liberia's civil wars when prodded. I toured the country with him, and found a man of enormous faith. He doesn't dwell on those who were lost in the wars, but instead, what his country can be once it gets back on its feet. He has forgiven the United States, because that is what he was taught as a Christian, but cannot forget the fact that the Americans never came especially when it comes to His son Shane.

Shane Brownell was born in the United States, but Lincoln Brownell says he will teach him to call Liberia, Africa, home, "he will never be a full American, a real American," Brownell told me fighting back tears. "He will always be a second class American."

Chapter Thirty-Two

The Minister and the Mass Murderer!

"In 1999 Reverend Pat Robertson, signed an agreement with Charles Taylor, to mine gold in Liberia through a company called Freedom Gold Limited."

Washington Post

In Africa, morality often times takes a back seat to money. Nowhere is that more important than the unusual marriage between one of Africa's worst mass murderers and one of America's most prominent ministers. In this case it is Charles Taylor, who is on trial at The Hague, for war crimes and Pat Robertson, the famous televangelist. (22)

In 1999 Robertson, signed an agreement with Charles Taylor, to mine gold in Liberia through a company called 'Freedom Gold Limited', an offshore company registered in the Cayman Islands. It was by all accounts a deal with the devil, giving Taylor, the mass murderer, 10 percent ownership in the company.

This is the same Charles Taylor who turned Liberia's children into soldiers and threatened to destabilize the entire region. This is the same Charles Taylor, who traded Liberia's diamonds for weapons and used that money to increase his military power and launch border raids into neighboring Sierra Leone.

The charges brought against Taylor include murder, war crimes, sexual slavery and enslavement. It doesn't get any worse than that. The teenagers that Taylor turned into killing

machines were forced to rape and plunder to carry out his
grand schemes of conquering the African continent.   In March
of 2008, CNN, reporting from the war crimes trials, quoted a
witness as saying that Taylor forced his child soldiers to, "eat
the bodies of their victims." (23)

For his part, Robertson, through various corporate reps
defended the action saying it would bring jobs and money to
Africa. A company representative told the Washington Post, in
2001, ""Freedom Gold has done more for the people in this
region in the last two years than any other company over the
last thirty years." No one talked to Dr. Lincoln Brownell or his
20 family members who died during Doe and Taylor's bloody
campaigns.

Televangelist Pat Robertson (24)

Dr. Lincoln Brownell sees things differently. "The
powers that be, I would want them to look into the eyes of the
children and basically rethink the greed, the genocide." I ask

him does he truly believe it is genocide. He answers," Oh I believe it is genocide...I believe it with all of my heart, I believe it is genocide. The powers that be decided who's going to live, who's going to die, who's going to eat, who's going to jump, who's going to have, who's not going to have...who's going to have HIV Aids and for how long."

No one in any U.S. administration has ever had to explain why the U.S. did nothing to stop the executions on the shores of Liberia on April 12th, 1980 or the senseless slaughter of Liberians in the days and months and years to follow. One would have thought that Jimmy Carter, a Baptist himself, would have taken special interest in the fact that William Tolbert of Liberia was also a Baptist minister.

Clearly America's historic ties to Liberia meant little when Liberian blood was being spilled across the continent. The fact that Liberia was founded by freed American slaves meant even less, and few Americas even know that Monrovia got its name from James Monroe, an American President.

Perhaps what Randall Robinson says is true, "All Americans saw is some Africans, who executed some other Africans on the shores, and here was Reagan welcoming the man who had done the deed!"

No one in the Reagan Administration has ever had to explain why Ronald Reagan saw fit to meet with a known war criminal in Samuel Doe. No has ever had to explain why the true reasons for that meeting were hidden from history for more than a decade. Why, if America's intentions in Liberia were so forthright, the need for secrecy? No one has ever had to explain why foreign policies toward America's oldest ally in Africa, made no mention of its people, only its natural resources.

No one in the Clinton Administration has been asked to explain how Charles Taylor, a black man, somehow managed to mysteriously escape from a U.S. Prison and wind up in Africa without the assistance of the CIA or other U.S. agencies.

So far, in Charles Taylor's trial, there has been no mention of any U.S. involvement in destabilizing Liberia. No one has been asked to explain why it took twenty years for the most powerful country in the world to come to the aid of the descendents of its former slaves.

Those are the questions Dr. Lincoln Brownell and the other Liberians want answered, but they are not holding their breath. No one in America has ever had to explain any U.S. involvement in Africa. It is as if the thousands of pages of documents that explain that involvement don't exist.

To this day, Liberians find it difficult to immigrate to our shores even though it is the one country in the world that can claim America as its ancestral homeland.

Charles Taylor (25)

Liberian Atrocities (26)

(27)

Chapter Thirty-Three

Rwanda

"Unless both sides can be convinced to return to the peace process, a massive (hundreds of thousands of deaths) blood-bath will ensure that will likely spill over into Burundi. In addition, millions of refugees will flee into neighboring Uganda, Tanzania, and Zaire."

Declassified State Department documents

On April 6th, 1994 the President of Rwanda Juvenal Habyarimana, and the newly elected president of neighboring Burundi, Cyprian Ntayamira, along with ten others, were assassinated when their jet was shot down. Most believe the jet was downed by rocket fire. The world watched what happened next. One hundred days later, as many as one million Rwandans had been killed; many of them hacked to death with machetes. Few of those who died took up arms against their enemies. They were men, women, children, and most were innocent.

A United Nations peacekeeping force was on the ground but ordered out of the country at the height of the killing. One of the most brutal massacres took place, in of all places, a church. What you are about to read, is the official record of what the United States did in Rwanda, or for the most part didn't do. It is a written record of how officials spent more time debating whether the deaths of hundreds of thousands of Africans rose to the level of genocide, because that single classification would demand immediate action. It is a record of how the death of hundreds of thousands of people was discussed over dinner, or on the way to the theater. It is a record of how the world reacts differently when those dying, are African.

In the end the record shows that while people were being hacked to death the most powerful country in the world stood by and did nothing. The president at the time, Bill Clinton, later apologized, but it meant little to the hundreds of thousands of mothers, fathers, sisters and brothers who will never see their loved ones again.

April 11th, 1994,

The April 11th, 1994 document was classified confidential. It was written as a briefing document for Under Secretary Frank Wisner, who was the third ranking official at the Pentagon who was planning to meet later that evening with former Secretary of State Henry Kissinger.

April 11, 1994
I-94/16533

EXECUTIVE SUMMARY/COVER BRIEF

MEMORANDUM FOR UNDER SECRETARY OF DEFENSE FOR POLICY

THROUGH: Assistant Secretary of Defense for International Security
                Affairs

FROM: Deputy Assistant Secretary of Defense for Middle East
                Africa
                Prepared by: LtCol Harvin:MEA:x78824

SUBJECT: Talking Points On Rwanda/Burundi (U)

PURPOSE: INFORMATION--Talking points for your dinner
                tonight with Mr. Kissinger.

DISCUSSION: (U) Action Officers in H&RA, PK/PE, and MEA
                collaborated on the attached talking points.

COORDINATION
ASD/SOLIC _____
ASD/SR&R   _____

Atch: a/s

The document shows that in those seven days after the downing of the plane that carried Rwanda's president, the U.S. knew a bloodbath was unfolding, and not just any bloodbath. The memo states in no uncertain terms that the United States new *"hundreds of thousands of deaths"* would occur. It also shows that the U.S. knew the United Nations was about to *"withdraw all forces,"* an action that would lead to that blood-bath. The bottom line, the U.S. position was to not get in-volved, *"until peace is restored."* The memo is shocking, as it paints a picture of apathy at the highest levels of government, but after all, *"This is Africa."*

"Will Burundi's newly democratic, Hutu-led Government fall?

"Probably.

"It is likely that inter-tribal killings will spread."

"Is the USG willing to get involved?" Not inside Rwanda or Burundi until peace is restored."

"Unless both sides can be convinced to return to the peace process, a massive (hundreds of thousands of deaths) bloodbath will ensure that will likely spill over into Burundi. In addition, millions of refugees will flee into neighboring Uganda, Tanzania, and Zaire."

"When the peace process is back on track, we should resume our security assistance program."

Classification: Confidential.

Declassified on November 18th, 1998.

RWANDA/BURUNDI

- **What is State doing now?**
  Just beginning to look at next steps (DCM Leader will brief at State tomorrow).
  Expect little beyond diplomatic statements.

- **What next in Rwanda?**
  Rwanda Patriotic Front (RPF) will maintain 48-hour cease-fire to allow ex-pats to depart.
  UN will likely withdraw all UN forces.
  Following the 48-hour cease fire period, RPF forces will attempt to take Kigali and will come into open warfare with any remaining French, Belgian, or UN forces.
  Civilians will increasingly be drawn into the conflict and fighting will likely spread to Burundi.
  AmEmbassy Bujumbura is under "Ordered Departure" and is drawing down from its 46 official/31 dependents to essential personnel only (planning on 22, could drop lower).
  Unofficial U.S. personnel normally number between 100-150, but many may have already departed.

- **Will Burundi's newly democratic, Hutu-led Government fall?**
  Probably. Given the close tribal ties to the parties in Rwanda, it is highly likely that inter-tribal killings will spread.
  A NEO should not be necessary given the prior warning foreign citizens are getting.

- **Is the USG willing to get involved?**
  Not inside Rwanda or Burundi until peace is restored.
  We played an important role in brokering the Arusha Accords.
  As the only "honest broker" left on the field (given the intense hatred of Belgium by the Rwandan Hutus and of France by the Tutsis) we could (and should) play a critical diplomatic role in urging the parties to adhere to the Arusha peace agreement.
  We would want to restart our security assistance program once the peace process is back on track.

- **What is happening at the U.N.?**
  Security Council is meeting today to discuss future of UNAMIR, probably will take no action--everyone waiting for UNAMIR Commander's recommendations. USUN has not been given guidance. There is some support in the USG for leaving the Commander and a small support staff in Kigali. He seems to be the only person who can talk to both sides.

- **What are the humanitarian issues, and what can DoD do?**
  Since last Wednesday, 5,000 refugees have fled Rwanda to Zaire, 5,000 Burundi have fled to Tanzania in anticipation of more violence, and UNHCR in Tanzania is expecting 100-250,000 more.
  UNHCR has refugee support food in Zaire for 10 days. DoD may be asked to airlift relief supplies. If State requests, H&RA can provide MREs, Humanitarian Daily Rations, consumable medical and other supplies for disaster relief.

Days later the State Department would declare, *"The United States shares the shock and outrage of the international community over the events in Rwanda in recent days….in the current environment in Rwanda there is no role for a United Nations Peacekeeping force…we endorse the decision of the*

UNAMIR UN Mission) contributors to withdraw their forces from Rwanda for their safety. " (28)

    According to an historian who wrote about the memos, "as the killing intensified, the international community deserted Rwanda." He goes onto say, "Despite overwhelming evidence of genocide and knowledge as to its perpetrators', United States officials decided against taking a leading role in confronting the slaughter in Rwanda."

~~C O N F I D E N T I A L~~ **UNCLASSIFIED**

RWANDA

DoD POLICY OPTIONS

• Because of the fluidity of the situation and the obvious requirement to focus on the NEO, State has not yet begun to look at its next steps re: U.S. Policy toward Rwanda and will not do so for a few days. DCM Joyce Leader will brief at State tomorrow. AMB Rawson will remain in Burundi for a few day. The Burundi Government wants the additional US Marines in Bujumbura to depart as soon as all AmCits are out of Rwanda-- we support that request. (State Rwanda TF)

• State will likely shut down its Rwanda Task Force NLT Wednesday morning. (State Rwanda TF)

• We believe State will initially limit itself to diplomatic statements in support of the UN, the French, the Belgians, and the necessity for both sides to resume the peace process. Of note: this crisis will likely raise questions at the UN about the wisdom of including lightly armed troops in a Chapter VI PKO instead of only unarmed observers (who would probably have been well-treated like most other un-armed ex-pats).

• Unless both sides can be convinced to return to the peace process, a massive (hundreds of thousands of deaths) bloodbath will ensue that would likely spill over into Burundi. In addition, millions of refugees will flee into neighboring Uganda, Tanzania, and Zaire, far exceeding the absorptive capacity of those nations. Since neither the French nor the Belgians have the trust of both sides in the conflict, they are unlikely to be able to convince the parties to return to the peace process--thus there will be role to play for the U.S. as the "honest broker."

• One of the primary U.S. representatives at the last round of peace negotiations was an ISA alum, LTC Tony Marley, who is assigned to the Africa Regional Affairs office at State. He is known and trusted by both sides and will likely be called upon to play a significant role once more if the peace process can be put in motion.

• When the peace process is back on track, we should resume our security assistance program:

Recent Security Assistance Summary ($ in Millions):

	FY91	FY92	FY93	FY94	FY95 (PROPOSED)
FMF	0.0	0.0	0.0	0.0	0.0
CIVIC ACTION	.135	.150	0.0	0.0	0.0
BIODIVERSITY	.525	N/A	.525	N/A	N/A
IMET/DIRECT TRNG.	.060	.070	.127	.075	.150
IMET Students	3	2	5	4	8

Prepared by LtCol Harvin, 11 April 94, X78824

CLASSIFIED BY: DIR, AFR REGION
DECLASSIFY ON: OADR

~~C O N F I D E N T I A L~~ **UNCLASSIFIED**

DECLASSIFIED BY AUTHORITY OF:
OSD
DATE: 18 Nov 1998
CASE #: 95-F-0894

There is one point in one of the documents where someone notes that a line stating the possibility of 500,000 deaths will be eliminated. It was as if someone inside the State Department was foolish enough to believe that 500,000 deaths was somehow unacceptable, while 300,000 might be more palatable.

Unknown to most, the issue of how America views death in Africa surfaced in the final line of the document, its title. The file name for the documents:

NONAMERWANDAKILLINGS, or non-American-Rwanda Killings.

Thus the written record leaves no doubt that when presented with genocide on a scale that hadn't been seen since WWII, the United States watched Africans die by the thousands and did nothing. Instead it continued to separate African death, from the death of others.

A footnote to the sordid ordeal is of little comfort to the thousands of men, women, and children who will never see their loved ones again. The President of the United States at the time, Bill Clinton, apologized.

Rwandan Atrocity Photos (29)

(30)

(31)

(32)

Rwanda Documents (33)

126

OUTGOING CODE CABLE

JAN 11 1994

DATE: 11 JANUARY 1994   NIR 47

TO: BARIL\DPKO\UNATIONS NEW YORK	FROM: DALLAIRE UNAMIR\KIGALI
FAX NO:MOST IMMEDIATE-CODE CABLE-212-963-9852 INMARSAT:	FAX NO: 011-250-84273

SUBJECT: REQUEST FOR PROTECTION FOR INFORMANT

ATTN: MGEN BARIL	ROOM NO. 2052

TOTAL NUMBER OF TRANSMITTED PAGES INCLUDING THIS ONE: 2.

1. FORCE COMMANDER PUT IN CONTACT WITH INFORMANT BY VERY VERY IMPORTANT GOVERNMENT POLITICIAN. INFORMANT IS A TOP LEVEL TRAINER IN THE CADRE OF INTERHAMWE-ARMED MILITIA OF MRND.

2. HE INFORMED US HE WAS IN CHARGE OF LAST SATURDAYS DEMONSTRATIONS WHICH AIMS WERE TO TARGET DEPUTIES OF OPPOSITION PARTIES COMING TO CEREMONIES AND BELGIAN SOLDIERS. THEY HOPED TO PROVOKE THE RPF BN TO ENGAGE (BEING FIRED UPON) THE DEMONSTRATORS AND PROVOKE A CIVIL WAR. DEPUTIES WERE TO BE ASSASSINATED UPON ENTRY OR EXIT FROM PARLIAMENT. BELGIAN TROOPS WERE TO BE PROVOKED AND IF BELGIANS SOLDIERS RESORTED TO FORCE A NUMBER OF THEM WERE TO BE KILLED AND THUS GUARANTEE BELGIAN WITHDRAWAL FROM RWANDA.

3. INFORMANT CONFIRMED 48 RGF PARA COO AND A FEW MEMBERS OF THE GENDARMERIE PARTICIPATED IN DEMONSTRATIONS IN PLAIN CLOTHES. ALSO AT LEAST ONE MINISTER OF THE MRND AND THE SOUS-PREFECT OF KIGALI WERE IN THE DEMONSTRATION. RGF AND INTERHAMWE PROVIDED RADIO COMMUNICATIONS.

4. INFORMANT IS A FORMER SECURITY MEMBER OF THE PRESIDENT. HE ALSO STATED HE IS PAID RF150,000 PER MONTH BY THE MRND PARTY TO TRAIN INTERHAMWE. DIRECT LINK IS TO CHIEF OF STAFF RGF AND PRESIDENT OF THE MRND FOR FINANCIAL AND MATERIAL SUPPORT.

5. INTERHAMWE HAS TRAINED 1700 MEN IN RGF MILITARY CAMPS OUTSIDE THE CAPITAL. THE 1700 ARE SCATTERED IN GROUPS OF 40 THROUGHOUT KIGALI. SINCE UNAMIR DEPLOYED HE HAS TRAINED 300 PERSONNEL IN THREE WEEK TRAINING SESSIONS AT RGF CAMPS. TRAINING

127

2/2

FOCUS WAS DISCIPLINE. WEAPONS. EXPLOSIVES, CLOSE COMBAT AND
TACTICS.

6.   PRINCIPAL AIM OF INTERHAMWE IN THE PAST WAS TO PROTECT
KIGALI FROM RPF. SINCE UNAMIR MANDATE HE HAS BEEN ORDERED TO
REGISTER ALL TUTSI IN KIGALI. HE SUSPECTS IT IS FOR THEIR
EXTERMINATION. EXAMPLE HE GAVE WAS THAT IN 20 MINUTES HIS
PERSONNEL COULD KILL UP TO 1000 TUTSIS.

7.   INFORMANT STATES HE DISAGREES WITH ANTI-TUTSI EXTERMINATION.
HE SUPPORTS OPPOSITION TO RPF BUT CANNOT SUPPORT KILLING OF
INNOCENT PERSONS. HE ALSO STATED THAT HE BELIEVES THE PRESIDENT
DOES NOT HAVE FULL CONTROL OVER ALL ELEMENTS OF HIS OLD
PARTY\FACTION.

8.   INFORMANT IS PREPARED TO PROVIDE LOCATION OF MAJOR WEAPONS
CACHE WITH AT LEAST 135 WEAPONS. HE ALREADY HAS DISTRIBUTED 110
WEAPONS INCLUDING 35 WITH AMMUNITION AND CAN GIVE US DETAILS OF
THEIR LOCATION. TYPE OF WEAPONS ARE G3 AND AK47 PROVIDED BY RGF.
HE WAS READY TO GO TO THE ARMS CACHE TONIGHT-IF WE GAVE HIM THE
FOLLOWING GUARANTEE. HE REQUESTS THAT HE AND HIS FAMILY (HIS
WIFE AND FOUR CHILDREN) BE PLACED UNDER OUR PROTECTION.

9.   IT IS OUR INTENTION TO TAKE ACTION WITHIN THE NEXT 36 HOURS
WITH A POSSIBLE H HR OF WEDNESDAY AT DAWN (LOCAL). INFORMANT
STATES THAT HOSTILITIES MAY COMMENCE AGAIN IF POLITICAL DEADLOCK
ENDS. VIOLENCE COULD TAKE PLACE DAY OF THE CEREMONIES OR THE DAY
AFTER. THEREFORE WEDNESDAY WILL GIVE GREATEST CHANCE OF SUCCESS
AND ALSO BE MOST TIMELY TO PROVIDE SIGNIFICANT INPUT TO ON-GOING
POLITICAL NEGOTIATIONS.

10. IT IS RECOMMENDED THE INFORMANT BE GRANTED PROTECTION AND
EVACUATED OUT OF RWANDA. THIS HQ DOES NOT HAVE PREVIOUS UN
EXPERIENCE IN SUCH MATTERS AND URGENTLY REQUESTS GUIDANCE. NO
CONTACT HAS AS YET BEEN MADE TO ANY EMBASSY IN ORDER TO INQUIRE
IF THEY ARE PREPARED TO PROTECT HIM FOR A PERIOD OF TIME BY
GRANTING DIPLOMATIC IMMUNITY IN THEIR EMBASSY IN KIGALI BEFORE
MOVING HIM AND HIS FAMILY OUT OF THE COUNTRY.

11. FORCE COMMANDER WILL BE MEETING WITH THE VERY VERY IMPORTANT
POLITICAL PERSON TOMORROW MORNING IN ORDER TO ENSURE THAT THIS
INDIVIDUAL IS CONSCIOUS OF ALL PARAMETERS OF HIS INVOLVEMENT.
FORCE COMMANDER DOES HAVE CERTAIN RESERVATIONS ON THE SUDDENNESS
OF THE CHANGE OF HEART OF THE INFORMANT TO COME CLEAN WITH THIS
INFORMATION. RECCE OF ARMED CACHE AND DETAILED PLANNING OF RAID
TO GO ON LATE TOMORROW. POSSIBILITY OF A TRAP NOT FULLY
EXCLUDED. AS THIS MAY BE A SET-UP AGAINST THE VERY VERY IMPORTANT
POLITICAL PERSON. FORCE COMMANDER TO INFORM SRSG FIRST THING IN
MORNING TO ENSURE HIS SUPPORT.

13. PEUX CE QUE VEUX. ALLONS-Y.

United States Department of State

Washington, D.C. 20520

UNCLASSIFIED

~~SECRET/ORCON~~
DECL: OADR

TO: AF - Mr. Moose
          L - Mr. Harper

FROM: INR - Toby T. Gati

SUBJECT: Rwanda - Geneva Convention Violations

There is substantial circumstantial evidence implicating senior Rwandan government and military officials in the widespread, systematic killing of ethnic Tutsis, and to a lesser extent, ethnic Hutus who supported power-sharing between the two groups. The Rwandan Patriotic Front (RPF) has also killed Hutus in battle and has admitted targeting extremist Hutus whom it believes to be responsible for massacres of Tutsis. Unlike government forces, the RPF does not appear to have committed Geneva Convention defined genocidal atrocities.

                  *   *   *

Bloody, inter-ethnic struggles between Tutsis and Hutus date back to the colonial period. An estimated 20,000 Tutsis were killed between 1959 and 1964 during the struggle for independence when the Tutsi monarchy fell, but the recent killings far surpass anything in Rwanda's history. Since the April 6 downing of an airplane carrying Rwandan President Habyarimana and Burundian President Ntaryamira, massacres in Rwanda have claimed from 200,000 to 500,000 lives, according to international humanitarian organizations. [We believe 500,000 is an exaggerated estimate, but no data is available, if systematic killings began within hours of Habyarimana's death.] Most of those killed have been Tutsi civilians, including women and children.

INR is ruining this sentence

UNCLASSIFIED

UNCLASSIFIED

Some Rwandan government troops, Hutu militia and extremist Hutu youth squads often trained or armed by security forces are the main perpetrators. Killings by the predominantly-Tutsi RPF are much fewer in number and have occurred mainly in battle. There are credible reports that the RPF has summarily executed Hutu militia alleged to have been involved in the massacres and the RPF has admitted to such killings. While the RPF has generally protected Hutus within the territory it controls, Tutsis behind government lines continue to be killed by government supported militias.

<u>Geneva Convention Criteria.</u> The 1948 Convention on the Prevention and Punishment of Crime and Genocide establishes (there) criteria to identify acts of genocide: 1) killing members and causing serious bodily or mental harm to members of the group; 2) deliberately inflicting on the group conditions of life calculated to bring about its physical destruction in whole or in part; and 3) imposing measures intended to prevent births and forcibly transferring children of the group to another group.

<u>Killing and harm.</u> International organizations, foreign diplomats and indigenous eye witnesses have reported systematic executions of Tutsis in villages, schools, hospitals, and churches by Hutu militia, the Presidential Guard, and military forces. Many have been killed or gravely injured by machete-wielding militia members because they are ethnic Tutsi, have Tutsi physical characteristics, or support Tutsis. Government forces have also attacked sites where Tutsi civilians have sought refuge, such as the UN-protected Amahoro stadium in Kigali. They have prevented others from leaving a stadium in Cyangugu and have selected and killed some of those inside.

Numerous credible reports claim that government officials, including national and local, officials have also exhorted civilians to participate in the massacres, often utilizing the militant Hutu radio station, Milles Collines. The new government named following Habyarimana's death is comprised primarily of hard line Hutus opposed to compromise with Tutsis and includes individuals believed to have been involved in Tutsi killings. It has taken little, if any action to halt the killings, most of which have occurred behind government lines.

<u>Unbearable living conditions.</u> Campaigns of ethnic cleansing against Tutsis appear well-planned and systematic. Homes are often destroyed and looted after the occupants have been killed. Hospital staffs have witnessed the execution of Tutsi patients. An estimated one million persons have been displaced and another 350,000 Tutsis and Hutus have fled the country. Inadequate nutrition and

UNCLASSIFIED

UNCLASSIFIED
- 3 -

medical care are claiming additional lives and diseases such
as cholera and hepatitis threaten thousands more. Sources
of drinking water have become polluted by thousands of
corpses thrown into rivers, lakes and wells. Government
officials and soldiers have denied or limited access by
international relief workers to threatened groups, thus
preventing them from obtaining needed food and medical care.
Government forces and militia have killed dozens of UN, Red
Cross and other relief workers and attacked ambulances
bearing the injured.

   Measures to prevent births. Tutsi children, along with
their parents, are being mutilated and killed. In one town,
pregnant women at a maternity clinic were massacred.
International humanitarian agencies estimate from eight to
40 percent of the Tutsi population may have perished.

   Who Killed the Presidents. The assassins of Presidents
Habyarimana and Ntaryamira may never be known. The black
box from the airplane has probably been recovered by Rwandan
government officials who controlled the airport when the
plane was shot down or, according to unconfirmed reports, by
French military officials who later secured the airport and
removed the body of the French pilot from Habyarimana's
plane after the crash. Reports alleging that Hutu
government leaders have created lists of Tutsis and moderate
Hutus to be killed cannot be confirmed, but soldiers engaged
in specific executions of Tutsis and moderate Hutu officials
reportedly referred to lists and addresses. There are
credible, but unconfirmed reports that Hutu elements in the
military opposed to the Arusha Accords killed Habyarimana in
order to block the accords and eliminate the Tutsi-dominated
RPF and sympathetic Hutus.

UNCLASSIFIED

Drafted: AA/JMann/77698

Cleared: AA/JMann/77698

Approved: INR/PDAS: PCWilcox, Jr.

File Name: NONAMERWANDAKILLLGS.

UNCLASSIFIED

~~SECRET~~

NOFORN

Defense Intelligence Report

9 May 1994
J2-210-94

RWANDA:The Rwandan Patriotic Front's Offensive (U)

Key Judgments

(C) The Rwandan Patriotic Front (RPF) will almost certainly translate its military success into political power by demanding a larger role for its Tutsi minority than agreed to in the August 1993 Arusha Accords.

(S) The original objective of the RPF's offensive was twofold: to rescue and to reinforce its 600-man battalion in Kigali and to stop the slaughter of Tutsis and moderate Hutus by progovernment forces.

(C) In light of the RPF's overwhelming battlefield success, the Hutu-dominated government forces (Forces Armees Rwandaises, or FAR) will be hard pressed to reconquer lost territory. A FAR offensive, however, would most likely achieve some limited gains and prevent the RPF from taking total control of Rwanda. The RPF would probably retain control over most of the west, north, and east, while the government forces would be confined to the southern region centered around Gitarama.

(C) Both sides can be expected to eventually return to the negotiating table, considering their inability to overcome the military stalemate, due to logistic constraints, and the RPF's narrow political base.

~~SECRET~~

Background

(C/NF) The RPF is a political organization, originally based in western Uganda, comprising Rwandan expatriates and their allies inside Rwanda. Its members are primarily Tutsis; however, the organization includes many Hutus from Rwanda's opposition parties. The president of the RPF, Colonel Alexis Kanyarwenge, is a Hutu. Tutsis make up the majority of the soldiers in the RPF's military wing, the Rwandan Patriotic Army (RPA). General Paul Kagame, a Ugandan-born Tutsi, commands the RPA and is the de facto head of the RPF. Kanyarwenge serves as the RPF mouthpiece, while Kagame is the mastermind of RPF policy.

(C) The RPF was founded as an opposition party in 1979 as the Rwandaise Alliance Nationale de Unite (RANU). By 1987, expatriate Rwandans of Tutsi ancestry who had served in the Ugandan Army dominated the organization and changed the name to the Rwandan Patriotic Front. This military experience of RPF cadre, coupled with the link to the current Uganda government, are important factors in RPF gains over the past few weeks.

(C) After the Habyarimana regime refused to accept a peaceful resolution of the expatriate Tutsis' refugee status and their return to Rwanda, the RPF launched a conventional military offensive from Uganda into northern Rwanda on 1 October 1990 with approximately 2,000 troops. The FAR, with help from France and Zaire, pushed the rebels back into Uganda. The RPF Commander, Fred Rwigyema, died in the fighting. Former Ugandan Major Paul Kagame took command and reorganized RPF forces into mobile guerilla groups that could better operate from bases in Uganda into the border area's difficult terrain. This flexible force structure contributed to the RPF's recent success against the government.

(C) The rebel-controlled territory gradually expanded. The RPF possessed a little over 2 percent of the country when the rebels and government signed the Arusha Accords in August 1993. The RPF could then have based all its military units inside Rwanda; however, it continued to use Uganda and eastern Zaire for training

and logistic purposes. The force dispositions along the demilitarized zone (DMZ) enabled Kagame to rapidly mobilize his forces for the latest offensive.

(C) The United Nations and the Organization of African Unity (OAU) provided observers (UN Observer Mission in Uganda/Rwanda—UNOMUR) to monitor the cease-fire and patrol the DMZ in the north. In October, the United Nations adopted a resolution to send troops (UN Assistance Mission in Rwanda—UNAMIR) to provide security (2,200 soldiers) during the governmental transition.

Key Points of the Arusha Accords

- Creation of Hutu/Tutsi transitional government
- Multiparty elections, 1995
- RPF integration into and an overall reduction in the armed forces

Disposition of Forces Prior to 6 April 1994

(S/NF) At the time of the 6 April crisis, the majority of the forces of both sides were deployed in the north along the cease-fire line (see figure 1). Government military and paramilitary forces numbered approximately 39,000, while the RPF had approximately 15,000 combat troops with 5,000 administrative and support personnel, for a total of 20,000.

(S/NF) The bulk of the FAR combat units rotated into and out of the seven operational sectors, primarily along the DMZ. The sector name came from the location of each sector's headquarters (figure 1 shows dispositions in each sector). This disposition did not allow for a defense indepth and explains how the RPF was able to infiltrate units to Kigali prior to its major defeat of government troops along the DMZ.

(S/NF) The total strength of government forces arrayed along the northern front was approximately 18,700 soldiers and gendarmes. Military and paramilitary forces stationed in the capital numbered approximately 5,200-6,350. The troops stationed in Kigali served as

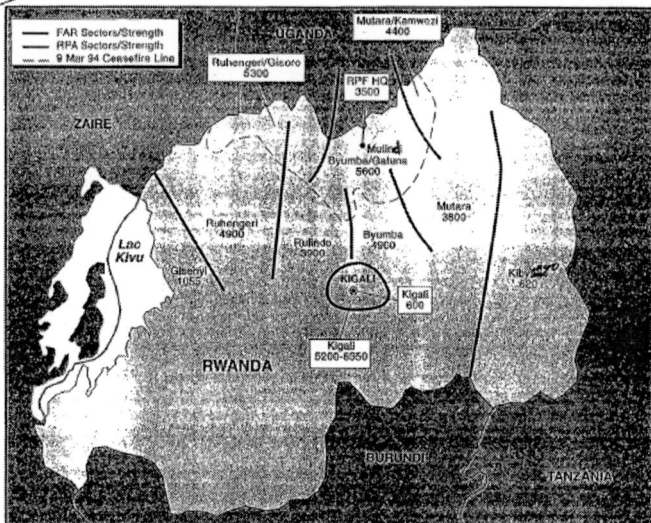

(C) Approximate Distribution of Forces Prior to 6 April 1994.

the Strategic Reserve. The government forces were better equipped than the RPA and, prior to the 1990 civil war, were very competent by regional standards.

(S/NF) As a response to the civil war in the north, the military expanded from 7,000 to 31,000. The new conscripts received little training, which severely reduced the military's overall effectiveness. Thus the RPF, a much smaller and less equipped force, has been able to achieve significant gains in its latest offensive. The government is expected to replace its losses through rapid conscription, which will further degrade the quality

of government forces. Numerical superiority in this case does not equate to battlefield success in Rwanda.

(S/NF) The government's elite units tend to be better led and disciplined and remain relatively effective organizations. These units allow the government to hold onto portions of Kigali, particularly the airport. They are key to government survival; should these elements be rendered combat ineffective, little will stand in the way of a total rebel military victory.

(S/NF/WN) The RPA is predominantly a light infantry force armed with a variety of small arms and infantry support weapons. It deployed its forces in three sectors in northern Rwanda, while keeping its logistics and training units in Uganda and eastern Zaire (see figure 1). The RPF located its headquarters in Mulindi. In Kigali, a special RPA battalion was based near the National Assembly for security of RPF officials negotiating with the government. The RPA is a highly disciplined and cohesive fighting force with reasonably good leadership. Replacements for combat losses will probably come from the huge Tutsi refugee population still in southern Uganda.

Crisis Overview

(C) President Habyarimana supported a reconciliation but delayed forming a transition government. Hutu hardliners were against the Accords, and the Armed Forces were not favorable to integration and demobilization. It is believed that including a high number of Tutsis in the new military fueled antipathy to the President among hardline elements within the army, particularly the Presidential Guard. It is believed that the plane crash that killed the Rwandan and Burundian presidents and their entourages was actually an assassination conducted by Hutu military hardliners.

(S) Almost immediately after President Habyarimana was killed, in Kigali the Presidential Guard began the systematic execution of prominent Tutsi and moderate Hutus sympathetic to reconciliation. Multiple sources indicate that the violence by the Presidential Guard and various youth militias was not spontaneous, but was directed by high-level officials within the interim government. It appears that, in addition to the random massacres of Tutsis by Hutu militias and individuals, there is an organized, parallel effort of genocide being implemented by the army to destroy the leadership of the Tutsi community. The original intent was to kill only the political elite supporting reconciliation; however, the government lost control of the militias, and the massacre spread like wildfire. It continues to rage out of control.

(S) In addition to civilian deaths, fighting erupted between the government forces and the RPF battalion in Kigali. The Presidential Guard and rebel com-

pounds were within 500 meters of each other, near the Parliament complex. The RPF had little choice but to launch an offensive to rescue its besieged battalion in Kigali and to stop the wanton slaughter of civilians. Rebel elements seized the high ground between central Kigali and the airport and began to consolidate their positions until help could arrive from the north.

RPF Offensive

(S/NF) Around 8 April, the RPA Commander decided to launch an offensive with two objectives: to reinforce the Kigali battalion and to stop the massacre of Tutsis and moderate Hutus. The RPA attacked along the entire front to penetrate government lines and then to infiltrate troops south into Kigali. The force in Kigali attacked to expand its position and tie down government forces to prevent reinforcements from moving north. The original government force disposition prevented a defense indepth, so upon penetration of the front line, the RPA rapidly expanded its territorial control and moved quickly to Kigali.

(S/NF) By 12 April, rebel forces had gained control of most of Mutara province and positioned a battalion-sized force approximately 12 kilometers from Kigali. On 14 April, this force had linked up with the troops in Kigali. Additional RPF units attacked from the southwest and isolated the airport from central Kigali. The majority of government forces withdrew from the capital toward Gitarama, the seat of the interim government, while the paracommando battalion, gendarmes, and some Presidential Guard elements challenged RPF gains. The paracommando battalion counterattacked, and it appeared that the RPF attack had stalled; however, the RPF was consolidating and reinforcing its gains.

(S/NF) Both sides declared cease-fires early in the week of 26 April. They appeared to be posturing for the final battle for Kigali, the prize for the political elites battling for control of Rwanda. It appears that the battle began on 6 May as the RPF seized additional areas on the periphery of Kigali. As of 8 May, their forces were 300 meters from the vital western intersection to Gitarama and had taken the high ground to the northeast of the airport. On 9 May, rebels attacked

the Kanombe barracks, key to the government's defense of the airport. The RPF must figure out how to eliminate the government forces at the airport without hitting the UNAMIR troops there and, at the same time, not to destroy the airport, which is critical for humanitarian assistance. Figure 2 shows the RPF-controlled areas and RPF thrusts as of 9 May.

(S/NF) According to the U.S. Ambassador prior to the offensive, RPF-controlled areas were devoid of civilians because of Hutu distrust and fear. It appears that this perception of the RPF by Hutus is changing because displaced persons have been moving into rebel territory. Though lacking sufficient forces to

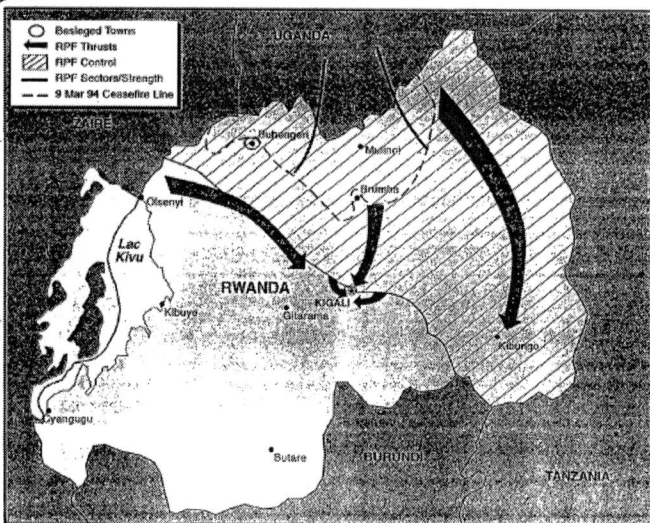

(U) RPA Offensive Thrusts and Occupied Territory as of 9 May 1994.

occupy every town, as the RPF moves into an area, the massacres stop.

Political and Military Implications

(S/NF) The RPF is making an effort to expand its power base among the Hutu and has taken steps to change the Hutu perception that it will massacre them. If it is viewed as the provider of basic needs by Hutus and Tutsis alike, the RPF's political power base could expand beyond that of Tutsis and moderate Hutus of the opposition parties. Furthermore, refugees have

been seen moving north into RPF areas. Unless the government can stop the massacres, it will lose its legitimacy as the stabilizing force in Rwanda. In addition, humanitarian aid organizations are reluctant to venture into government areas to assist the hundreds of thousands of displaced persons. According to the U.S. Ambassador to Rwanda, the routes through RPF territory will be the best way for humanitarian assistance to reach the displaced people left in Rwanda.

(S) Even if the RPF fails to capture Kigali, which would be a decisive military and political victory, its

FAR and RPA Force Composition and Location of Government Forces

Major Tactical Units	Strength	Location
25 Infantry Battalions	13,000 (900-800 each battalion)	Seven operational sectors
2 Commando Battalions	1,000	Ruhengeri and Gisenyi sectors
1 Paracommando Battalion	1,000	Kigali
1 Armored Reconnaissance Battalion	690	Kigali
Presidential Guard Battalion	600	Kigali
Headquarters/Support Units	4770	Kigali
Training Battalion	600	Butare
Subtotal	23,460	
10 Gendarme Territorial Groups	5,300	One group per prefecture
1 Gendarme Territorial Company	400	Kigali
2 Gendarme Intervention Battalions	920	Kigali
1 Route Security Company	200	Kigali
1 Gendarme Air Assault Company	200	Kigali
1 Gendarme Headquarters	200	Kigali
Subtotal	7,260	
Major Unit Total	30,660	
Total Forces Available	Approx. 39,000	
RPF Forces		
5 Light Infantry Battalions	5,800 (about 1,000 each battalion)	Ruhengeri/Gisoro sector
5 Light Infantry Battalions	5,600	Byumba/Galuna sector
4 Light Infantry Battalions	4,400	Mutara/Kamwezi sector
RPF Headquarters/Security	3,600	Mulindi
Kigali Battalion	600	Kigali
Administrative/Support Troops	5,000	Uganda/Northern Rwanda
Total	Approx. 26,000	

6

current military posture allows it to bargain from a position of strength at the inevitable peace talks. It is virtually guaranteed that the RPF will emerge with a larger portion of the spoils than previously attained from the Arusha Accords. The RPF has stated that its objective is a resumption of the transition process begun by the Arusha Accords. In addition, it wants those responsible for the massacres brought to justice. These will be the initial positions at the peace talks. Being a minority party makes the RPF dependent on coalition politics if it wants to adhere to its stated policy of support for democracy in Rwanda. The country's deeply rooted ethnic animosity and its tenuous security conditions make it nearly impossible for the RPF to govern by itself, despite its military victories. Any new Rwandan government that would hope to reestablish order and obtain the loyalty of the military and security forces would have to be broad-based and include a majority of Hutus. While understanding the basics of Rwandan politics, the RPF's role in a reorganized armed forces is the most problematic, yet this critical issue precipitated the current crisis and has to be addressed in any meaningful peace accord. Because of its military dominance, the RPF will quite naturally expect wider representation (especially in key command positions) in the new force drawn from the 20,000-man, predominantly Tutsi RPA and the 30,000-man Hutu FAR. In this way, the RPF could ensure its safety and preempt Hutu plotting. The military issue will probably be the biggest hurdle for achieving a long-term settlement to the Rwandan problem.

(U) Each classified title and heading has been properly marked; all those unmarked are unclassified.

(U) This document contains both sensitive compartmented and collateral information. Individual portions are marked to indicate specifically individual classifications and control markings applicable to their content, including WNINTEL when appropriate for collateral-level portions.

(U) This report contains information as of 9 May 1994. Questions and comments may be addressed to MAJ R. Orth, USA, J2M-2A

Chapter Thirty-Four

The Congo

According to a 2008 report by the International Rescue Committee, as many as 5.4 million people have died in the Congo since 1998, making it the bloodiest continuous conflict since World War II.

What would have happened to America had the British succeeded in killing George Washington, or Thomas Jefferson, or Benjamin Franklin? What would have happened to the United States if Lincoln had been assassinated earlier, and the South won the Civil War?

Much of what happens in Africa is reduced to trivial speculation because we are blinded by the lens through which we view the Continent. If we examine Lumumba and the other African leaders through the lens of a Tarzan movie it is easy to discount their deaths. Then we are talking about the death of savage men in a savage land. Men, who like the others in the Tarzan movies, probably could barely read or write. America or the Belgium's simply killed another African leader with a bone through his nose, who cowered in the shadow of a white man in a leotard.

These, however, are not the stories of white men in leotards. In most cases those pulling the triggers were soldiers in uniforms who were either trained by, or allies of the U.S. Like all soldiers they knew the rules of engagement. The people they shot were no longer a threat. The only crime they committed to deserve such a treatment, was that they were black. Patrice Lumumba was no different. Lumumba was the leader of the Congo, he was their leader, their Washington, and

Lincoln, and Jefferson, and Nkrumah all rolled into one. Not one African leader has ever been offered the chance to surrender. They are, instead, killed.

That means when Patrice Lumumba was assassinated, the heart and soul of an emerging African nation died with him. Imagine the United States after the death of John F. Kennedy, or Dr. Martin Luther King, or Malcolm X, or Robert F. Kennedy. Like him or leave him, Patrice Lumumba was all that to the Congo. He was their future. (34)

According to a 2008 report by the International Rescue Committee, as many as 5.4 million people have died in the Congo since 1998, making it the bloodiest continuous conflict since World War II. As many as five million more died in the years immediately following the assassination of Patrice Lumumba. That means, ten million Congolese men, women and children have died since we decided to dispatch '*Joe from Paris*' to assassinate Patrice Lumumba. Each month another 45,000 die according to the report. It is death on a scale to rival the holocaust, and yet, because it is in Africa, the world watches and wonders why so many Africans keep killing each other. All of this in a country where relatively few are college educated, and no guns are made. Were we responsible? Did we break the Congo, and therefore should we fix it? There is evidence we did, and that we continue to ignore the consequences of our deeds.

Is there blood on America's hands? Randall Robinson, the former head of TransAfrica, says yes. Robinson who came to fame securing the release of Nelson Mandela from Africa says, "It is unconscionable what the western powers have done in Africa." He is not alone.

Roger Morris answers the question even more succinct. When asked if there is blood on America's hands he says, "of course," reaches down and to pick up the glass of ice tea sitting on the table next to him and then, in a matter- of- fact manner, he blames the Unites States and its allies for, "perhaps the greatest human rights catastrophe in the history of the planet."

The question is why? Why did we do it? The answer came long after Lumumba's death. It is the reason American's may owe the Congo more than money. We owe them our very existence.

The Atomic Age is born

Ask any school child and they will tell you the two bombs that were dropped over Japan destroyed the cities of Hiroshima and Nagasaki. Some can tell you how many Japanese died, and others can name the scientists who worked on the once Top Secret Manhattan Project to build the bomb. Few can tell you where the uranium used to build those bombs came from. That information was classified before and long after the death of Patrice Lumumba. Still it may have had more to do with his death than any single factor.

In an article entitled 'Congo Uranium and the Tragedy of Hiroshima', two researchers from the University of Copenhagen document that which for years was unknown.

They write:

"In the summer of 1939, while Hitler was preparing to invade Poland, alarming news reached physicists in the United States. In addition to articles on uranium fission published in Naturwissenschaften and Deutsche Allgemeine Zeitung, two meetings of German atomic scientists had been held in Berlin under the auspices of the Research Division of the German Army Weapons Department. Furthermore, Germany had stopped the sale of uranium from mines in Czechoslovakia".

The world's most abundant supply of uranium, however, was not in Czechoslovakia, but in Belgian Congo. Leo Szilard, a refugee Hungarian physicist living in the US, was deeply worried that the Nazis were about to construct atomic bombs; and it occurred to him that uranium from Belgian Congo should not be allowed to fall into their hands."

Enter Albert Einstein

The mission to save the U.S. nuclear program fell into the hands of Albert Einstein who was a personal friend of Elizabeth, the Belgian Queen Mother. Einstein fled Europe when Hitler came to power in 1933 and went to work at the Institute of Advanced Studies at Princeton. It was Einstein's job to use his personal influence with the Belgium Royal Family, to make sure the Belgium uranium did not fall into the hands of the Nazis.

A top secret decision was made for the U.S. to secretly purchase most of the Belgium Congo's uranium. The die was cast in Africa, and was stamped 'Top Secret'. The Congo's uranium became the lifeblood of what were to become the roots of America's cold war. As a result, when Patrice Lumumba travelled to Washington to meet with the Eisenhower administration he was little more than a sitting duck. He saw them as the beacon of democracy that might one day shine in Africa. They saw him as the African, with communist leanings, a black man who couldn't be trusted with the natural resources the U.S. needed most.

"Oh boy the Congo!" Roger Morris smiles as he realizes we are about to discuss what amounts to ground zero in America's war on Africa "The Congo was seen from the very beginning as strategic heart of black Africa...not only because of its wealth but because of its locale, its location. It is huge it's potentially rich; it is the dog that wags all these tails around it. It was also seen as a kind of front line state. So the Congo was seen as a strategic wedge in population and size."

He gets nothing by way of disagreement from Randall Robinson, "Congo was rich in these things the western world covets. It was big, strategically located and I think that was the death knell for the Congo. Heaven help you when the U.S. decides to help you. When the U.S. decides to help you, run. Run ... fast."

In the end however, the Congo may have had the last laugh. When terrorists flew planes into the World Trade

Center in New York City, the U.S. suddenly realized how many of its weapons were sitting in and around the third world, especially Africa. It was then officials made a startling discovery. The Congolese mine where the uranium was obtained during World War II was no longer secure. Africans, trying to feed their families had reopened the mine and were selling its contents to the highest bidder. The uranium that the U.S. coveted to end World War II, now posed a threat in what some believe has become the Third World War.

Would those Africans treat the U.S. better than it treated Lumumba?

Chapter Thirty-Five

The New Slavery

"Africa is important to us. Coffee, cobalt, cocoa, iron, diamonds, come from Africa, thirty to sixty percent of our consumption and for our European allies the figures are even higher."

Henry Kissinger in declassified State Department document

Slavery never died, it just switched continents and, in many cases, grew, as more and more children now find themselves slaves to a culture they will never know. They toil in unspeakable conditions so we can live the lives we lead. They are unaware of us, and we are blind to their suffering.

As evidence, at any given time there are numerous humans rights investigations unfolding on the African continent. So why, if these conditions are so horrible do they exist even to this day? Because, whether we like it or not, we need Africa for our very survival. A fact that was stated by none other than Henry Kissinger, the author of NSSM 200, upon his return from the continent in the 70's.

"Africa," he states, *"is important to us."* He goes in the document to spell out exactly why:

"Coffee, cobalt, cocoa, iron, diamonds, come from Africa, thirty to sixty percent of our consumption and for our European allies the figures are even higher."

We needed Africa and the White House knew it. Still, they had a choice to make. They could have negotiated with African leaders for their natural resources the same way they negotiated with leaders in France, Germany and Britain. They didn't. Instead, it was easier to enslave an entire continent that depended on the West and its allies in order to survive. Africa had the goods, but we had the guns and money. What happened next was nothing more than economic apartheid, where African nations found themselves slaves to western greed and businesses that would do everything and anything to deliver products at the lowest of cost, even if that mean forced labor on a scale that rivaled the slave trade.

Del Walters

3

Africa is important to us, many key products -- coffee, cocoa, cobalt, chrome, iron ore, diamonds -- come from Africa, thirty to sixty percent of our consumption; and for our European allies, the figures are even higher. The radicalization of Africa would turn the Europeans, vis-a-vis Africa, into commercial enterprises rather than governments.

In the face of this situation we attempted to do the following:

Find a platform on which we could rely that would arrest the armed struggle in southern Africa, preclude foreign intervention, and give the moderate regimes something to hold on to and the radicals something to think about. The strategy was to slow down the struggle and get control of the process as we did in the Middle East.

I saw Nyerere first, and I told him that if there was Cuban and Soviet involvement we could stop it and that if he would work with us we would find some way to make progress on solving the problems of southern Africa. That was why it was important to make my Lusaka Speech, to give us a platform on which we could stand. There was really very little that was new in that speech. We have always supported majority rule -- you have said it yourself many times, Mr. President, -- supported repeal of the Byrd Amendment, and supported UN sanctions.

In return for our commitments Nyerere, Kaunda, Machel, and Khama have agreed:

1. There will be no call for Cuban troops.

2. There will be no direct dealings by outsiders with the liberation movements, a decision designed to prevent the communists from influencing the Rhodesian struggle.

3. All arms shipments are to go through the neighboring govern-ments.

4. While they could not prevent armed struggle, Nyerere said that that struggle had to be ended by negotiations.

5. It was agreed that we would deal more actively with South Africa and that we would not continue to treat them as pariahs. Thus we have gained more freedom of movement with respect to South Africa.

I talked to Nkomo and he told me that the issue in Rhodesia is that if he takes over through negotiation there will be civilian rule in Rhodesia, that if the military takes over through force there will be a regime in Rhodesia like that in Mozambique. He said that if a negotiated settlement

In 2007 the a reporter for the Canadian Broadcasting Corporation traveled to the African nations of Togo, Ghana and Mauritania where he reported witnessing slavery and human trafficking firsthand. A published report indicates that in this

country of 11 million, as many as 870 thousand are enslaved.
(40)

Hillary Anderson, a BBC correspondent published a
story entitled, *"Born to be a slave in Niger."*

He writes, *"Slavery in Niger is not an obscure thing,
nor a curious relic of the past, it is an intrinsic part of society
today. A Nigerian study has found that almost 8% of the
population is enslaved. You wonder how this can be in the 21st
Century and why people do not know about it."*

How indeed. (40-41)

The slavery I saw during my visit to Africa, was the
traditional model of slavery the developed world once used and
continues to exploit to take advantage of those who will do
anything to get a job. Even if it means working themselves to
death. I saw the evidence of modern day slavery during my
trip to Liberia and a perilous trip to the plantation run by the
Firestone Tire and Rubber Corporation.

Chapter Thirty-Six

Firestone

"We pay our workers $3.39 cents a day, which is pretty good
by Liberian standards!"

Firestone spokesman, February 2007

For years, the sign outside the 'Firestone Plantation' in Liberia
greeted all who traveled there, declaring it was the spot of the
"World's largest plantation." A century ago, Firestone was
given a lease in Liberia for one million acres of land, at six
cents an acre which included mineral rights.

In the film *'Pepperbird Land,'* narrated by Sydney Pot-
tier, Firestone workers are shown carrying latex to the various
processing stations by hand, happily headed off to work. The
problem is, fifty years later, they are still transporting the latex
the same way, and this time, there are no smiles on their faces.
After it was learned that we had taken pictures of the sign as
part of *Apocalypse Africa, Made in America*, the sign has been
taken down.

The conditions remain the same. It is a plantation in
every since of the word. It has slaves, slavelike conditions and
human misery on a slavelike scale. (43-44-45-46-47)

Imagine the backbreaking task of carrying two 70
pound buckets filled with latex, attached only to a pole that
over the years digs into your back. Now imagine doing so five
hundred times a day. Imagine you are a child who cannot go to
school because you have to help carry those buckets in order to
keep your family afloat financially. Such is life in Liberia on
the 'Firestone Plantation'.

"One man cannot make it, his wife and children all have to join in together if not the debt will go against them." That was the state made to me by a Firestone employee who spoke on condition of anonymity. He told me that in order to meet his quota of latex, his wife and children had to help out meaning those children could not attend school even if they were lucky enough to get into one of the few schools available.

For his back breaking labor Firestone admits he is paid, $3.39 cents a day, which according to a Firestone spokesman, "Is pretty good by Liberian standards." Consider this however, the average cost of a single tire for a suburban housewife's Ranger Rover is $250 dollars, $1000 dollars for a set of four, considerably more than the average Firestone worker will make in a year.

"Social Security costs, firewood cost, health care cost, before long you are left with nothing," the worker told me. He lives in a shack.

According to the International Labor Rights Forum, Firestone workers continue to live in cramped shacks that haven't been renovated since 1920, and while some are being renovated, the vast majority of Firestone workers living in shacks with no indoor plumbing or, for that matter, a stove to cook on. A worker we spoke to had the same to say.

"The people at Firestone, they live in a chicken basket, it is a chicken basket at Firestone there." Again he did not want his name shared.

In its defense Firestone points out that Liberia's civil wars stopped renovations that began in 1990. They maintain that in a country torn apart by conflict Firestone is a safe port in the storm. What is more difficult to explain is why Firestones management lives so well, compared to its workers.

In sharp contrast, Firestone management lives in houses with all of the modern amenities. There is also a golf course on the Firestone Plantation, where U.N. workers can be seen hitting the links with Liberia's poor as their caddies. The

United Nations inspectors who visited the compound saw the
same things we did.

    According to a U.N reports as many as 60-65 percent of
the children living on the Firestone Plantation do not go to
school.

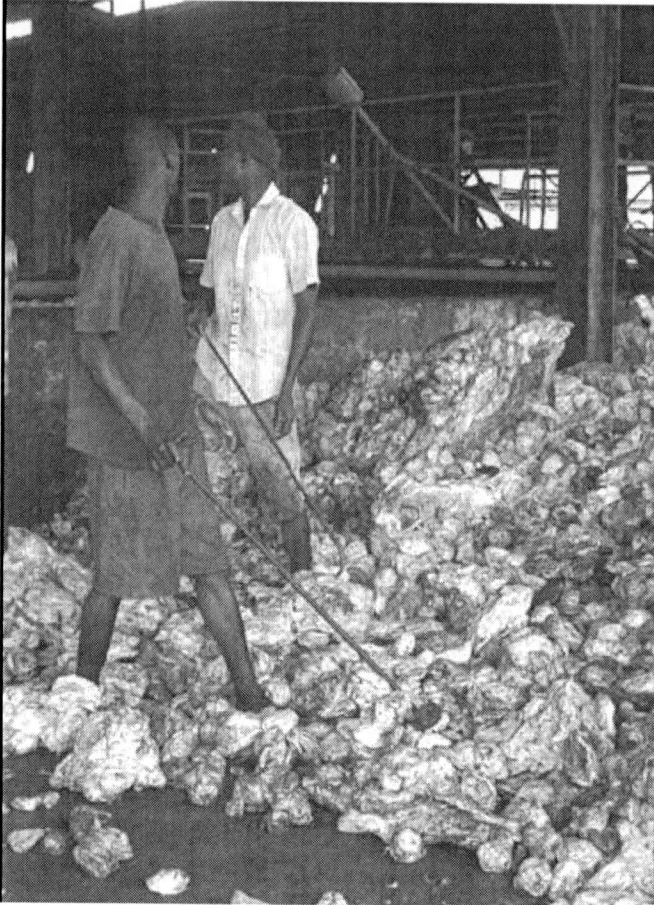

Firestone Photos as taken from 2006 UN Report

Firestone Photos as taken from 2006 UN Report

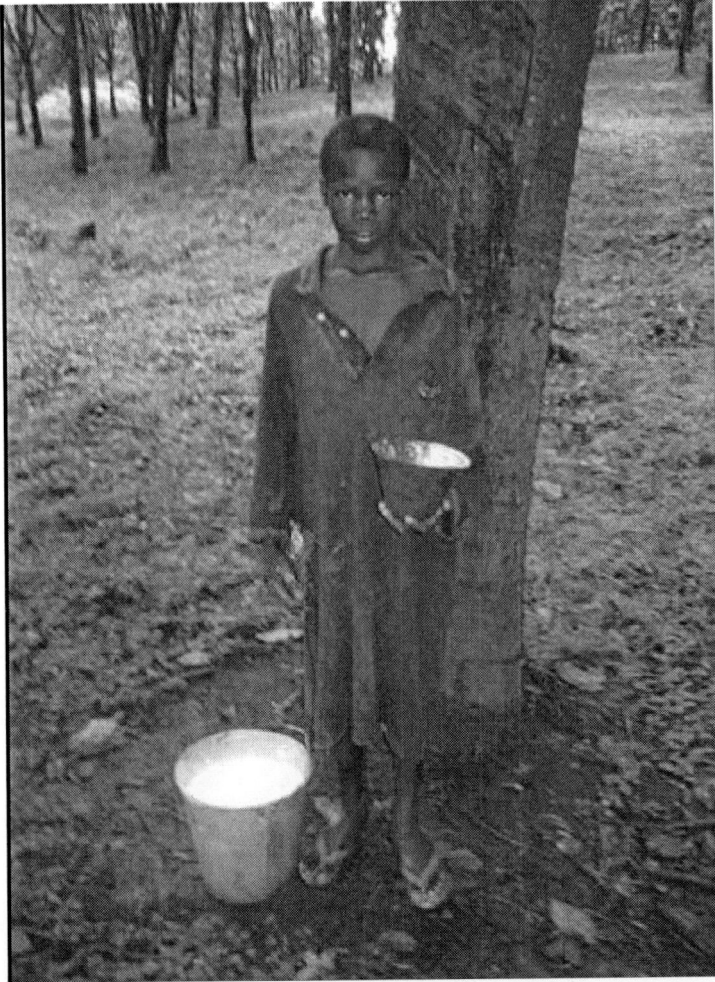

Firestone Photos as taken from 2006 UN Report

Firestone Photos as taken from 2006 UN Report

Firestone Photos as taken from 2006 UN Report

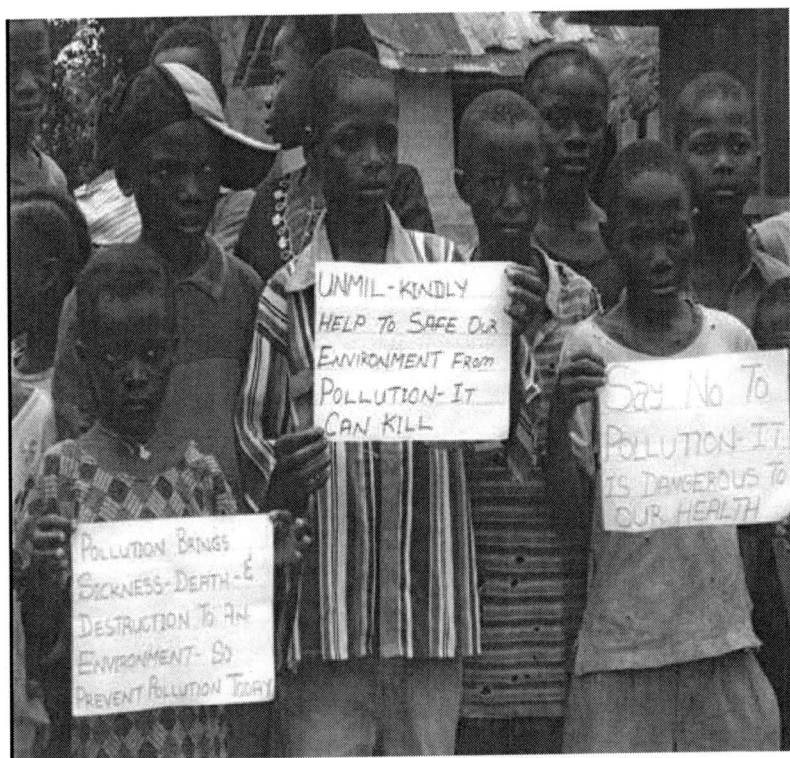

Firestone Photos as taken from 2006 UN Report

Chapter Thirty-Seven

"Cocoa Children"

Cote d'Ivoire/Chocolate Slavery
"The legal minimum age for a child to work in Cote d'Ivoire, is 12"

The United States State Department

Forty percent of the world's cocoa comes from the West African nation of Cote d'Ivoire, where, according to some reports, as many as 109 thousand children work under slave like conditions. Like Liberia, farmers in Cote d'Ivoire are forced to use their children to "get the job done." Children, who often work hours that would be torturous for adults, suffer under the grueling heat of Africa's sun and backbreaking work around chemicals that can kill. Those children, like their counterparts in Liberia, have never seen the insides of a classroom. They will work, live, and die in the same fields that will claim the life of their parents. (48)

The legal minimum age for a child to work in Cote d'Ivoire, is 12, according to the US State Department. Some independent groups have documented children in the fields as young as 9. The State Department places the number of child laborers at 15,000.

Those 9 year old children often use machetes to open the "cocoa pods" and work around dangerous chemicals. Imagine your nine year old child doing the same. If you find it unimaginable then why is it acceptable in Africa? Perhaps because it is not.

An estimated 10,000 more children in Cote d'Ivoire are subject to other forms of slavery including human trafficking. Efforts to remedy the situation in 2005 went unheeded. Much of the slavery continues today.

Sadly, we still aren't finished with Africa. Enter once again, the CIA.

The World Bank and IMF Policies in Cote d'Ivoire:
Impact on Child Labor in the Cocoa Industry

Africa has become the "forgotten continent"[1], left behind in the globalization race. Most African countries have the highest level of poverty in the world. The legacy of the colonial past, corruption of the rulers, and the dependence of Sub-Saharan African economies on primary commodities are some of the many theories that exist to explain this phenomenon. However, the advent of structural adjustment policies (SAPS) imposed by the World Bank and IMF in the region within the last two decades has exacerbated social and economic problems. Their attempt to bring the African countries onto the world stage has only resulted in reversal of development there.

Cote d'Ivoire is a perfect example of a country where the socioeconomic situation deteriorated with the arrival of the World Bank and IMF. Cote d'Ivoire was a relatively stable country and possessed the largest economy in the West Africa Monetary Union,[2] until it began engagement with the World Bank and IMF in 1989. In exchange for aid and loans, the international institutions imposed structural adjustment policies that were harmful to the poor. Specifically, their policies have exacerbated the child labor problem in Cote d'Ivoire's cocoa farms.

Before linking the policies of the international institutions to the deterioration of Cote d'Ivoire's socioeconomic environment, a brief introduction to the World Bank and IMF, and their policies will be given. It is followed by description of the impacts of these policies on poverty, education, health, and ultimately child labor in Cote d'Ivoire.

I. The World Bank and IMF: Reversing Development

The World Bank and IMF are US-created, international development/financial institutions that were started in 1946 in Bretton Woods, Massachusetts, to assist countries recovering from the devastation of World War II. While the World Bank took to financing development projects, IMF provided financial policy advice to donor countries. Their aim was to stabilize national currency and balance of payments in order to encourage foreign investments. They also provided aid and loans in exchange for structural adjustment policies (SAPs) the donor countries had to implement. The policies include reduction in government expenditures, monetary tightening, elimination of government subsidies for food, privatization of state owned enterprises, and reductions in barriers to trade, foreign investment, and ownership.[3]

[1] Mkandawire, Thandika & Soludo, Charles. *Our Continent Our Future: African Perspectives on Structural Adjustment*. New Jersey: Africa World Press, Inc. 1999.
[2] The World Bank Group. *Countries: Cote d'Ivoire, April 2002* (visited May 15, 2002) <http://www.worldbank.org/afr/ci2.htm>.
[3] Naiman, Robert and Watkins, Neil. "A Survey of the Impacts of IMF Structural Adjustment in Africa: Growth, Social Spending and Debt Relief." Center for Economic and Policy Research April 1999.

Chapter Thirty-Eight

Nelson Mandela: what if Alive and Well and Free in South Africa

"During my lifetime I have dedicated myself to the struggle of the African people. But if needs be, it is an ideal for which I am prepared to die."

Nelson Mandela

In September of 1986 the government, the CIA, proved that it had learned nothing in the 29 years after it had launched the efforts to destabilize the Congo and assassinate Patrice Lumumba. This time, however, Lumumba was long dead, Mobuto had died in exile, Doe was executed by his own countrymen, Taylor was at large and scholars like Nkrumah were long since gone. This time it was Nelson Mandela, a man who sat in prison, who posed the greatest threat to life as western authorities knew it. (49)

What to do with this African leader who somehow managed to avoid the coups and "survive!" Clearly, from the early days of Lumumba, no one ever thought about what would happen to Africa's *surviving* elite. What would happen if one of the leaders from Africa's "greatest generation," somehow survived? No plans were made, perhaps because they all had been targeted for assassination. Perhaps that is hidden inside the thousands of pages of African related documents that are still classified.

Once again, Langley, the headquarters of the CIA had a problem to contend with. What would happen if Nelson Mandela *survived* and was alive and well and free in South

Africa? Would Mandela and his followers do unto Africa what America and its allies had done unto them? How would Mandela react to a U.S. government that had done little, prior to public outcry, about his imprisonment. What would he do to a government, whose CIA helped imprison him in the first place by tipping off South African authorities to the fact he was hiding out in Algeria? It is one of the great paradoxes in South African history: so many know how long Nelson Mandela suffered in prison, so few realize why.

March 21, 1960 The Sharpeville Massacre,

On March 21st, 1960, black South Africans who were protesting racially biased "pass laws" were suddenly fired upon by police near Johannesburg. When the shooting stopped, 72 protestors were dead and as many as 200 were injured in the riots that lasted two days. It was a pivotal moment in South African history. In many ways it was similar to the opening shots fired in the days of the American Revolution. But once again, men like Nelson Mandela and the others in the ANC, weren't viewed as revolutionaries like George Washington, and Thomas Jefferson, but instead communist revolutionaries like Nicolai Lenin or Joseph Stalin. They were branded communist because, quite simply, they believed that Africa's wealth belonged to its people. Its gold, diamonds, uranium, and other assets that should have assured Africa's status as one of the wealthiest continents on the planet, instead of one of the poorest.

August 5ᵗʰ, 1962

On August 5ᵗʰ, 1962, acting on a tip from the CIA,
(who told them his whereabouts and disguise) South African
police arrested Nelson Mandela, the leader of the African
National Congress, who had been on the run for seventeen
months. Mandela had become the face and name of the violent
effort among blacks in South Africa, who opposed the brutal
regime known as Apartheid, whereby a white minority ruled
the black majority with an iron, an often brutal fist. He was a
freedom fighter.

Nelson Mandela (50)

A self-proclaimed person of non violence, Mandela came to the realization that a peaceful end to Apartheid was no longer possible   In his statement to his supporters from the dock at the opening of his case Mandela said the following,

"During my lifetime I have dedicated myself to the struggle of the African people. I have fought against white domination, and I have fought against black domination. I have cherished the ideal of a democratic and free society in which all persons live together in harmony and with equal opportunities. It is an ideal which I hope to live for and to achieve. But if needs be, it is an ideal for which I am prepared to die."

For the next 18 years, Nelson Mandela was a prisoner on Robben Island. Like the other inmates, he was forced to do backbreaking labor under the sweltering African sun working in the lime quarry there. The problem is, unlike many, Nelson Mandela could not be broken. The longer he sat in prison, the more he grew in stature and popularity.

Authorities feared he would become a martyr if he died in prison, and feared what he would do should he be released even more.

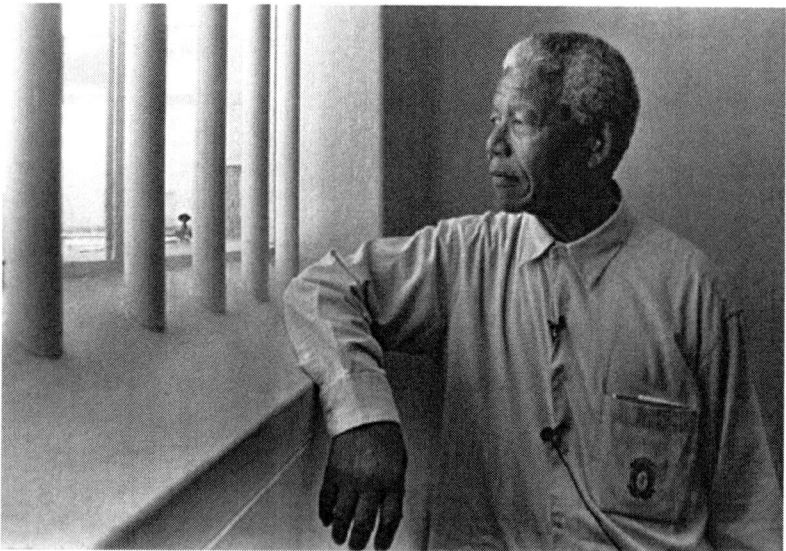

Nelson Mandela in prison

On the streets of the United States, the fervor to free Nelson Mandela from prison had reached a fever pitch. Celebrities and others were protesting in front of the South African Embassy with TransAfrica's Randall Robinson leading the charge. Finally, it seemed as if African American got it. Something was seriously wrong with the situation in South Africa. Privately, the White House knew it had a problem and so did the CIA. Once again the agency had backed the wrong horse in Africa, and once again something had to be done.

In September of 1986, the CIA commissioned a study entitled *'Nelson Mandela: what if alive and free in South Africa'?* The document was prepared for the Directorate of Intelligence. In it the CIA proves thirty years of getting it wrong in Africa meant nothing and they were prepared to get it wrong again. Instead of looking at Nelson Mandela as a man, who quite possibly was wrongly imprisoned, the memo examined the possibility Mandela was still, somehow, associated with Communist Russia:

> *"Before his imprisonment Mandela worked closely with many South African Communists."*
> *"Many observers have labeled Mandela a communist because of his close working relation with South Africa's communist party."*
> *"Pretoria, which has never been able to substantiate its charge that Mandela was a communist in court or otherwise."*

No one inside the CIA speculated that Mandela's attitude toward Russia might have had something to do with the fact they weren't the ones who had him arrested! To this day, we still don't know everything the CIA wrote. Five of the seven pages of the document are still heavily redacted.

DIRECTORATE OF INTELLIGENCE

26 September 1986

Nelson Mandela: What If Alive and
Well and Free In South Africa?

Summary

Imprisoned African National Congress leader Nelson Mandela is the most popular leader among South African blacks, many of whom view him as the "president-in-waiting" of a postapartheid South Africa. Mandela, who was in his midforties and already had well-established views when he entered prison in 1962, is an African nationalist and a socialist. Although time and incarceration have undoubtedly had their impact, his fundamental political philosophy has not changed. Before his imprisonment Mandela worked closely with many South African Communists (most of whom were not black), but the evidence on whether he is a Communist, although not conclusive, tends to support his claim that he never joined the South African Communist Party.

This memorandum was prepared by ▮▮▮▮, Office of Leadership Analysis, for the Secretary of State's Advisory Committee on South Africa. Information available as of 26 September 1986 was used in its preparation. It was coordinated with the Directorate of Operations. Comments and queries are welcome

Confidential
Noforn

If the 68-year-old Mandela were released from prison without conditions--as he has insisted--he very likely would immediately emerge as the acknowledged leader of most South African blacks. He probably would also reassume a top position in the ANC. If Pretoria agreed to negotiate, we would expect Mandela to support the suspension of violence and to seek the dismantling of apartheid; the creation of one-man, one-vote representation; and the implementation of a socialist economy. He would probably leave some room for compromise, particularly concerning the role of whites in a black-ruled South Africa.

Introduction

No single individual enjoys more popular support among South African blacks than Nelson Mandela, whose popularity crosses all ethnic and geographic lines. Public opinion polls indicate that most blacks regard him as their "leader" and that they still identify him with the outlawed African National Congress even though he no longer holds an official position in the organization. During 24 years of imprisonment he has become an almost mythical figure to blacks, embodying their aspirations and goals and becoming a symbol of black strength and black resistance to the white regime. He has also become a "cause celebre" for international critics of the South African Government. His image has been transformed from that of a prominent leader of a protest movement to that of the unofficial "president-in-waiting" of a postapartheid South Africa.

South African officials have been considering Mandela's release primarily because they fear that the death in prison of the aging leader (he is 68) would trigger massive upheavals and would intensify international criticism.[1] Pretoria has other reasons to consider releasing him. Some officials believe that his release could produce a public relations bonanza. It also might exacerbate existing ideological divisions in the black community and throw the ANC and other opponents off stride as they adjust to his return to the political fray.

The government has toyed with the idea of banishing Mandela to his native Transkei (one of four independent black homelands) or expelling him from the country, but he has steadfastly refused to consider these options. He has stated that his release must be

1

2

unconditional, and he has rejected State President P. W. Botha's offer to release him in exchange for his renunciation of violence.

We do not think that Mandela will change his mind on the issue of his unconditional release. He almost certainly believes that his remaining in prison serves the black cause better than his accepting a conditional release. He evidently calculates that his continued imprisonment keeps international attention focused on the South Africa problem and discredits government reform efforts that do not include him. He also probably believes that, if Pretoria released him unconditionally, it would be prepared to negotiate with him. We expect, given his statements, that Mandela would insist that his release be accompanied by the legalization of the ANC.

There are several scenarios under which Mandela could be released, including that involving a drastic deterioration of his health. What follows is both an analysis of what we know about Mandela's ideology and views and a projection of how we believe he might act if he were released unconditionally and he and Pretoria agreed to negotiate. It is in this latter scenario that we believe he would have the greatest impact on the resolution of the South African crisis.

Many observers have labeled Mandela a Communist because of his close working relationship with many members of the South African Communist Party. He had ample opportunity to join the SACP before his incarceration, but he has stated that he never did so, possibly because the ideology did not mesh with his deep attachment to nationalism and to the socialist, quasi-democratic ideals that he believes characterize traditional African culture.

which has for years accused Mandela of being a Communist, has never been able to substantiate its charge, in court or otherwise, despite its considerable intelligence collection capabilities and its unconcealed desire to display such proof before the West. The government, in fact, now appears to be backing down from its allegation. Minister of Law and Order Louis Le Grange this year publicly distanced himself from Pretoria's contention that Mandela was "Communist controlled" (the term the government had begun to use) and stated his belief that Mandela was a "nationalist."

4

Confidential
Noforn

5

Confidential
Noforn

Confidential
Noforn

6

CONFIDENTIAL
NOFORN

CONFIDENTIAL

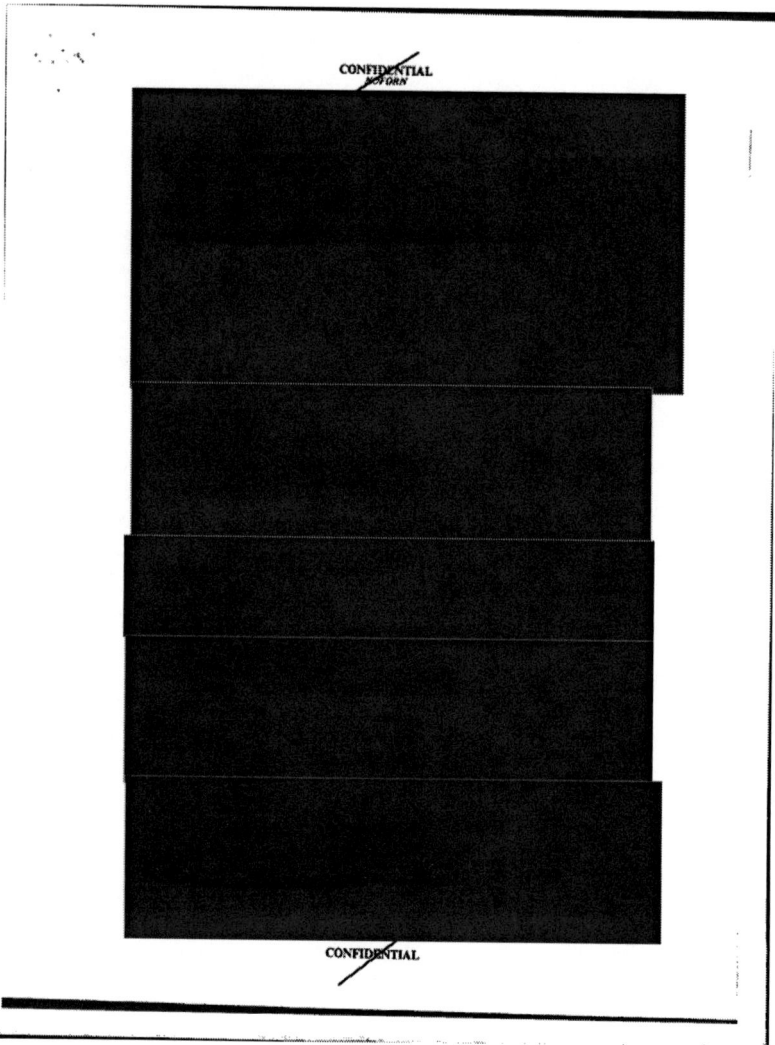

History proved, the CIA once again got it wrong in
Africa. The world watched when on February 2nd, 1990, F. W.
De Klerk reversed his nation's ban on Mandela's African
National Congress and other anti-apartheid organizations. At
that time he declared that Nelson Mandela would finally be

released from prison.

Nelson Mandela after being freed from prison (51)

Nine days later on February 11th, while the world watched, nelson Mandela walked away from Victor Versten Prison a free man. In his speech to the nation, Mandela once again declared he was a man of peace, but if necessary was prepared for war:

"Our resort to the armed struggle in 1960 with the formation of the military wing of the ANC was a purely defensive action against the violence of apartheid. The factors which

*necessitated the armed struggle still exist today we have no
option but to continue. We express the hope that a climate
conductive to a negotiated settlement would be created soon,
so that there may no longer be the need for the armed struggle."*

Nelson Mandela took office as South Africa's President, in 1994, at the age of 77. What happened next defied
decades of CIA and State Department bigotry. Mandela,
instead of punishing his foes, called for 'Truth and Reconciliation' hearings. Those whites, who had committed horrible
evils against blacks in South Africa, would be forgiven if they
would fully confess their actions.

The fact that five of the seven pages of the CIA's report
are blacked out speaks volumes as to how much the culture
inside the CIA has not changed. While South Africa's whites
may have had to confess their sins, the CIA is not quite ready
for such an admission.

Confidential
Not orn

7

CONFIDENTIAL
NOFORN

2
CONFIDENTIAL

Chapter Thirty-Nine

The Family Jewels

"Reading these memos is like sitting in a confessional booth and having a string of former top CIA officials say, 'forgive me father for I have sinned."

Tom Blanton, who heads the National Security Archive

On June 26, 2007 at 11:30 a.m., the CIA released its collection of documents known as "The Family Jewels." We would say, 'the Agency' finally aired its dirty laundry. The documents described how 'the Agency' spied on journalists, opened mail, played a role in Watergate, and even plotted against Beatles great John Lennon by funding anti-war activists. 'The Agency' trained foreign police on bomb making, and sabotage. And oh yes, "tried to poison Congo leader Patrice Lumumba." Those same documents revealed 'the Agency' also wanted to make sure that black leaders on this side of the Atlantic, never connected with African leaders on the other side of the ocean.

The New York Times declared, *"Files on Illegal Spying Show CIA Skeletons From Cold War."* Karen DeYoung and Walter Pincus of the Washington Post wrote under the banner, *"CIA Releases Files on Past Misdeeds."* Richard Willing of USA Today penned his column under the headline *"CIA discloses past abuses."* While NPR's All Things Considered, *"CIA Releases 700 Pages of 'Family Jewels.'"*

Historians noted, correctly, that most of 'the Agency's' dirty deeds originated during the Johnson/ Nixon years. According to both the Washington Post and the New York Times, the investigation into the CIA's bag of dirty tricks was launched in 1973 by then CIA Director James Schlesinger. Schlesinger was reportedly told by Henry Kissinger that the public would demand "blood" if they ever learned what the agency did in the name of protecting the average American. Schlesinger, the newspapers report, was "appalled" at domestic break-ins and other illegal activities launched during the Nixon years.   But the New York Times maintains the agency was actually following orders. They point to an incident involving President Lyndon Johnson:

"In 1967, for instance, President Lyndon B. Johnson became convinced that the American antiwar movement was controlled and financed by Communist governments, and he ordered the C.I.A. to produce evidence.

His director of central intelligence, Richard Helms, reminded him that the C.I.A. was barred from spying on Americans.

In his posthumous memoir, Mr. Helms said Johnson told him: "I'm quite aware of that. What I want for you is to pursue this matter, and to do what is necessary to track down the foreign Communists who are behind this intolerable interference in our domestic affairs."

The Subsequent domestic surveillance project code named 'Chaos' went on for seven years under both Presidents Johnson and Nixon. As part of Operation Chaos CIA agents grew long hair and infiltrated anti war groups both domestically and abroad:

The agency compiled a computer index of 300,000 names of American people and organizations, and extensive files on 7,200 citizens. It began working in secret with police departments all over the United States.

Upon releasing the documents, the CIA's director declared that their release was part of 'the agency's' "social contract to give those we serve a window into the complexities of intelligence." But Tom Blanton, who heads the National Security Archive, a private group that filed the FOIA (Freedom of information act) back in 1992 that forced the CIA to finally come clean told the newspapers he was "underwhelmed." Blanton said, *"Reading these memos is like sitting in a confessional booth and having a string of former top CIA officials say, 'forgive me father for I have sinned."*

Despite that, when the documents were released, there was little attention to the fact that in the case of Patrice Lumumba, the CIA got away with murder! No one wrote that the CIA's efforts to assassinate Lumumba plunged an entire nation into five decades of chaos. There was little if any mention of the fact that the CIA's efforts to destabilize the Congo, as part of the 'Family Jewels' may have been the indirect cause for millions of deaths in a country that has seen more of its citizens die than died any single nation since World War II. In fact, one major broadcast network spent a week in the Congo, without ever mentioning the fact that it was 'our CIA' that fired the first covert shots. Africa had become invisible once more. But there was also something that the documents proved;

America's presidents lied, often under oath and in one case, in front of a watching nation.

1960 Presidential Campaign

In the fall of 1960, at the height of a very contentious presidential campaign, Richard Nixon squared off against John F. Kennedy on the issue of foreign affairs. Nixon, at the time, was Vice President during the Eisenhower years.

Kennedy, during the debates argued that the United States should be there as an ally as Africa emerged from colonialism. He argued that the United States needed to increase its investment in the continent, and step up efforts to see to it that Africans wishing to learn could have access to the colleges and universities America had to offer.

Nixon, on the other hand lied. Nixon looked squarely into the lens and stated, "We must remember that the people of Africa, and Asia and Latin America, don't want to be pawns in a struggle between the United States and the Soviet Union. "We must let them know," he said, 'that we care about them, that we are on their side."

Nixon made no mention of the fact that even as the words were coming from his mouth, plans were already underway to assassinate Patrice Lumumba. He made no mention of *"Joe from Paris,"* or "poisoned toothpaste." To an outsider, Nixon made it seem as if the bigoted words that he would utter privately on White House Tapes were a fluke.

Roger Morris says Nixon knew Lumumba was about to be assassinated."He knew that there was a contract out. Nixon knew that we tried to kill (Fidel) Castro too. Nixon knows a lot of what's going on, he had to swallow his pride not to give away the family jewels." But did he lie? "Of course, of course!" Morris states emphatically. Nixon lied, the Congo died and Nixon walked away from it all never having to answer for either his lies, or his sins. In fact in the later years of his life, Richard Nixon was hailed as a foreign policy genius.

In the days leading up to the release of the Family Jewels papers, the news media in Washington was a twitter.
They were finally going to be able to peek inside the deepest
darkest recesses of the CIA and find out what really happed.
And yet, in the days and weeks that followed there were no
calls for investigations, even though in the case of Patrice
Lumumba, someone got away with murder. Not one foreign
government asked formally for an explanation as to why the
CIA, acting under orders of the President of the United States,
would seek to bring about change in a democracy, by executing
its leader. There was no outcry on the streets of Africa for
justice. Instead, the release of the CIA's deepest darkest
secrets produced...nothing!

Will we ever know why the agency wanted Patrice Lumumba dead? Probably not. The 'Family Jewels' offered only
one page on the Lumumba assassination that wasn't already
public. As I mentioned in the early chapters, the man who
should have stood trial for his murder, Dr. Sidney Gottlieb died
a national hero. After all, the enemy was communism.

The fear was that great men like Lumumba, Nkrumah,
Mandela and the others were out to destroy America. The
problem is, if the U.S. was right and the threat was communism
why were most of the casualties of this cold war black? Why
did more African's die in the cold war than Americans or
Soviets? Why did, as the documents show, the Chinese and
Americans sit across from each other and try to figure out how
to get weapons across Africa? Why were most of the countries
that were targeted countries where *"people of color"* lived?
Why are we still at war with Africa?

Roger Morris says until America looks in the mirror, it
cannot look back on its history with any degree of certainty,
especially when it comes to Africa. "I thought it was one of the
most tragic aspects of dealing with African ambassadors and
political figures...especially the younger ones that had an
idealized image of America. But this is true of a lot of people

in the world. It was true of the Arabs until recently … they had an idealized image of us being different than the European colonials." Morris says the world pleasantly forgets America's past … a past that included enslaving millions of Africans all in the name of economic prosperity. "They somehow managed to overlook that we were this incredible slave holding culture through half of our history and we had this unhealed view of racism in American life North, South, East and west that still bedeviled us. That was not something that we had healed or coped with … and yet there was this incredible indomitable hope that America was going to be different. They believed in our myth in many ways as much as we did."

H. Rap Brown, the famous sixties radical once told me that racism was "as American as cherry pie." When I corrected him saying he meant 'apple pie' he laughed. He said, "Cherry pie" because he maintains that, "the American myth is based on a lie." Rap Brown says that America created this image of itself as "the good guys" and never ever seeks to examine reality.

That American dream came face to face with reality with the release of the "Family Jewels." The United States, the country that was charged with being the beacon of democracy worldwide, was prepared to, and in the case of the Congo, did whatever it took to make sure the only democracy that survived was ours or at least those democracies where the leadership had the same skin color as those who occupied the White House. The sad fact is, they did it all across Africa.

Chapter Forty

A Marshall Plan For Africa

*"You are going to be the proud owner of 25 million people.
You will own all of their hopes, aspirations and problems.
You'll own it all."*

Colin Powell / Former Secretary Of State

Colin Powell, faced President George W. Bush who wanted his input on whether to invade Iraq and reportedly said, "You are going to be the proud owner of 25 million people. You will own all of their hopes, aspirations and problems. You'll own it all." He was warning the president of the consequences of invading and ruining another nation.

Powell then cited what has become known as the 'Pottery Barn Rule'... "You break it, you own it." In truth, there is no such rule, and the same can be said about what America invades and breaks. The paper trail is beyond debate, the U.S. had a major role in Africa's destabilization, and like the invasion of Iraq, money, greed and "strategic interests" were the real causes. The question is what to do next? Does the U.S. owe it to Africa to rebuild its infrastructure? Or is it simply a matter of, to the victor go the spoils? On this issue, history points to the former.

The Marshall Plan

By some estimates as many as 60 million people lost their lives during World War II, 20 million soldiers and 40 million civilians. Cities across the European continent were laid bare and Europe was in ruins. Japan, especially the cities of Hiroshima and Nagasaki where the first two atomic bombs were dropped, were decimated. Fields that once spawned fertile farms were littered with bombs, craters and tank tracks. There was an estimated 500 million cubic tons of waste in Germany alone.

People across the continent wandered the streets. There was no place to work. The factories were destroyed, bombed first by allied planes and no place to call home. Thousands who survived the war starved to death, others committed suicide. It was at that time that the U.S. Secretary of State announced on the steps of Harvard University a bold plan. He unveiled "The Marshall Plan," his plan to rebuild Europe. There was but one major problem. His plan called for rebuilding the homelands of the people we had just gone to war with.

Millions of Americans were either killed or maimed fighting that war. The blood of sons and in some cases daughters, from all fifty states had been spilled on European Soil. The Japanese attacked Pearl Harbor. It was, as Franklin Delano Roosevelt told us, 'A day of infamy." American soldiers fought against the Germans, the Italians, and the Japanese. American bodies littered the landscape and filled cemeteries in Henri St. Chappell, Normandy and other infamous burial sites.

Now, after all of that bloodshed, here was a U.S. Secretary of State suggesting U.S. taxpayer money could be used to rebuild the land of our enemies. Think about it, less than a year after America's soldiers stood face to face, barrel to barrel with Nazi soldiers in Europe, or a Japanese suicide bomber in Japan, here was a U.S. secretary of State saying we should rebuild the cities of Europe.

The resulting plan to rebuild the continent became known as "The Marshall Plan." It was signed into law on April 3rd, 1948 by President Harry S. Truman and passed with bi-partisan support. In signing the legislation Truman said, "Few presidents have had the opportunity to sign legislation of such importance ... this measure is America's answer to the challenge facing the free world today."

Four years later some 13 billion dollars in U.S. economic aid and technical assistance had flowed to sixteen European countries. We were, in essence, leading the charge to rebuild the homeland of our enemies.

(52)

America chose to rebuild Europe on the heels of a war that came on the heels of the Great Depression. Isolationism spread like wildfire across the U.S. Despite that "The Marshall Plan" worked.

This Quote appeared in Kiplinger magazine, the bible of the business world:

"The Marshall Plan is very much a business plan. At its root is an office and factory and warehouse job. The Marshall plan means work, and you will be on of the workers."

According to the U.S. State Department the plan worked not only for Europe, but for America as well. *"During the program's four years, participating countries saw their aggregate gross natural product rise more than thirty percent and industrial production increase by 40 percent of prewar levels."* (53)

Before and after photographs show the Mönckebergstrasse business district in Hamburg, Germany, as it appeared in 1945 and in 1950, following it's rebuilding with Marshall Plan aid.

The Washington Post, 1947

Two years after the war Stuttgart's inner city still reflected the destruction of urban centers during wartime bombing. | 1947 1955 | Marshall Plan funds helped provide for the rebuilding of cities. Photos on these two pages were taken from the same spot.

FOR EUROPEAN RECOVERY
SUPPLIED BY THE
UNITED STATES OF AMERICA

Labeling used on aid packages

Country	1948/49 (millions)	1949/50 (millions)	1950/51 (millions)	Cumulative (millions)
Austria	232	166	70	468
Belgium and Luxembourg	195	222	360	777
Denmark	103	87	195	385
France	1085	691	520	2296
Germany	510	438	500	1448
Greece	175	156	45	366
Iceland	6	22	15	43
Ireland	8	85	40	133
Italy and Trieste	594	405	205	1204
Netherlands	471	302	355	1128
Norway	82	90	200	372
Portugal	0	0	70	70
Sweden	39	48	260	347
Switzerland	0	0	250	250
Turkey	28	59	50	137
United Kingdom	1316	921	1060	3297
Totals	**4,924**	**3,652**	**4,155**	**12,721**

Countries that received aid as part of the Marshall Plan

Chapter Forty-One

The Marshall Plan in Black and White

"Some of those black soldiers returned home and found themselves sitting in the back of theaters behind German prisoners of war."

From the investigation: A Soldier's Story

Failure to heed history's warnings makes us doomed to repeat them. On July 26th, 1948, President Harry S. Truman, signed the executive order integrating the army. He was the same U.S. President that months earlier decided to rebuild the homeland of our enemies, finally signed the law to integrate the U.S. army that relied on its black soldiers to win the war.

Some two thousand black soldiers fought alongside General Patton in the Battle of the Bulge, while others served with distinction in other branches, most notably the Tuskegee Airmen. Those soldiers, however, returned home to a country that required they sit in the back of movie theaters, drink from separate drinking fountains and dine at separate lunch counters. America was black and white, and its green power was being used to rebuild the countries of our enemies.

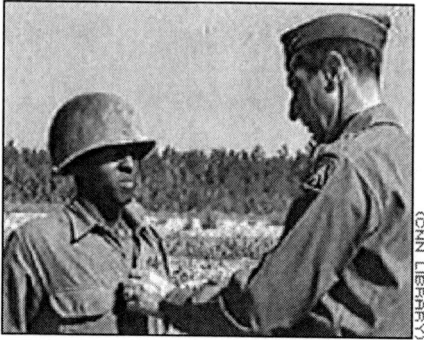

Some of those black soldiers returned home and found themselves sitting in the back of theaters behind German prisoners of war. Now, the U.S. wanted more than their blood, it wanted their sweat and tears as well.

A young man, living in the Bronx at the time of Truman's order, would later occupy the highest military office in the land. Colin Powell, who went onto become Secretary of Defense, and later Secretary of State, told G.Q. magazine:

"Black people had served for 300 years, going back to the early Massachusetts militia. They had served the nation even when the nation had not served them. They chose a way to show their commitment to the nation, and that was to shed the same red blood that their white fellow citizens had shed. They did it time after time, through every one of our wars. And they did it knowing that while in the military, they would be discriminated against. Truman changed that by executive order, because he knew that Congress would not approve it."

In short, Powell told G.Q. that the same Congress that approved rebuilding the lands of our enemies would have voted against allowing blacks in the military. Those who bled for the U.S. had once again taken a back seat to those who had drawn our blood.

That is why Colin Powell's warning to President George Bush is so applicable here. Powell, a student of history and war, was asked by President Bush whether he supported the U.S. Invasion of Iraq. Powell realized that the U.S., by its past history would have an obligation to rebuild the lands it destroyed. It was, after all, history.

"You are going to be the proud owner of 25 million people," he told the President. "You will own all of their hopes, aspirations and problems. You'll own it all. You break it you own it."

Do we not owe Africa a Marshall Plan? Not one African nation in modern times ever raised arms against the U.S. Liberia offered us its airports and military support. Monrovia was home to the CIA's Omega Spy Station. Robert's Field was used to resupply U.S. planes during World War II and the Cold War.

Africa was ready to fight for us, and yet we secretly declared war on them. We secretly committed U.S. troops to the Congo, while Lumumba believed us to be an ally. We supplied the weapons that killed thousands in Liberia, and Angola, and South Africa, and a host of other African nations. We launched the coups and secretly drafted the studies that revealed our intentions to keep a continent in the dark. They were policies that were driven by bigotry that went unexamined for decades and have yet to be fully explored. We have never been asked why there is so much violence on a continent that has never taken up arms against any of its invisible enemies.

Chapter Forty-Two

AFRICOM: Trojan horse

After the Trojans drag the horse inside their city walls, Greek soldiers sneak out of the horse's hollow belly and open the city gates, allowing their compatriots to pour in and capture Troy.

Webopedia

There is a well known saying, "beware of Greeks bearing gifts." The saying comes from one of the greatest military strategies of all time, *the Trojan horse*. When faced with an enemy that would be impossible to overcome or infiltrate, the Greek's decided that sometimes a well planned strategy can defeat an ill timed conflict. They came up with what became known as *the Trojan horse*.

The Trojan horse was a massive wooden carved sculpture that was delivered to their enemy. By some estimates, as many as 3,000 Greek soldiers hid inside the belly of the offering. While their enemies slept after a night of wine and women, the soldiers opened the inside of the Horse and launched one of the most famous attacks in military history.

For decades African leaders have been wary of "Greeks, or Americans bearing gifts, in the form of military assistance." By the CIA's own accounts the African continent was growing at a steady rate of 5% as it emerged from the colonial period. When African leaders reached out to the U.S. and its allies they were offered aid, but with strings attached. We now know those strings included military assistance, and population control. The impact both strategies had on the

African continent is without debate. The continent was devastated and has yet to recover. Enter AFRICOM.

AFRICOM

According to the governments own website, "The United States Africa Command, also known as AFRICOM, is a new U.S. military headquarters devoted solely to Africa. It is one of the Defense Department's six regional headquarters." There is no getting around the fact that AFRICOM is also, military and militaries have guns.

AFRICOM is a concept of the Bush administration. The same George W. Bush administration that launched the war in Iraq. Iraq, we now know, was based on a lie. So is AFRICOM according to many.

According to the Defense Department, "Africa Command is the result of an internal reorganization of the U.S. military command structure, creating one administrative headquarters that is responsible to the Secretary of Defense for U.S. military relations with 53 African countries." The question is why?

According to resist AFRICOM.org, "If reorganization were the only goal, there would be no reason to oppose the command. What goes unsaid in the above definition is the fundamental shift in the roles of the State Department and the Department of Defense. Many duties such as building schools and digging wells will now fall under the jurisdiction of the DoD." Why does the U.S. want its military digging wells? If African's didn't trust Americans wearing suits and ties, what makes the administration believe it will trust Americans wearing military uniforms? Perhaps the Bush administration is right, but a close examination of history should be cause for concern.

According to Resist AFRICOM.org, "Donald Rumsfeld, a man expelled from office for his failed policies in the

Middle East, approved the creation of this command.
AFRICOM is designed to fulfill the immediate special interest
of the United States with little heed to the implications for the
people of Africa."

It is the same Donald Rumsfeld who was in the room
when Richard Nixon referred to Africans as *"just out of the
trees,"* and *"niggers."* Despite that the government maintains
that fears of another U.S. military presence in Africa are
unfounded. "Africa Command will focus on war prevention
rather than war-fighting. Africa Command intends to work
with African nations and African organizations to build regional security and crisis-response capacity in support of U.S.
government efforts in Africa." this the same government that
gave us 'peace keeper missiles,' and 'Operation Iraqi Freedom'!

Still, according to several groups hostile to the creation
of AFRICOM, the bottom line is once again money. "In
several meetings, briefings and statements, high-level officials
have said that AFRICOM has three main goals.

1.) To counter terrorism on African sol as part of the Global War on Terror.

2.) To protect oil resources, recognizing that the U.S. may
purchase as much as 25% of its oil from Africa by
2015.

3.) To counter China's growing economic investment on
the continent.

The problem is, at a time when Africa needs books and
buildings to house its students, it is once again being offered
bullets and bombs. The Southern African Development
community which represents 14 Southern African nations has
publically denounced AFRICOM. The only government that
seems to be cooperating with the U.S. on the matter is Liberia.

Consider these facts. The same cast of characters heading the Bush administration are many of the same players in

charge during the Nixon Administration. When Richard Nixon resigned, NSSM 200, which declared war on the third world was passed on to the administration of his Vice President Gerald Ford. Ford made NSSM 200 and 201, actionable. Donald Rumsfeld, the man who said nothing while Nixon attacked Africa was Fords Chief of Staff. He was preceded by Alexander Haig, who listened while Nixon said there hadn't been a fair election in Liberia since Slavery. That is the same Liberia that the U.S. now wants to welcome AFRICOM. Donald Rumsfeld was followed by Dick Cheney the man who would become Vice President during the George W. Bush administration. Both men went onto become Secretary of Defense, overseeing the budgets and procurements that destroyed Africa. Which once again begs the question, is AFRICOM a *Trojan horse?*

According to the Department of Defense, "Africa is growing in military, strategic and economic importance in global affairs. However, many nations on the African continent continue to rely on the international community for assistance with security concerns. From the U.S. perspective, it makes strategic sense to help build the capability for African partners, and organizations such as the Africa Standby Force, to take the lead in establishing a secure environment. This security will, in turn, set the groundwork for increased political stability and economic growth."

Donald Rumsfeld meets with Dick Cheney and President Ford April 28th, 1975 (54)

The military says it is consulting with the African nations to alleviate any suspicions. I am, however, reminded of a scene in my documentary *Apocalypse Africa made in America.* The documentary contains a clip from another film entitled, '*A time for celebration'.* Shot by the United States Information Agency, or USIA shows Air Force One, the Presidential Plane, coming into frame, as it prepared to touch down in Liberia.

A short time later, as the Grambling Marching Band, which was flown to African by the Nixon administration played, Patricia Nixon walked down the stairs. There she was greeted by William Tolbert, Liberia's President. Thousands of Liberians stood watch as her motorcade wound through the streets of downtown Monrovia. There were no bombed out buildings, or child soldiers, just smiling Africans who turned out to greet a visiting dignitary.

With Pat Nixon smiling at his side, William Tolbert welcomed her as an emissary of, "his good and personal friend President Richard M. Nixon." The crowd cheered. Months later, a secret audio taped conversation between President Richard Nixon and Alexander Haig told a different story:

"Liberia, you call that a contested election, hell they haven't had an election there since the slaves went over."

Richard Nixon with President and Mrs. William Tolbert (55)

Africa trusted an American president, and decades later learned it had secretly been burned. For William Tolbert, it was even worse. By all accounts William Tolbert was killed and disemboweled in his bed while he slept. Who killed him remains the subject of debate. America, however, did not come to his rescue, nor did his "great personal friend Richard Nixon."

On august, 5th, 2008, appearing before a Truth and Reconciliation Commission in Monrovia, a government official said it was not Samuel Doe who killed Tolbert, but instead a

288

Del Walters

white CIA agent who shot and killed him. *The White Hand* in Africa surfaced again.

Snowflakes

On Tuesday November 1st, 2007, the Washington Post reported Defense Secretary Donald Rumsfeld wrote what he called, *"Snowflakes."* They were short talking points to pass along to others in the government. One of those snowflakes seemed eerily similar to the strategies of coups in Africa. *"Keep elevating the threat,"* Rumsfeld wrote. *"Talk about Somalia, the Philippines, etc. Make sure the American people realize they are surrounded in the world by violent extremists."*

Substitute *terrorism* for *communism* and just how far have we come?

A footnote: shortly before the film *Apocalypse Africa, Made in America* premiered at Cannes, I received a call from a source inside the National Archives saying a "military Colonel" came to the archives and Demanded to see all of the films that I used to make the documentary. One of the films was of Pat Nixon's trip to Liberia. It seemed there was an *"angle"* that was not used in the official government documentary of the trip. The reason this particular raw footage was never used is because it was taken from the "wrong angle." Sources who looked at the film say "that angle" would have revealed the CIA agent sent to destabilize Liberia, a Special Forces Soldier who was tasked with carrying out the mission, and "the Coup Leader."

Was Air Force One touching down in Liberia in 1971 a *Trojan horse?* Is AFRICOM? You decide.

Does AFRICOM threaten the sovereignty of other nations?

No. U.S. Africa Command will in no way infringe on the sovereignty of any African nation. Africa Command is an administrative reorganization of long-existing U.S. military relationships with African nations and organizations, just as the

U.S. Defense Department coordinates relationships with nations and regional organizations throughout the world. **(Taken from the U.S. DoD. Website)**

Chapter Forty-Three

The Debt

Let's just lance the boil. We hate ourselves. Not all of us, but too many. Most of the rest of us have leaden doubts about our worth.

Randall Robinson/ The Debt

We ... and I am speaking as an African American, should not try and fool ourselves. Africa exists as it does today because of *us*. Few visit the continent, instead choosing to travel to Europe or Mexico, or some other "safe" location first. Tarzan has taken its toll on our lives as we have become the greatest purveyor of myth versus reality when it comes to the African continent. *We* blame their leaders, but rarely, if ever explore how those leaders rose to power and the U.S. role. *We* blame the Africans themselves, rightly so, for picking up the guns the various powers provided and killing each other. *We* do not pause for a moment to consider this simple fact: In nations like Liberia entire generations are now in their twenties, and never set foot inside a school. *We* have the privilege of not only the attending best schools in the world, but can't name five countries in Africa. *We* should, but we never blame ourselves.

As I write this I am preparing for the annual rite of passage in Washington D.C., known as the "Congressional Black Caucus Weekend." When I first arrived in town, the "Caucus" was described as one of the "hottest tickets" in Washington. Little has changed since then, with the exception of the mission. Great black men who championed the cause of Africa like the late Mickey Leland, of Texas who died in 1989 delivering food to Ethiopia, and Ron Dellums of California who championed the cause of ending Apartheid, have been replaced by a generation of black leaders affectionately nicknamed, "generation overcame." They are, a generation of black men who act like they grew up watching Tarzan on TV. The caucus with a cause has been replaced by a party with little or no purpose, at least one that the public can readily identify. As of this writing it has been four years after the calamity of Hurricane Katrina. "The buzz," as they like to say in Washington is about Barack Obama. Katrina and the people of the ninth ward of New Orleans is talked about but not actively protested.

Need I say more?

To date I have received several invitations to some of the most lavish cocktail parties known to man. Ironically I have received only one to an event focusing on the plight of Africa, and it came from the white rock star Bono's One.org. Make no mistake about it, should Bono grace the Caucus weekend there will be a stir. The same stir that would be caused should George Clooney, or Angelina Jolie, or Brad Pitt show up. White faces have become the "faces of Africa." To be fair there are African American actors like Don Cheadle who starred in the movie "Rwanda," who has taken an active role in Africa. Those actors, however, fail to garnish the same headlines as their white counterparts.

Chapter Forty-Four

The Black Hand In Africa

The world is black and white, with only one color dead.

Songwriter Peter Gabriel, from Biko

X, Y and *Z* exist. They are the people you sit next to in church, sing in the choir and discuss current affairs with in the barbershop. For their own safety I have agreed to never disclose their identities. They are people who either worked, or still work inside the agency. They are also African American...African Americans, with very guilty consciousnesses. Imagine if you will the obvious. How could the U.S. to carry out its missions in Africa without people of color?

"White people stuck out like a sore thumb," *X* once told me. *X* is a former Special Forces soldier who helped destabilize Angola and the Congo. While we are the same age, he appears as if he were ready for duty in a moment's notice. *Y* and *Z* are '*Agency people*', a husband and wife team that spent most of their adult life in the Congo. They would seem to be more at home doting over their grandchildren, and then telling tales of clandestine activities.

The truth is, they are three of at least twenty individuals who have approached me over the past three years during the filming and release of my documentary to confirm I got I right. Each has his or her own story to tell. Most hinge on one emotion...guilt.

X

X walks over to me while I am doing research and places an aging black and white photo on the table. The photo shows four people underneath the Angolan flag. One is an African American wearing a U.S. Special Forces Uniform, the other two are white men in short sleeve shirts. "Do you recognize anyone in the photo?" he asks.

Almost immediately I recognize the younger version of X.

"Do you recognize anyone else" he asks.

"Is that John Stockwell?" I answer. John Stockwell was the former CIA Station Chief in Angola, who later wrote the U.S. efforts in that country had little to do with stopping communism.

"You've done your homework, "he says smiling and then walks away. I ask him why he was there, and then it dawns on me. He turns... pauses momentarily... and smiles again. It is one of several chance encounters I had with X while working on the film and the book. He has proven invaluable over the course of my research. He has been the glue to the many missing pieces of the puzzle that exist when it comes to Africa.

"It always began with a whisper campaign," he once told me. It was the coup d'état. X maintained that by the time the shooting began, the covert action was over as far as the Agency was concerned. The "boots on the ground" as he put it had already done their job. "The whisper campaign," he told me went something like this.

Leader A approaches the United States Government seeking financial assistance in rebuilding his country. He wants 200 million but is told he will get 500 million instead. When he protests he is told the balance should be spent reinforcing the airport for larger planes. After all, the leader is told, his country is going to welcome "Heads of State" and other foreign dignitaries. In addition, those dignitaries will need a place to stay. A palace literally fit for kings and queens. Still he objects, but they insist.

The headlines declare the U.S. has been a most gracious host and he returns to Africa a very successful emissary on behalf of his people. Then the 'whisper campaign" begins. Agency people, *X* tells me, are in the outlying areas sowing the seeds of discontent.

"You know he is building an expensive palace for him and his family," an agency member tells a hypothetical chief.

"The road only goes from the airport to the palace," another chief is told. *"That is where all of the money is going. That, which isn't headed for his Swiss bank account,"* the covert operative adds. Always, in Africa, it is money that would be best spent *elsewhere*. That is the problem in Africa, there is always an *elsewhere*.

"That's where my guys came in," he once told me. Sometimes "his guys" wore uniforms most of the time they did not. They were Special Forces soldiers who were black and in some cases actually spoke the local language. They were the black faces the Africans could trust. After all, everyone in Africa knew the black man in American was still fighting for equal rights and facing discrimination. If anyone understood the plight of the Africans it was the African Americans. Surely, people who looked like them would not be the 'Brutus' in this equation. Africa couldn't have been further from the truth.

"How do you think they got their stripes," he once said. Those words continue to haunt me. *X* described a military that rewarded those who did the "deed" with a promotion. He described a situation not unlike the organized crime families I had covered, in which "made men" were those who were forced to do unmentionable acts the others would hold over their heads. It is not true, what they say. There is honor among thieves.

African American soldiers who wished to rise through the ranks often took on African assignments according to *X*. All too often those assignments included the various coups of which we have become all too familiar. They became the military's version of "made men" or soldiers who sold out their own for a star on their shoulder.

Y and Z

Y and Z worked in Africa for *'the Agency'*. They confirmed on two separate occasions all that, *X,* told me. I met them at one of the dozens of screenings for my film...this one down south. When the film was over, the question and answer period began. Always there are those who ask plenty of questions and those who ask none. I am usually more interested in those who don't ask questions than those who do...especially when they stick around.

Y and Z sat together in a corner and waited for all of the others in the room to leave. Both approached me at the same time.

"You got it right," *Y* said.

"You were very thorough," *Z* said. A few days later, *Z* sent me his resume. He was no longer with *'the Agency'* but proudly listed it on his resume. Still, that resume said nothing about being in Africa, only that he was some sort of accountant. It made no mention of coups, or assassinations or other clandestine assignments. It left the impression that *Z* spent his days toiling behind a desk inside an embassy. *Z* made it clear to me on more than one occasion, that couldn't have been further from the truth.

Judas

There is a third group of people I have met while on this journey. Those in this group betrayed Africa from within. They were African. They sold out. My favorite is a man who works for one of the largest corporations in Africa. He ate at my house and insulted my senses. His name is not important but his story is one that occurs all too often.

I will call him *'Judas'*. *'Judas'* defends the rape of Africa. he says his company has done all it can in providing for Africans in a war torn environment. "Without _____(fill in the company) they would have had nowhere to go," he tells me in between sips of coffee. I smile knowing the coffee beans probably came from a country his company betrayed. The company pays them a fare wage by African standards and provides shelter, even if there is no running water or toilets.

When I counter that what he is sanctioning is slavery, he responds "This is Africa." "You," he is quick to point out, "don't understand."

'*Judas*' is paid well for his betrayal. He has homes in two African nations. At one residence he pays his workers $50 per month. A paltry sum by U.S. standards, but he says the money is buttressed by the fringe benefits that he provides. He pays their rent in a place that would make a Manhattan slum-lord happy, and makes sure that they have a "bike" to get to and from work.

'*Judas*' maintains that it is wrong for "Westerners" like me to assume that Africa will get better overnight. He reminds me, as so many others have, that Africa didn't get this way overnight and its problems will take time to solve. I remind him that the Marshall Plan in Europe saw results in far less time that wars in Africa last. I remind him that I watched the Olympics in Sarajevo only to watch that country plunge into chaos and back to economic stability while Liberia struggled to survive. I remind him that I am a child who watched the U.S. go to war in Vietnam, and watched Vietnam welcome the aging American GI's back as tourists. He is silent. He is, however, far from finished.

"You don't understand," he says as he makes his way toward the door.

"Perhaps it is you who don't understand," I tell him quickly closing the door on this chapter of the story. "When so many Africans have died, there is little time or room for understanding."

The last I heard from '*Judas*', was when he offered, on behalf of his bosses to buy my film. I refused. Like the "*White Hand*" in Africa, the "*Black Hand*" is seldom seen. But every African knows behind every coup there is someone who looks like them, and has once again sold Africa into slavery. One hand orders the assassinations, the others pull the trigger. It matters little which is which. The end result seldom varies, those dying are African.

The last time I saw *X*, he handed me a small piece of paper with the names of three African countries on it. The names on the list: Kenya, Somalia, and Zimbabwe. Six months later all three were experiencing either coups or some sort of economic turmoil.

Chapter Forty-Five

Cannes/ The World Premier Of NSSM
Guns…Greed…Genocide

"20,000,000 dead and counting ...."(Appeared on screens
across Cannes France)

Apocalypse Africa, Made In America

My film premiered at Cannes, France, at the Cannes International Film Festival to a packed theater. Several people in the crowd could be heard weeping openly, as they witnessed the true horror of what happened to Africa. Some laughed, an uncomfortable laugh, as a segment aired that revealed most African Americans we interviewed couldn't name "three countries in Africa," as Randall Robinson put it. They cringed when they heard the words of an American president caught on tape, referring to Africans as "just out of the trees," and "the little black bastards."

Afterwards those who watched gathered in the hallway outside the theater to continue the discussion that began inside following the film. They wanted to know more about the film, and more about why it all was allowed to happen. They wanted to know how an American president could sound so backward and stupid, and get away with it.

Several of the Europeans who came to watch said only one word, "finally." The Europeans who gathered outside told me that they had been forced to confront their evils in Africa long ago, mostly because of books written by American authors. Many of those authors, they pointed out, like John

Stockwell the former CIA Station Chief in Angola, once worked for *'the Agency'*. They wondered why the American media ignored such obvious truths. They wondered why African Americans weren't outraged by those truths. They wondered. So did I

Next came the marketing phase. This involved an endless series of meetings with the men and women of Hollywood, (America) Bollywood (India) and Nollywood. (Nigeria) These people come to see your film for one very simple reason. They want to make money. To a person, most of the people who viewed the film said it was one of the most powerful documentaries they had ever seen.

A person who worked at the USA's Discovery Network told me, "It *was* the most powerful documentary he had ever seen." He then added, "But they won't show it on my network."

A representative of one of the most powerful black movie moguls in the United States told me that his boss was interested only in "comedies and dramadies," which are movies where black people act stupid but try and impart some serious uplifting theme. She was apologetic as she dismissed my movie. It was as if she felt she owed me an apology for her rejection. Not me, but Africa. They were all polite and all walked away.

All told, my company invested thousands on big screen advertising showing the images of a starving black child with the numbers **"20,000,000 dead"** thundering onto the screen. We handed out hundreds of leather bracelets, all made in Liberia, each with the same information stamped inside. We called them "holocaust bracelets." Everyone wanted them.

I personally delivered a package containing the information about NSSM 200 to one of Hollywood's most vocal starlets on Africa. The worlds cameras clicked away as she received the package and the members of the media were given their own information packages by way of explanation. I have yet to hear from her or any of the assembled press. We are now entering the second year since the film premiered. I have given up hope. It's easy to show African's suffering, it hard to face the fact that perhaps, we had something to do with it. American is, after all, the good guys. We are the nation that gave the world Tarzan!

A young woman with a very big heart, who I will call 'Mary', took an interest in the film. She asked for several copies and vowed to find a "Hollywood name" that would be crucial for the marketing of the film. I asked why it was that in Hollywood the truth wasn't sufficient. I am still waiting for *'Mary's'* answer. *'Mary'* mentioned some of the biggest names in Hollywood. Some of them were black, some were white. We kept up with each other telephonically for three months after Cannes. Then, I never heard from her again.

It's easy to quit when the subject is Africa.

The fact is Africa dies because most of us want an easy answer to a very complex problem. We want, as she suggested, an hour and a half film that ends with a series of solutions listed at the bottom of the screen that make it easy to write a check to fix that which was broken. Sadly, that is not the case.

That is not to say I walked away empty handed. The film, which premiered at Cannes under the title, NSSM, Guns, Greed … Genocide was picked up by Cinequest Films in San Diego, California. Cinequest prides itself on "empowering the maverick." I met the representatives from Cinequest at Cannes and received one of the most welcome phone calls of my filmmaking career almost six months later. They wanted "rights" to the film. The rest is up to those who see it.

Chapter Forty-Six

The Debt

"We're interested only in comedies and dramadies."

Spokesman for head of major African American
broadcast network

In his book "The Debt," Randall Robinson, who I interview for the film, maintains we as African Americans simply don't like ourselves. Robinson writes, "Let's just lance the boil. We hate ourselves. Not all of us, but too many. Most of the rest of us have leaden doubts about our worth."

I remembered reading those lines and wondering aloud could it be true? Was Randall Robinson right? Do African Americans indeed hate themselves? The evidence points to one simple and troubling truth. The answer to all of those questions is yes! How else can you explain the deaths of millions of Africans in some of the most brutal conditions imaginable with little or no cry of outrage coming from the African American community?

Was the representative of the African American movie mogul right when he said we were only interested in "comedies and dramadies?" Does the Hollywood starlet do just enough or does she simply not know. Worst still, now that she has the package, does she simply not want to know. She is not alone.

In 2008, CNN, a major American News Network, spent a week in the Congo. CNN sent Anderson Cooper, one of their biggest stars. Cooper reported the truth about the Congo. He told his audience that millions of Congolese were dying and

that it is one of the world's worst and least reported on trage-
dies. He talked about blacks killing blacks. He talked about
blacks raping blacks, and he talked about how the world
watches as the Congo dies. He didn't however; mention
anything about "our" role in the collapse of the Congo. Is it
that he didn't know? Or did his researchers inside CNN fail to
do their homework? One of those producers visited me in
Cannes. She watched my film and walked away.

Clearly, Lumumba's assassination is no secret, nor is
the U.S. role in that assassination. It is, as one CIA agent said
once on TV, "like you're standing there holding a smoking gun
over a smoldering body admitting to kidnapping but saying
you had nothing to do with the death." If CNN couldn't get it
right in the Congo, who will?

The endless string of documentaries that stream out of
Africa all have one thing in common, they blame the violence
in Africa on the Africans. Again, this is not to absolve the
Africans from their share of the blame, or the African Americans, which I will get to later, but it is to point out the subject is
not so simple. How can so many perish from guns that are not
made on the African continent? Where to the tanks come
from? Where do the planes come from? Where to the bullets
come from? As Randall Robinson says, "we see people in rags
but with sophisticated expensive weapons but Americans never
stop to ask, where do these guns come from? These are the
weapons sold largely by U.S. suppliers. The United States is
the leading supplier of guns to these thugs."

CBC

I am sitting at my table at the Congressional Black Caucus. It is
no different than any of the other dinners I have participated in
during my 22 years as a working journalist in this town. There
are two wines, and two entrées. One is always meat, the other
fish. When I first arrived in Washington the waiters were
black, then Hispanics became the wait staff of choice, and now

immigrants from the various African conflict countries I have outlined make up a large portion of the wait staff. I have noticed that Liberia seems to be the country most represented. As I look around the room at the wealthiest, most connected African Americans in the world I wondered about the people I left behind in Africa. Do they have running water yet? Is there food enough to feed the various families who made a living inside a bombed out hotel? What would they say about this gathering?

Clearly the Caucus will argue that they are doing all they can. They will point out the millions of dollars in U.S. aid that is spent, much of it wasted, on African countries. They will point to their fact finding missions abroad and argue what next? Some of those sitting at the table are ministers whose congregations have built schools, dug wells, and sent millions of dollars in textbooks to the African continent. There are the media types who have built schools, adopted children and done all that they can. Then there are people like me who continuously scratch their heads and wonder how we can celebrate when so many die? How can we celebrate when so many live in huts?

There is a scene in my film that causes so many to pause. It shows Liberia in 1971 before the coup d'état that brought about the downfall of the administration of President William Tolbert. He was the one who was disemboweled by rebel forces loyal to Samuel Doe, whom Ronald Reagan welcomed to Washington with open arms. Tolbert is seen smiling in the film arm in arm with Patricia Nixon, the wife of Richard Nixon who was sent to Liberia as a "goodwill ambassador." What Tolbert didn't know is that some of those who got off the plane with Nixon were members of the CIA and Special Forces that would bring about his demise. But there they are, smiling, dancing, he in his white dinner jacket, she wearing a sequin gown. Others join in, in what is known in

Liberia as the "Grande Marche." It is a time of celebration. All seems well.

The movie then cuts away from 1971 to a shot taken in 2004. It shows a little girl, five or six years of age, teetering on the brink of falling off the ledge in a bombed out building in downtown Monrovia.

Tolbert is dead, as are most of the people in the film. The girl represents a generation of Africans born into war and raised in poverty. Somehow I find it difficult, as I look around the room, to imagine this could happen here, but then again, the Liberians believed all was well too. I write this book for that little girl.

Chapter Forty-Seven

Holocaust

"Unless and until the philosophy that holds one race superior and another inferior is finally and permanently changed, everywhere is war."

Haile Selassie Emperor of Ethiopia,
He died in a bloody coup.

Africa is the holocaust that is happening on our watch. The death camps have names like Liberia, Sierra Leone, Rwanda, Darfur, Sudan, Ethiopia, Chad, Eritrea, Kenya, Zimbabwe, the Congo, and the list goes on and on and on. The weapons of mass destruction in Africa are misinformation, and the coup d'état. The world continues to believe, wrongly, that the United States and its allies were trying to protect Africa from communism. They continued to do so even though there are hundreds of internal documents that reveal that as early as 1969 the United States knew that was not the case. Still, U.S. presidents up to and including Ronald Reagan used communism as the defense of U.S. actions in Angola, and Liberia and the Congo. Perhaps the only thing that historians believe in is that the "Third World War" was fought in Africa, and all of the casualties were black.

According to the historical record and people with firsthand knowledge of events like Roger Morris, Randall Robinson, and a host of African leaders the coup d'état was the weapon of choice. One by one African nations were toppled in CIA led coups with little or no regard to what the end result might be, so long as Americas "strategic interests" were protected. Strategic interests that were protected even if it meant propping up "Tinhorn dictators" like Idi Amin, Samuel Doe, Charles Taylor, and Joseph Mobuto, who single handily, massacred their populations by the thousands. So long as we believed the violence was tribal in nature, few, reacted with outrage.

It is as if death inside a tribe is different than death outside. There is little mention in the history books about the ordinary people who lost their lives, and their livelihoods at the end of weapons sold to those "Tinhorn dictators." There is no mention of the Dr. Lincoln Brownells of the world. Peaceful people who watched their entire families die because of American or soviet made and American supplied weapons.

Instead, the world looks at Africa and wants to blame Africa for its problems. Those Africans can't feed themselves. Why do those Africans keep killing themselves? Why does the United States continue to provide aide to those people if they can't one day learn to feed themselves?

Roger Morris says the "blood debt" owed to Africa is incredible. "Oh my God we owe them horrendous blood debt for what we allowed to happen over the last half century. We owe them trillions in aid."

Morris and others believe America's ignorance about Africa dates back to Tarzan. He says, in addition to the "blood debt" owed to Africa, Americans must be educated out of their ignorance. "We owe them much more education of our own people. We owe them awareness and consciousness. We owe them sensitivity."

Randall Robinson agrees, "You cannot take from a people, language, culture, religion, mother, father, sister and brother, you cannot deconstruct a people…." Robinson says as a result of that ignorance the world sees Tarzan when it thinks of Africa. Or, as he puts it, "a man who can scarcely read a one word bulletin, was king of the jungle, we thought Africa was jungle, lord knows there are few places where there is actually rain forest."

Brian Clowes believes Africa's apocalypse began with a single document, NSSM 200. "We want these natural resources for ourselves. We see Africa as a young and vigorous continent, unwilling to accept the leadership of these companies and governments."

To understand the cause and effect of what has occurred you need only look at a map of Africa prepared by the CIA in 1969. The document points out all of Africa's strengths and weakness as it emerged from colonialism. Most of the skilled labor positions in the colonial period were filled by white foreigners. Most of the money came from selling the products those countries produced to the U.S., Europe and its allies. Despite that, Africa emerging from colonialism was fiscally strong, if those powers "did the right thing" when they turned the keys to Africa over to the African people. The money that was being made and turned over to "white" European governments would have done the same for Africa as it did for Europe. But instead of treating Africans like equal, they were treated time in time again, in secret, as lesser. They were treated like slaves.

Perhaps the most haunting aspect of the CIA's 1969 study is the map that shows where Africa's vast natural resources were located. It is that map that serves as a blueprint for the destruction of an entire continent. Where there is something of value, there was war.

74-0085 #4
Intelligence Data

DIRECTORATE OF
INTELLIGENCE

Intelligence Memorandum

Economic Trends in Black Africa

THIS COPY TO BE FILED OR
DESTROYED BY THE RECIPIENT

ER IM 69-1
January 1969

Copy No. 60

D - 863/69
Attach 7

Figure 2

Forty years after that document was written, the fact
remains the U.S. and its allies wanted what Africa had then,
and still do. The companies accused of the most horrific
human rights abuses on the continent still do business un-
abated. The U.S. and its allies still sell millions of dollars of
weapons to African leaders torn between protecting themselves

and rebuilding their infrastructure. And the White House refuses to repudiate NSSM 200.

In 2004 Brian Clowes group, Human Life International, approached the George W. Bush administration and asked the administration to renounce NSSM 200. As of this printing they are still waiting for an answer. Population Control has supporters in the highest ranks of American private and government life. To put it mildly, we still don't believe Africa should profit from it own natural resources.

The fact that NSSM 200 and NSSM 201 even exist are frightening in their own right. Are we so bent on controlling the world's resources that we will do whatever it takes to control the world's populations? Do we have the right to tell families in Africa how many children they can, or should have? Should we facilitate abortions? Sterilization? What gives us that right? Who?

History has allowed the Lincoln Brownell's of the world to become invisible. Their deaths are no longer counted outside of Africa. Instead the world counts the dead in Africa country by country, instead of family by family. We talk of death tolls, but not human loss. We seek ways to explain the numbers as if "one death" is not "one death" too many.

In June of 2006 the Associated Press reported that as many as 100 million Africans could die of AIDs by the year 2025. You probably read that last sentence not realizing what it said. It is so important it bears repeating; In June of 2006 the Associated Press reported that as many as 100 million Africans could die of AIDs by the year 2025.

So what happened? Did the world become immune to death in Africa on a continental scale, just as the Hutus and Tutsis did in Rwanda? Did the U.S. commit genocide in an effort to survive World War II and the Cold War? Were Africa's natural resources become the defector fuel that allowed us to become the military power that we are? And finally, as the *"Eight stages of Genocide"* suggests, are we now in a state of "denial?"

Roger Morris and others say, the chickens have come home to roost. "One would have thought that September 11th would have prompted the question: Why do men fly jets into buildings? It isn't because they hate our freedoms or that they disagree with Hollywood. This is a profound protest at American policy. This is a war that America has been in without knowing it for almost a half century."

Many believe the principles that allowed the U.S. to pillage Africa, played out in the Iraqi theater of war decades later. They say, as was the case with Africa, the U.S. government lied about a threat to national security to commit troops to foreign soil, when all that was really wanted was Iraq's oil. History will be the judge there, but in Africa the paper trail is complete.

There was no Soviet threat. Great men like Dr. Kwame Nkrumah, and Patrice Lumumba, and Nelson Mandela were targets simply because they were black. There was bigotry in the highest levels of the United States government. Bigotry that was ignored then and still ignored today. Tarzan did make us numb to the reality in Africa. Without Africa we, the United States and its allies would not be here. We owe Africa everything and facing that reality will cause us to take a long look in the mirror and face the horrors of the continent we left behind getting to where we are now.

Twenty million people who look, dance, eat, and act like me are dead today. Most died anonymously in a world that simply didn't give a damn. They never found a cure for cancer or dreamed of walking on the moon simply because they were African. They were men, women, and most importantly children. And they are still dying today.

This is the true story of the holocaust that has happened in half century of my life.

Chapter Forty-Eight

Deaths in Wars and Conflicts in the 20th Century

"Indeed we have no excuses anymore. We have no excuses for inaction and no alibis for ignorance. Often we know before the very victims of conflict that they will be victimized."

United Nations Secretary-General Kofi Anan from Death in Wars and Conflicts in the 20th Century. February, 1998.

The true story of Africa's holocaust can be found in the numbers and nowhere are those numbers more frightening than in a report entitled *"Deaths in Wars and Conflicts in the 20th Century." (56)*

The report was compiled by Milton Leitenberg from the Cornell University peace studies program. It is a blow by blow, number by number accounts of all the wars fought in every country in the 20th century. Most of those wars took place on the African continent. The numbers don't lie and in this case, if anything, understate the problem.

My film, *'Apocalypse Africa, Made in America ends'*, with these numbers thundering onto the screen. I broke down in tears while loading them into the computer because it seemed like the task would never end. I kept typing, and typing and typing. It was 2:00 in the morning when I finished. Many of those who have witnessed the death tolls at the end of the film burst into tears. It is emotional to see how many people have died in one's lifetime, especially when those numbers are so often overlooked.

Here are the numbers at the films end, as compiled by Milton Leitenberg and the others at Cornell University.

Country and year	Death Toll
Sudan 1955-1972	750,000
Nigeria/Biafra	2 million
Uganda ca. Idi Amin 1971-1978	300,000
Burundi ca. 1972	250,000
Angola 1980-1988 ca. 1980-85 1995-2000	300,000 1 million 100,000
Burundi 1972 1988 1993	80,000 200,000 200,000
Cameroon 1955-60	32,000
Chad 1965-1989	25,000
Ethiopia 1962-1989	150,000 1 million

1998	100,000
Ghana	
1981	1,000
Guinea- Bissau	
1972-74	15,000
Kenya	
1953-63	300,000
Liberia	
1980-2000	250,000
Mozambique	
1965-75	30,000
1980-81	900,000
Namibia	
1967-89	13,000
Nigeria	
1967-70	2 million
1980-1999	16,000
Rwanda	
1960-65	105,000
1990-95	1 million
Sierra Leone	
1991 – 2000	50,000
Somalia	
1980-1993	310,000

South Africa
1985-90   5,000

Sudan
1955-72   750,000
1983-90   510,000
1990-95   500,000
1995-2000   1 million

Uganda
1966-1985   605,000

Uganda continued:
1981-1990   150,000

Zaire Congo
1960-2000   1.8 million

Zambia
1964   1,000

Zimbabwe
1972-87   14,000

Algeria
1954-2000   1,132,000

Morocco
1953-56   3,000
Tunisia
1952-54   3,000

Photo as Prologue

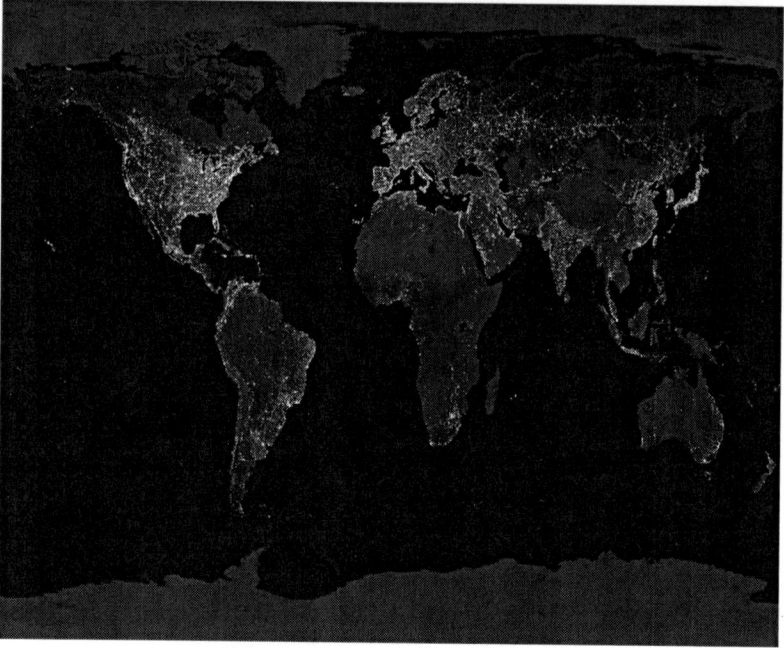

"You break it, you own it."

The Pottery Barn Rule

LaVergne, TN USA
18 August 2010
193717LV00005B/6/P

9 780982 282229